On the Highway
of the Stories of the Gods

Martin Edmond

LASAVIA
PUBLISHING

Published by Lasavia Publishing Ltd.
Auckland, New Zealand
www.lasaviapublishing.com

ISBN: 978-1-991083-41-8

Contents

Introduction

Once we had decided on February nineteenth as the date we would begin our sojourn in Japan we had to work out what we would do when we arrived there. We couldn't stay indefinitely at Mayu's mother Yoshie's apartment in Yoyogi, Tokyo, because it was too small; and we couldn't go immediately to our place in the mountains of Honshu because it wasn't ready. It had been a cold winter up in Shinanomachi and the architects, Sato Komusho, said the snow was still waist high; they hadn't yet been able to put the finishing touches to their rehabilitation of the *akiya* we had bought, our little cabin in the woods. Mayu thought of various strategies to delay, in the most enjoyable way possible, our relocation there; the one she decided upon was a road trip around Kyushu, in the south of the archipelago, where the weather would be warmer and where we could spend a few weeks travelling and sight-seeing. 'A holiday,' she said.

I was happy to go along with this and happy also to leave it to her to plan the itinerary, which she did with characteristic rigour and a meticulous eye for detail. I also believe she had certain themes in mind. I didn't inquire too deeply into what she was envisaging because I trust her judgement and also because I liked the idea of not knowing exactly where we were going and what we were doing: each day would bring its own surprises. Plus she speaks and reads the language and I don't; so I limited my contribution to an offer to pay for the hire of the rental car and a promise to drive her anywhere she wanted to go. She was shooting material for a film so I called my task *Driving Miss Mayu*, not without irony but not without affection either. We were very much in love. We still are. And so, ten days after we arrived in Tokyo, on March first, we flew to Kumamoto.

A word about the title: there is indeed a road of that name, loosely rendered, in south-eastern Kyushu but the official translation is Legendary Road, with the implication that the stories of gods told upon it are, if not exactly fictions, then folk tales. We did travel along parts of that road, from Takachiho to Miyazaki and beyond; elsewhere we encountered gods other than the *kami* of the Shinto pantheon or gods in other forms. In southern Kyushu, for example, we discovered vestiges of the worship of the emperor as a god which sent nearly four thousand young men to their deaths as *tokkotai*, kamikaze pilots, during the Pacific War. And in those parts of western Kyushu where the Portuguese influence was strongest there were many roads along which you hear stories of Christian gods and, if you include the Virgin Mary, goddesses too.

Stories of the Gods

Kyushu | March | 2023

Flying to Kumamoto

We were early for our flight so we hung out at a café in the terminal at Haneda until it was time to board the plane — which an official announcement kept saying might have to return to Tokyo because of poor visibility over the airport at Kumamoto. This was, we surmised, Japan Airlines erring on the side of caution. To the GNP and the GNC (Gross National Cool) we added the GNA — Gross National Anxiety; all three are high. I was intrigued by a pot plant in the café which appeared artificial even though it was real. The reverse of the usual attempt to make the unreal look real. I was also intrigued by a mannequin in a beige dressing gown in the adjoining boutique, with his back to us, looking a bit like the young Marlon Brando, brooding over the concourse as if examining the crowd for fashion mistakes or wardrobe malfunctions. When we boarded at last, we were seated right at the back of the plane, without a window. I read Turgenev: *Fathers & Sons*.

The rental car we picked up at a depot outside of Kumamoto was a late model Nissan Note and, like most cars these days, half way towards being driverless. You enter into a relationship with it like that which you have with your computer or your phone. I found it difficult to handle at first, but not nearly as intimidating as Mayu's sister Mioko's brand new BMW. We had just been staying at Hakone, near Fuji, where we had gone to look for one of the places Yoshie had been sent to live as a child during the war and, during a brief stint at the wheel, the beamer alarmed me in a way vehicles never usually do. Now I drove the Note easily enough through intensively cropped flat land and then, after crossing a river, down narrow valleys where the houses were all built in traditional style, albeit with tiled not thatched rooves. Then we climbed up into the mountains.

It was dusk when we arrived at the hotel, near the opening of Kikuchi Gorge, built along a high bank on the north side of the river. There was a view from our room of blue and white water boiling over rapids below and then pooling, deep green, beneath mossy cliffs. It reminded me of the Manganui o te Ao in New Zealand, on the banks of which, at Ruatiti, we used to picnic when I was a child. Our room had its own outdoor *onsen* where we could bathe together overlooking the Kikuchi. I grew up beside another river, the Mangawhero, and have always slept happily when I can hear the sound of water flowing outside.

Kikuchi

My nephew Max and his wife Shinoka were living in Kikuchi, the old castle town of Waifu, in a low, rambling house on a street behind a convenience store. It was part of Shinoka's *jikka*, her family place. Next door lived her grandmother and her aunt, who were in a relationship resembling that between Yoshie and Mioko. An eighty-something year old being looked after by her fifty-year old daughter. However, Shinoka said her aunt had never left home, which isn't the case with Mioko, who lives a cosmopolitan life and often travels for her work to London, Milan and other places. We drank tea and talked. I gave Max his own grandmother's autobiography and her selected poems, which was something of a relief. I didn't have to carry Lauris around with me anymore. I also gave him the two cakes of Whitakers dark chocolate and two jars of marmite he'd requested.

We went out for a walk and, at the local museum, saw restored Jomon pots and tiny, delicate, flaked stone arrow heads and spear points, and much else besides. An intact ceramic receptacle for receiving the bones of the dead. A beautiful hand drawn map of the river, from the source to the sea, set high up in wood panelling and running both sides of the beam. It was exquisitely coloured, predominantly in greens, blacks and whites, and included geographical features as well as human settlements. All of the many castles in central Kyushu in the Edo period (1603-1868), when the Tokugawa shogunate ruled, were drawn in; there must have been at least twenty of them. Another cabinet displayed pictures of local dignitaries, artists, writers and musicians, including a painting of a venerable old teacher, who looked at us, resigned and faintly quizzical, down the years.

There was a street fair on, with stalls selling hot food; but, as Max remarked, it was mostly just fried squid. Desultory crowds drifted from shop to shop, eyeing without enthusiasm the generic souvenirs for sale. We paused at a plain modern building which had a *Noh* theatre within; but it was closed. Pretty soon we went back to their place for a lunch of eggs, homemade bread baked with shitake mushrooms, salad, cheese (fetta and a sharp blue), roasted home grown pumpkin, kimchi and pickled daikon. It was many years since I'd seen Max and in the interim he had grown into a fine young man of thirty-two, capable, generous, fluent in Japanese and full of plans for the future.

After lunch he and Shina took us to the *kominka*, an old house from the Meiji era (1868-1913) which they, with others, had assumed ownership of, for nothing but the taxes, in order to restore it as an arts centre and café. A big old family home which stood on a square block of land in another part of town, it had been abandoned by the last of the descendants with everything they owned still inside. A remarkable place. Some parts of the house were infested with white ants but the structure was largely intact. The barn, in which there was still some hay, had been partially burned in a fire. There were two old wooden carts parked there, probably horse drawn, but small enough to have been harnessed behind a donkey or a goat. There was also an implement shed made of mud and wattle, the walls of which had gone a lovely yellow ochre colour. It too was dilapidated but not beyond repair. A small stone buddha sat beside the disused well.

Inside the house pictures still hung upon the walls, for instance an old, faded map of the world in which only the territories coloured green — Argentina, the United States, Alaska, and the Congo — could still be made out. In another room a scroll showing the white figure of Sakuya, the Blossom Princess, hung next to a ghostly Fuji, left there as an after-image now the original picture had gone — if it was not drawn directly onto the wall. There was a poem written upon the scroll but I neglected to find out what it said. In a bookshelf stood a complete set of the Encyclopaedia Britannica, in Japanese — the famous 1911 version so beloved of Jorge Luis Borges.

In another cabinet were photograph albums with the family photos intact therein — beautiful, glossy, black and white prints from the early twentieth century; their abandonment so full of sorrow I couldn't bear to look at them. I only opened one, on a formal portrait of a bespectacled, dignified older man, then quickly closed it again. Diaphanous pale green and pale yellow fishing nets hung from the walls, used in river fishing and, because they were made of nylon, not susceptible to decay. Upstairs, before a window, stood a massive, antique wooden loom also in need of restoration. Max pointed out a couple of nineteenth century monograms from the hilts of *samurai* swords, high up, nailed to the wall. They are now worth quite a lot of money on the second hand market.

When he first saw the place there was a single futon on the floor of one of the rooms where a man had been sleeping; now, in the same place, lay piles of clothing, mostly cheap suits, far more than any one person could wear. The fellow had fallen on hard times and returned to camp in the house before finding his feet again elsewhere; the property had reverted to his sister, who lived in another town and didn't want it. Max and his co-owners were sorting what they would keep from what they would throw away; a task made complex by the vast number and bewildering variety of the household goods. Cutlery, crockery, pots and pans, old tools, books, papers . . . the detail vertiginous and unassimilable, poignant, fascinating, strange.

In the high blue air over the town, three raptors — most likely black kites — wheeled before the daylight moon. Down in the yard, where someone had already begun to plant a vegetable garden, the stump of an old sour plum tree had put out a few new shoots, which were flowering white — an apt image of their enterprise, I thought. It seemed quixotic to me. When I suggested to Max it might take years to come to fruition, he looked at me with alarm. He thought they could have it up and running in eighteen months to two years; and it turned out he was right.

Shina had to go to the town office for her work (she's a videographer) and Max wanted to show us the library. The head man, Kobo, was one of his partners in the house restoration project. He and his wife lived next door to it, they were the ones who started the vegetable garden. He was a bit older than Max, a serious man in his forties, who said his library had been voted one of the twelve most relaxing in the world. It was discreet, modern, with sweeping curved blond wood shelving and white appurtenances; and that hushed murmur of rapt attention libraries do so well. Mayu went to the children's section to look for folktales of Kyushu, and Max disappeared somewhere else. Outside, in the lobby, in a glass case, I saw a pigment-stained saucer, two brushes, three tubes of paint and a modest wooden palette with muted traces of pinks, whites, ochres, greens and greys upon it. It had belonged to French Polish artist Balthasar Klossowski de Rola, otherwise known as Balthus. His wife, Setsuko, was Japanese.

Max and Shina came to the hotel for dinner that night and afterwards had an onsen in our private pool. Shina told Mayu, in the restaurant, when they were speaking Japanese, that she and Max met in a gay bar in Tokyo in the years when he used to cross-dress, and that her other job was as a pole dancer at a local club in town. Some of the books on her shelves were manuals explaining how to make pornographic videos — a lucrative career path for Japanese film makers. After their bath, they called an *unten daiko*, a service which brings two drivers in a single car: one to drive you home in your own car, the other to pick up the other driver afterwards. The drink driving limit here is so low it might as well be zero; and the penalties for breaking the law extreme. You can be sent to jail; and Japanese jails are notoriously grim.

Towards Mount Aso

In the morning there were four white-headed ducks on the river and two little black and white wren-like birds feeding in the green weed that skirted the rocks in the stream. I had watched one of them working along the stones in a canal in town the day before. We checked out and headed up the gorge where, the fellow at hotel reception told us, it was always cold, even in high summer. 'It is also one of the best places in Japan for forest bathing,' he added. The road ran uphill through a mass of trees and, towards the top, took a tight bend over a bridge; to the right was a spectacular fall of water. We turned around and went back to the car park, where the forest bathers leave their cars, and left ours there too.

It was cold but not bitingly so. Wild camellias, with small pinkish red flowers and yellow centres, glowed among the cedars, the larches, and the pines, along with the blush of new growth on the wild *sakura*, the cherry blossom trees, which had already finished their spring flowering. The river was loud, incessant and the falls very beautiful. Their formal name, Kakemaku Falls, compares them to theatre curtains, which they did indeed resemble; but locally they are named after two brothers, charcoal burners, who lived up here long ago. You could feel their presence too, lighting fires against the cold in their little house above the river.

We carried on, up and over the crest of the range and onto the Milk Road, which ran through a spectacular landscape of high rolling plains where acre after acre of golden *susuki* grass, with its gracefully inclining cream seed heads, all facing the same way, grew. Some of the unfenced fields had been harvested already and the hay gathered into stooks like those you see in Monet paintings; others were yet to be mowed. Further along we came out on to a ridge and saw far below us a broad plain in which stood a large town surrounded by orderly fields and scattered houses. This too looked as improbable as the fields of golden grass, like something out of an old tale.

Between the high yellow fields and the wide plain below grew rank upon rank of cedar trees, with their billowy pyramidal shape, some russet with new growth, others still carrying the evergreen of winter; and on the far side of the plain a volcano smoked in amongst a number of other peaks, most of them shattered cones after ancient explosions had blown their tops. We lunched in the town of Aso then circumnavigated that nest of volcanoes on the western edge of an immense caldera, one of the largest in the world, also called Aso. On a good day you could drive right to the lip of the crater of Nakadake, the peak we had seen smoking on the horizon — but not today. The road was closed because the volcano was at level two activity, on a scale of one to five. That meant: do not approach the crater. Five meant evacuate.

We stopped at the point where barriers had been set up across the road and found there a grimacing buddha with sinister knife-bearing figures on either side and a relief of a horse's head on his headpiece: the plaque upon the plinth said it had been erected by a local horse lord in memory of a favourite animal. There were also several headless or otherwise damaged buddhas lined up along a broken wall, and an abandoned shrine crumbling away behind a much larger, brand-new shiny one. Shrines are never demolished, they are just left to fade away. The rocks around the crater were a strange grey-green colour, like the verdigris that accretes on copper or bronze; and behind the wall along which the headless buddhas stood was a sturdy bridge to nowhere. I saw several people taking selfies inadvertently drop their camera phones to the ground, as if afflicted by the otherworldly atmosphere of that place.

On the road around the mountains we passed deep ravines with intricate stone or cement works along them, scaling upwards, to prevent erosion. We also passed outcrops of rock, frozen in the bizarre shapes the last eruption had made, all within fields of golden grass or else stands of red and green cedar trees. Not long after the mountains dropped suddenly from view we came in to the little town of Takamori. Here we stopped to visit the famous Shinto shrine of Kamishikimi Kumanoimasu, dedicated to the creator gods Izanagi and his sister / wife Izanami, said to bring good luck in marriage. We climbed up, through huge cedar trees and in between ranks of hundreds of moss-covered *toro*, stone lanterns, a thousand steps to the shrine near the top of the hill.

Behind the main hall, up a zig-zag path, was a sacred rock called Ugetoiwa, in which, just below the summit, an oval opening, like an eye, metres wide, gave on to a view of distant ranges, each a paler blue than the last. Legend has it that this opening was created by a demon escaping from his prison; if such a thing is possible, people say, then any obstacle may be overcome. Thus Ugetoiwa has become a symbol of the achievement of difficult goals. Indeed, getting up that far was hard enough. By the time we reached the eye in the stone I was light-headed and beginning to wonder if the feeling you get here, a sense of godly presences everywhere, was an effect of the place or a by-product of the exhaustion of the climb. We made our devotions then wandered back down to where we left the car, perhaps illegally, in the carpark next to a small roadside post office.

We drove on to our hotel down narrow back roads, through dairy farming country where cows were being fed hay in muddy paddocks or grazing on the golden grass; a solitary white horse stood in a field. Most animals are kept inside most of the time, which is not to say they are badly treated; the opposite may be the case. Wagyu beef cattle are cherished, they are massaged, sometimes with beer, to improve the quality of the flesh. Horses too are cherished, and also eaten; the meat is a pink delicacy sometimes compared to cherry blossom. Under-performing thoroughbreds are sometimes sold for food; horse flesh is also imported from Australia, among other places. I ate it once, inadvertently. I have also eaten whale, but did not know what it was either, until afterwards. Like horse meat, which it resembles, whale is pink, delicate in flavour, mild, not gamey, with a texture like thinly sliced raw tuna.

Senomoto

I was feeling a bit stressed when we arrived at Senomoto. It was the weariness after a day's driving, exacerbated by a bump I'd given myself on the head in the morning — failing to stoop low enough to walk through the wooden gateway that led to the parking lot at the hotel in Kikuchi Gorge. Max told me the standard building code here assumes five foot seven is the average height and I am six feet tall. I felt like I had received a blow from a Zen master, rebuking me for my chronic lack of attention. I had a lump a few centimetres long just back from my hairline which I kept fingering, wondering if I might come away with blood on my hands. Once we were in our room, in the old wing of the hotel, sixties style, with lots of blond wood, I opened a can of beer and immediately felt better.

The hotel seemed remote, isolated, strange. It was built on a ridge on the eastern side of the floor of the ancient caldera and looked across to the five volcanoes on the western rim. As we came in, we saw groups of brightly dressed young women walking through golden grass to some swings set up on a small rise that also looked over the valley to the mountains. There was something timeless in their swinging to and fro as evening came on and the sky clouded and darkened over the lava plains. We bathed indoors, in the bowels of the building; large, hot, tiled, the baths had that faded glamour of old resort facilities. The tiles were stained with rust or lifting off the walls, the window surrounds bizarrely corroded and the landscape outside occluded to fancy or legend by condensation on the glass.

Next morning Mayu resumed the laborious task of downloading the moving pictures she had taken the day before to her laptop. Because she was filming with a new iPhone, the sequences had to go up to the cloud before coming back down again. It was a slow process made even slower by the weak internet and the intermittent phone signal. When either connection failed part way through each ten-minute-long download, she had to go back to the beginning and start again. There was much weeping and wailing and gnashing of teeth when that happened.

At lunchtime she took a break and we drove off the main highway, down narrow switchback roads, through valleys of small farms, to a *soba* restaurant where the food was excellent. My serving included a small *wasabi* root, about the size of my little finger, which I could grate and add to the dipping sauce for the buckwheat noodles, made on the premises and served cold. I love the taste of wasabi but often find the commercially prepared paste, adulterated with horse radish, too hot for my liking. Au naturale, it was delicious. The reason you find these sophisticated restaurants and imposing hotels in such out of the way places is of course the onsen, the hot springs. Everything follows from that.

On the way back to the hotel we stopped at a shop in another narrow valley off the main road so that Mayu could spend the rest of her daily coupons. Travel incentives in Kyushu, post-pandemic, included discounts on accommodation (as much as 20% off) and vouchers which you were required to spend at local shops or businesses, which were then compensated for the cash amount represented upon them by the state. Our lunch cost us nothing and there were still some ¥3,000 ($30.00) left over. Mayu bought two jars of face cream made from horse oil and I acquired a couple of polished star-shaped pieces of hard wood to turn in my hands for exercise.

The outdoor onsen also looked out across the valley to Mt Aso. The first time we went there, four girls in blue *yukata*, carrying orange parasols, preceded us along the path between low topiaried bushes; the pools in the onsen were paved with stones the colour of lapis lazuli.

We went several more times. Once, when Mayu finished bathing before me, she asked a fellow who had just come out of the men's bath if I was still in there. 'Yes,' he said, 'he is looking at nature and being healed.' A lovely thing to say, even if he was being gently ironic, and this from a man who hadn't engaged in conversation with me, nor I with him. We had bathed together in companionable silence. At the evening bath, I saw an old fat fellow I met buying beer at the vending machine earlier. He had come here with his wife by bus and was thus carless and bewildered by the lack of facilities nearby. 'How do you stay here?' he asked me, plaintively. He seemed much happier once he'd had a bath.

In the pool I fell into conversation with a young pilot in the air force. His English was good, and when I remarked upon it, he said he'd learned the language in Italy where he had gone to train for a year under some kind of exchange program. I assume he worked with the Americans, or perhaps the British, there. He hoped to be sent to Australia next but wasn't keen on going to Darwin. He aspired to become a big game fisherman and preferred somewhere on the Pacific coast where you could angle for marlin or tuna or something of that sort. I told him about the many big silver fish I saw once rising from the milky blue depths of the sea off the wharf at Port Darwin to gulp down the food scraps, mostly potato chips, outdoor diners threw to them.

Beppu, Oita

On the road we passed a deer enclosure in a topiary park and stopped to have a closer look. The four or five *shika* deer in the steep, muddy paddock looked forlorn yet hopeful, as if we might be going to feed them. We couldn't; the roadside stall that sold snacks was still closed, nor was there any sign of the topiarist who had clipped well over a hundred small conifers into the shapes of birds, animals, humans, monsters, even a boat with a mast and sails. By far the largest number of trees were made into birds and in that bare volcanic landscapes they looked eerily like flocks of moa. They were actually cranes; some of the more elaborate had their wings spread. Several fearsome looking warriors, one with a face made out of an animal skull, also featured, along with baseball players with real caps and bats, a gorilla, a bear and a herd of giraffes.

Through the mountain pass we went, heading east, and came across another set of volcanoes, some of them smoking, above yellow hillsides where steam escaped from vents in the ground.

The road station where we stopped for a drink wasn't open yet either so I bought a can of hot sweet coffee from a vending machine and Mayu drank roasted green tea. Later in the morning we came down an avenue of small, skinny fan palms into the city of Beppu. Someone had told me the palms of Beppu are fake, a comment I didn't understand because they are undoubtedly real trees. Perhaps she meant they are not natives of Japan, but of the Ryukyu Islands away to the south.

Beppu is famous for its hot springs. Mayu had booked us seventy-five minutes in a family bath at an onsen which branded itself with a logo based upon a gourd. A large, carved, gourd-shaped stone, taller than I am and several times as round, was set up at the turn off and gourds of various descriptions were everywhere in the complex, which included restaurants, cafés, relaxing rooms and many private baths. There was a small fountain where you could boil your own eggs in a metal basket immersed in a stone basin full of hot spring water and a line of excited kids were doing just that.

We went through a low door and down a paved path to our bath. A small, misshapen winter cherry tree was flowering and, in amongst the blossoms, a number of tiny, green-winged birds fed on the nectar, chirping softly and causing white petals to fall onto the stones below. The pool was small and hot and it was nice to be bathing together again. A budding camellia leaned over the amber coloured water and bamboo stems left spiky shadows on an ochre wall. Red stamens from the cherry blossom floated on the meniscus. There was a small, squat, grey structure, a steam room, inside of which you could sit for as long as you could bear, about thirty seconds in my case. Ferns grew alongside rust encrusted pipes.

After we bathed we had lunch in one of the restaurants and then spent some time in the relaxing room where there was a floor made of *tatami* mats, futons and cushions to lie upon. There were chairs for the old and infirm and copies of a 1950s Japanese pictorial publication roughly equivalent to *Life* magazine. We became absorbed in a story about a peasant farmer who had, in 1952, murdered his neighbour and rival with a hoe. There were black and white photos of the dead man lying face down on the ground next to the wheel of his medieval wooden cart; and simulations of what took place in the court room, as suited lawyers and other interested parties attempted to demonstrate exactly how the culprit had struck the fatal blow, and why it could not be considered to have been an accident.

Leaving Beppu, we nearly had an accident ourselves. I was turning right onto the coastal highway when a van I thought was turning left into the same road came straight through the intersection at speed. He swerved. I braked. Calamity was avoided. We were heading south down the coast to Oita where Mayu was going, improbable as it sounds, to have her hair done by her old hairdresser from Sydney. Minori left Kayo, the salon where she worked in Chatswood, eight years before, intending to return to Oita to live with her mother and father and to open her own business.

This she has done and it was to her salon, called 'Oh My Hair!', that Mayu walked on Sunday afternoon. She passed the skateboard park, where the chimes played *Auld Lang Syne*, and went on through city streets for her appointment in a part of town where there are many government offices and the headquarters of big legal firms — both good sources of business for Minori. She took us out to dinner that evening, to a private room in an expensive restaurant where a dozen or so dishes, all protein based, were served in succession, while she drank *shochu*, Mayu *saké*, and I red wine from Spain and Argentina. I had never before eaten the tough meat of the mollusc that makes the turban shell.

It seemed to me that the meal would have cost Minori far more than she would have made from the haircut and the styling —

which were both simple and sophisticated. Afterwards she and Mayu wrapped their arms around each other as we walked back to the Blossom Hotel, next door to the railway station where Minori was to catch her train home. A simple, open, direct and sweet-natured person, when something pleased her, as it often did, she laughed and clapped her hands. She was delighted that Mayu had sought her out after all this time. When I remarked that it was a long way to come for a hair appointment, Mayu smiled and said she was already scheduling the next one.

Taketa

Our room at the Blossom Hotel was on the thirteenth floor, looking across the city to the pale blue ranges where volcanoes fumed and smoked. Seven floors above us were the baths. The outdoor bath consisted of a large hot infinity pool which also looked towards the mountains in the west. Next to that was a cooler bath of blue carbonated water which was good for your skin. The indoor pools, only slightly less spectacular because they were behind glass, were on the floor below and faced north over the port. In the carpark, as we were leaving, I saw some of the extraordinary plumbing that makes such wonders possible. It is as remarkable in its way as the national electricity grid — intricate, ubiquitous and frequently arcane in its appearance. Engineers and industrial designers are considered artists here and even pumps and pipes may have an aesthetic, or at least an expressive, component to them.

We had more vouchers to spend and our quest to find a place to do so led us, serendipitously, to the town of Taketa — an enchanted place. Here, the ruins of a castle on a high hill overlook a town where old and new mingle harmoniously together. Oka Castle, once thought to be impregnable, was built in 1185, improved in 1332 and again in 1584. An earthquake toppled the *tenshu*, the castle keep, in 1769 and a fire went through two years later. The castle was decommissioned, as so many were, after the Meiji Restoration, and its buildings dismantled stone by stone. Now only the foundations, massive as they are, remain. We saw them across the valley from a small hilltop park where, despite warnings about the presence of wild boars, we climbed for the views.

Mayu had noticed an optometrist's shop on the way in to town. We went there after we'd been to the hilltop park. A thin man in a dark suit, a pink tie with pastel dots upon it, and shiny black shoes, fixed my sunglasses for nothing by screwing back on the wing that had fallen off. He used a Philips head screw and I learned that here the two kinds are called the plus and the minus screws for reasons which are obvious once you think about it. While he worked on my Ray-Bans, at the other two counters little, bent-over old people were being fitted with hearing aids. It made perfect sense that you could get aids for vision and hearing at the same place.

After lunch at a French themed café called *La Pause* we walked further into the old town, down narrow streets, past samurai houses, with their ochre and tiled walls, their topiarised trees, low wooden gates, and compounds where once horses would have been stabled and now Kei vehicles parked. A turn in the road took us up a hill to a place where there was, on the right hand side, a red shrine to Inari, the fox god or goddess. On the left a path lead past bamboo-clad walls to a cave where, once upon a time, Hidden (or Secret) Christians worshipped after their faith was proscribed by the Tokugawa shogunate in 1614, early in the Edo period.

A small chapel had been hewn into the rock. Halfway up the zig zag path was a stone cistern, with a spring, and two ladles left for those who wished to purify themselves. The chapel, shuttered, was reached by a flight of timber steps. The altar was like a tiny church itself, pink and blue, with a square and then a rectangle, inside of which a miniscule, faded crucifix could be seen. A small white paper offering, a *gohei*, stood on the ground before it. A priest had sheltered here in the seventeenth century and the local *daimyo*, or lord, for unknown reasons, tolerated his presence. So must everyone else have done. Taketa is small; people must have known about this chapel at the time, yet said nothing about it.

At the railway station Mayu went to redeem more of her vouchers while I walked down to the river bank and found several wide flights of stone stairs descending into the water — as if there had been mass baptisms; or festivals where it was necessary to cleanse yourself. It seemed like something you would be more likely to see in India than in Japan; but then again, what do I know? I found Mayu down at the railway station shop, trying to make up the ¥8,000 in credit with postcards and sweets. The woman serving her said that local businesses were grateful for the scheme and that the compensation they receive in cash from the government was crucial and helped them stay afloat.

We drove on, through cedar forests, past roadside depots, where the logs were stacked in neat piles, all trimmed and sorted according to their circumference, which was painted in red numbers on the big end of each trunk, awaiting the trucks that would take them hence. Some plots of trees were clear-felled, leaving the usual devastation behind, but among the stumps and the debris of the slash line the seedlings of their successor trees were already growing. In the Edo period you had to ask permission before felling a cedar tree; if it was granted, you had to plant another in its place. Unauthorized felling of a tree was punishable by death.

Takachiho

The Shinto gods, called kami, resemble, in some respects, the gods of Olympus, in that they make up a family, with complex, often difficult, relationships with each other; like the Greek gods, they often behave as badly or worse than humans do. There are multiple versions of their stories too, with local variations which are usually held to be, and never are, definitive. The sovereign deity in the Shinto pantheon is, however, unlike the Greek and other Indo-European pantheons, female: Amaterasu, the sun goddess. It is from her that the unbroken imperial line, which still rules today, descended. For some reason, many of the stories about her are clustered in and around Takachiho.

The town is built on a slope descending towards a deep and spectacular gorge; the hotel was on the left about a third of the way down. Our room was on the second floor of a traditional *ryokan*, with tatami mats on the floor, beautiful woven bamboo ceilings and pale green venetian blinds which filtered the winter light to a pattern of shadows on the ochre walls. There were no lifts and no onsen either. An ordinary bath did duty instead, a simulacrum, filled with water heated on the premises and including some mysterious additives which, the chatelaine told us, were good for the body. After a couple of immersions, I decided she was probably right.

The next morning we drove a few kilometres out to Amanoiwato, on the Iwato River, to see if we could find the place where, long ago, the goddess Amaterasu had hidden herself away after an argument with her younger brother, Susanoo, the storm god, left her feeling angry and ashamed. There are two sanctuaries at Amanoiwato, an east and a west. They stand among groves of ginkgo, magnolia and other sacred trees. There are some fine examples here of *Magnolia compressa*, an evergreen and a native, called, in Japanese, Ogatama, 'summoning spirits'. As we paid our respects at the West Sanctuary, I saw a woman and a man, side by side, praying. They finished, clapped their hands twice, and turned away. Even though she was smiling, the woman's face was wet with tears.

I heard a cock crow, with a long melancholy after cry, sounding the unutterable sorrow of the world. Two splendid roosters perched on a railing next to the sanctuary; later, with another cock and a hen, they wandered across the path and went foraging, or dust bathing, in the gardens on the other side. I'm not sure what kind of bird they were, perhaps *satsumagori*, a local variety used in cock-fighting. They actually resembled the jungle fowl, the ultimate ancestors of all domesticated chickens; but were more likely bred, over many centuries, from exotic Chinese or South East Asian stock. Their presence was explained later, when I heard the rest of the story of the return of Amaterasu from her self-imposed exile in a cave in the cliffs above the river.

After the sun goddess sequestered herself in the cave, darkness fell upon the earth. The other gods gathered together to work out what they were going to do. They met in another cave further up the river and there was a path you could take to see this cave. It ran beside the rushing Iwatogawa, deep in the ravine below then, as we climbed, tumbled over rapids beside us. People had gathered small stones to make cairns; they were everywhere, on the rocks beside the river, on the big boulders which lay scattered here and there, on the muddy surrounds of the path. Some were tiny and some quite large; some approximated, how I do not really know, the shape of a buddha. All were ingenious and somehow tender too. They represented wishes or prayers.

The cave opened under a vast proscenium and when I stood at the altar of the shrine within for a moment or two, the air was still and cold and the presence of the other world, just centimetres away, beyond the stone curtain, very strong. When I looked back into the sublunary world, I could see the pale red flowers with yellow centres on a wild camellia tree whose branches bent over the cave mouth. I could easily imagine the clamorous meeting of the gods, numbered in the thousands or even millions, distraught because of the darkness of the sun that had fallen upon the world.

We still hadn't found the cave where the goddess had hidden herself. It turned out to be on the opposite bank of the river, and the only way to see it was to take a guided tour. We waited, with about twenty others, on seats beneath a canopy until a tall, aloof young man dressed in white robes joined us. After purifying us, he unlocked a gate, and we walked around the back of the West Sanctuary to the Far Precinct, a lookout, and gazed across the river at something that resembled a rock fall more than it did a cave. There had been many changes since the goddess sequestered herself here: floods, earthquakes and other ravages of time. Once there had been a path along which you could walk to the cave; but the stones of the path had disintegrated and fallen into the river and now it was closed.

When the gods met in the cave up the river, Omoikane, the god of wisdom, was asked to come up with a plan to entice Amaterasu out of her self-imposed exile. He gathered some roosters, whose crowing announces the sunrise, and hung a mirror and some jewels in the branches of a sakaki tree, a flowering japonica, growing in front of the cave. Then the goddess of dawn, Uzume, began to dance. Her movements became more seductive, more lascivious and when she showed her breasts, and perhaps her other parts too, the gods roared their appreciation. Amaterasu became curious. She couldn't help wanting to know what was happening. 'How,' she asked, 'can the gods still celebrate in a world plunged into darkness by my absence?'

She was told it was because they had found a goddess more beautiful than she was, which made her even more curious, and she came out of her cave to see who her rival was. However, instead of Uzume, she saw her own image in the mirror hung amongst the jewels in the branches of the sakaki tree and became entranced by her own beauty. While she was thus distracted, the gods threw a *shimenawa*, a sacred rope made of rice straw, across the cave mouth to prevent her going back in. Then Tajikarao, god of strength and power, picked up the stone that had closed the cave and threw it so high, wide and far that it came down on Honshu, far to the north. That door became the great wall of mountains at Togakushi, near Shinanomachi, where we live now.

The Takachiho Gorge on the Gokase River is a far more spectacular place than the relatively homely surrounds of Amanoiwato. It was also more populated with tourists, amongst whom there were some *gaijin* — the first we had seen on Kyushu. You could hire boats and row them into the gorge below the waterfall, a pastime popular with young lovers. The wooden dinghies looked precarious to me, especially in the hands of amateurs, and I noticed there was a safety officer, with a motor boat, stationed on the water in case of emergencies. He was looking at his mobile phone.

Here too, when you walked upriver, the path had been wrecked by a recent flood and closed off. The gorge had been formed, at some distant date, by an eruption of Mt Aso — some inconceivably large event, like the past eruptions of the caldera that is Lake Taupō in New Zealand. Grey, hexagonal, basalt columns plunged into aqua water; in an artificial pond, the shadowy shapes of river sturgeon, big as sharks, ghosted below a meniscus scattered with fallen petals. Outside the restaurant where we ate lunch, in vertical tanks full of turbulent water, a profusion of silver fish destined for the table twisted and turned as if trying to escape their inevitable fate.

That night we went to a performance at the local shrine, up a stone staircase towards the bottom of the main street of town. Kagura Hall was a handsome building with a stage at one end. About a hundred people gathered, sitting on cushions on the floor, to watch four out of a cycle of thirty-three dances, sometimes performed in its entirety at a local village. Such performances begin in the early evening, go through the night and continue on until the middle of the next day. Masked and gowned figures, with minimal props, to flute and drum accompaniment, turned slowly and repetitively on the bare stage.

We saw the Dance of Tajikarao, who was looking for Amaterasu's hiding place; the Dance of Uzume, the goddess of dawn, who finally enticed her out of her cave (although in this iteration it did not seem in the least bit suggestive, let alone erotic); the Dance of Removing the Door (Tajikarao again); then, as a coda, and light relief, the Goshintai Dance, starring a couple dressed as peasants representing the creator gods, Izanagi and Izanami. They mimed the making of saké, the drinking of it, and their subsequent drunkenness. In a village show, at this point, they would begin to flirt with members of the audience and things might get raucous, not to say salacious. Here, however, they just went, decorously, abstractedly, through the motions.

Between dances the band leader gave detailed explanations of what they meant. 'When the dancers wear masks,' he said, 'their bodies belong to the gods and the gods speak through them. When, however, they dance without masks, they dance in order to honour the gods.' A curious distinction. Alas, it was one of the longest hours of my life. I had — but I don't know how — injured my left knee walking up the one hundred stone steps to the hall. When it became too painful to sit on the floor I stood up and leaned against a pillar at the side of the room instead. Even so, the prolonged period of immobility made the injury worse: going down the steps afterwards was far more agonising than climbing up them had been. I limped, in the cracking cold, back up the hill to the ryokan.

On the Highway of the Stories of the Gods

Takachiho is famous for its beef, and at the local market, where we paused for a hot drink before setting out to drive south down the Highway of the Stories of the Gods, there were two big black shiny statues of a bull and a cow, the bull behind the cow, the cow smaller. Sometimes on the road we passed byres where these animals are kept. They were long low sheds with shallow peaked roofs and wall panels that could be opened or closed. Warm in winter but not so salubrious in summer perhaps. I never saw where pigs were kept, nor chooks, even though pork and chicken feature on nearly every restaurant menu. Mutton, more usually called lamb, however, because it is such a strong meat, isn't popular; people would rather eat horses. Or whales.

We were on our way to Saito, where there are burial mounds from early in the Common Era, called the late Yayoi and the Kofun periods. It was another fine day, with a porcelain blue sky overhead as we drove through the outskirts of the city and then into a landscape of dry yellow grass, with mounds everywhere, interspersed with fields where canola, tea and other crops were growing. There was something pleasing about the preservation of ancient monuments among working fields. The tea, which I'd never seen before, was grown in long rows of low rounded hedges, immaculately manicured, like topiary. I picked a couple of leaf tips and tasted them: bitter, astringent, certainly tea. It was destined to become green tea, of course or, roasted, brown; not black, which few Japanese people drink.

At the end of the road was the Saitobaru Archaeological Museum, a brutalist structure with a square main building like a military fort made of blocks of stone, a low administration area to one side and a flight of stone steps leading upwards on the other to some unknown beyond. The entrance mimicked the doorway into a tomb and, once we had bought our tickets and gathered our pamphlets, we found that the displays were all underground, in complex, strikingly lit spaces in which you could trace the progress of various ancient cultures through time.

People lived here before the great volcanic eruptions of 20,000 years ago and thus also before the last Ice Age. Human occupation of the archipelago probably first began forty or fifty thousand years ago, when there were land bridges both in the north and south. The Sea of Japan was a lake, and you could walk from what is now Korea, or what is now Siberia, into these islands. Quite probably two different populations did in fact follow those two routes; they were both most likely big game hunters, following herds of elephant and moose. After the ice came six horizons (a scholarly construct) of Jomon people, who were themselves various, not uniform, and who inhabited the land for an estimated 15,000 years. They were hunter gatherers who also cultivated fruit and nut bearing trees, including peach trees; the lacquer tree; and domesticated soy and azuki beans. What language(s) they spoke isn't known.

One of the maps from late in the Jomon period showed there was once a trade in shells, specifically scallop shells, to and from the Pacific coast of Kyushu via the Ryukyu Islands, Taiwan, the northern Philippines, coastal New Guinea and western Melanesia. Later, according to linguistic evidence, there was contact between Jomon people and speakers of Austronesian languages. It's now thought that the ancestors of the Austronesians came out of coastal China into northern Taiwan around 4000 BCE and spread rapidly south from there into South East Asia, west as far as Madagascar, east as far as South America where they left some of their chickens behind and picked up the sweet potato called the kumara. It's inconceivable, it seems to me, that these people didn't also come to Japan.

The Jomon were succeeded by the Yayoi, descendants of people who, fleeing long term drought and consequent desertification, moved from northern China eastwards into the Korean Peninsula, from which they were pushed out by further waves of people escaping the geographic processes which formed the Gobi Desert. The Yayoi were farmers who pioneered wet rice cultivation in Japan early in the first millennium BCE. There is some evidence that they arrived at, or just after, a time of extreme privation, if not famine, among the Jomon caused by a prolonged wet period during which people who lived away from the coast were reduced to subsisting upon nuts and berries.

The Yayoi are thought to have spoken a Japonic language and to be ancestral to the Japanese people of today. There is still controversy as to whether they replaced the indigenous inhabitants or merged with them; the latter is the preferred version among Japanese prehistorians. In this museum there were some fairly dubious displays in which skulls were used as a basis for reconstructing how people looked, including one which purported to show the merging of Jomon and Yayoi features to make the 'typical' Japanese physiognomy. However various modern Japanese people may look, studies consistently show that 10-20% of their genome comes from the Jomon.

The tombs at Saito, called kofun, date from the third to the sixth century CE, an era also known as the Kofun period; like their predecessors, these people seem to have entered the archipelago from Korea. The Yayoi built square mounds for their great dead, surrounded by ditches, sometimes with protruding corners, whereas the Kofun mounds are usually circular, key-hole shaped, or made of two conjoined rectangles. There are examples on the Pacific north coast shaped like scallop shells. They are found all over Japan, including on islands in the Sea of Japan; more than a hundred and fifty thousand of them are extant, an extraordinarily large number it seems to me.

Chinese sources from early in the Common Era describe the Japanese of the late Yayoi or early Kofun as people they called the *Wo* or the *Wa*. They lived on raw fish, vegetables and rice served on bamboo or wooden trays, clapped their hands in worship (as is still done at Shinto shrines today) and made earthen grave mounds. The Wa cultivated mulberry bushes and silkworms, maintained master-vassal relationships, collected taxes, built granaries, held markets and mourned their dead. They were warlike, and violent struggles between neighbouring principalities were common. So was decapitation: headless skeletons have been unearthed at Yoshinogari, a large Yayoi archaeological site in Saga Prefecture in north eastern Kyushu.

Most of the tombs we saw at Saito were circular, though there were examples of keyhole shaped ones there too. Some were quite substantial, others tiny. Many remain unexcavated and their contents, perforce, unknown. There was one you could go into. It was a large round mound raised inside what had once been two concentric moats. You reached it by climbing a staircase over a rampart then going down the other side and along a broad path to the entrance. Unlike most of the tombs at Saito, it lacked an inscribed stone marker on the top indicating who was buried there. Legend says it was made in a single night by an ogre lamenting the death of the woman he loved.

Through the dark door there was a plain, rectangular chamber with massive stones set in the roof, smaller blocks making the walls, and a cobbled floor which may or may not have been original. It was cool inside and you felt faced with the simple fact of mortality: only the bones and the accoutrements of whoever the person had been could occupy such a small space. This one was from the late sixth century CE and by then the graves tended to be full of military hardware, including iron swords and daggers, rather than the mirrors and jewels which were common earlier.

⛩

On the outskirts of the city of Miyazaki, in a forest of pine trees, is the pond in which Izanagi purified himself after he returned from Yomi-no-Kuni, the underworld, where he had gone to rescue his sister / wife Izanami, who died from her burns while giving birth to the last of their children, Kagutsuchi, the god of fire. In his grief Izanagi beheaded their son and cut his body into eight pieces, each of which became a volcano. Then he went to rescue Izanami. He found her in the underworld, seemingly the same as she had been in life; but when he broke his promise not to look directly at her, he saw that her body was in fact rotten, maggot-infested and stinking. She had, like Persephone, eaten food while in the land of the dead and so become corrupted.

Izanagi fled. Izanami set off in pursuit, sending her retainers, her warriors, and the Hags of Yomi ahead; he distracted them with grapes, with bamboo shoots, and with peaches, which he threw down on the ground in front of them and which they stopped to eat. When Izanami herself came after him, he sealed the gates of hell with a boulder. In her fury she vowed to kill a thousand people a day. He countered by undertaking to create fifteen hundred new ones over the same period, and so it goes. He also declared the peach tree divine and sent it off to grow in the world of the living.

The pond, Misogi-ike, really a small lake, was oval, about a kilometre in circumference, and covered in light purple lily pads. In amongst them a solitary dabbler with a brown and white face fed upon lake weed, and on a couple of rocks half out of the water a dozen black turtles sunned themselves. They had a leathery look, and the black of their shells inclined towards the purple of the lily pads. The pine trees threw stark shadows across the brown grass of the pool's surrounds and at the four cardinal points gohei, bamboo poles with white paper banners on them, stood out in the water. It was while Izanagi was bathing here that he gave birth to the sun goddess out of his left eye, the moon god out of his right, and sneezed the storm god out of his nose.

鳥

On a hill in Miyazaki there are, in Heiwadai Park, about four hundred *haniwa* figures. Hollow and made of unglazed clay, they are displayed on mossy ground beneath the trees. They are replicas; the originals were funerary monuments placed upon or within burial mounds like the ones we had seen at Saito. They were common all over Japan, not just on Kyushu, and apart from human figures there were horses, sometimes armoured, birds, fish, boats and houses and many semi-mythological figures in human form. Those with wide open mouths, round eyes and one hand raised, greet and farewell you as you enter and leave Haniwa Garden. They represent dancing girls. Some of the figures are dignified, even tragic, but others are comical, and many look like they might have been actual portraits of real people, though we cannot of course be sure.

Haniwa are old and may originate as far back as the Jomon period, when *dogu* figures, small humanoid or animal effigies made of clay, were sometimes placed in graves. If they were human, they are usually seen as representing women, often pregnant. There are suggestions that haniwa may have been used as replacement figures when human sacrifice at the death and burial of a notable person was discontinued. Something similar happened with the Ancient Egyptians who, during the Old Kingdom, began to employ ranks of shabti figures, made of clay, instead of live sacrifices to serve their great dead in the afterlife.

In the Yayoi period earthenware figurines and bowls were placed on the tops of the tombs of leaders, sometimes in a circle: 'haniwa' in fact means clay cylinder or circle of clay. Most of those we saw in Haniwa Garden were from the Kofun period when, as well as human and animal figures, fans, weapons, shields, sunshades and pillows made out of clay were also used to decorate graves. Haniwa figures may have been thought of as repositories for the souls of the dead, and the other items as household goods they would use in the afterlife. They had an endearing, child-like quality, somehow suggesting that the afterlife might take place in a realm of make believe.

Near Haniwa Garden, over a circular lawn, a white magnolia tree was flowering, dropping its fragrant, anise-scented, pink lined petals onto the grass below. Two pigeons with green wings and blue beaks grazed on mossy ground beneath the trees. As we were walking back to the car, we came across an aviary in which half a dozen somewhat bedraggled white doves were kept. Over all stood a stone column, the Peace Tower, completed in 1940 at the height of Japanese imperial expansion, just before the attack on Pearl Harbour. The stones from which the tower was built were gathered from all over the nascent empire: throughout the archipelago, including offshore island groups; Korea and Manchuria; Sakhalin Island; the Ryukyus; Taiwan and Hainan; the Mariana, Marshall and Caroline Islands; and those parts of mainland China the Japanese controlled, from Shanghai to Nanjing to Wuhan.

The ostensible reason for its construction was to memorialize the instalment of Japan's legendary first Emperor, Jimmu, the direct descendent, some say, of the sun goddess. Its original name was Hakko-ichiu, 'eight crown cords, one roof', a mystical phrase signifying the divine right of the Japanese to unify the eight corners of the world and a martial slogan used by the Japanese Imperial Army. It was inscribed upon the tower itself. During the Occupation, however, the Americans told their puppet government — which included bona fide war criminals and unreconstructed right-wing nationalists — to remove the incendiary words from the tower and give it a new name. Hence, Peace Tower.

Aoshima

We'd had a week of fine clear weather until, on the afternoon we drove into Miyazaki, a haze began to thicken the air and, next day, we woke to light rain which became heavier as the morning wore on. Our hotel was beside the Oyodo River and from the seventh floor, looking seaward, I could count half a dozen bridges, including a narrow red railway bridge which was sometimes crossed, spectacularly, by trim, purple-black trains. Miyazaki was one of the sixty-seven Japanese cities firebombed by the Americans during the war but it looked as if downtown might have survived. The footpaths along the main street were shaded by hooped verandas made from a kind of opaque plastic which had gone a pinkish-yellow colour and evoked the glamorous 1920s; and when we drove in the misty rain out of the city, it was along a highway lined with immensely tall palm trees like the Mexican Fan Palms, *Washingtonia robusta,* you see in Los Angeles.

Aoshima (Blue Island) was half an hour away. The rain was so heavy the road was covered in sheets of water; but the downpour eased as we turned off the highway, drove into a small seaside village, parked the car and made our way out to the causeway which leads to the island. It was low tide and on either hand we could see a strange formation known as the devil's washboard: long parallel lines of knobbly raised and tilted rock. These structures were made of mud and sand laid down on the ocean floor in the Miocene, seven million years ago, then uplifted. The hard sandstone and the soft mudstone eroded at different rates under the ebb and flow of the tide and thus the washboard pattern was formed.

A cold northerly blew across as we walked along the causeway towards the big red *torii* gate to the sacred precinct. The characters for 'torii' can be translated as a resting place for birds and perhaps that's what they originally were; to walk through a torii, as we did, is to leave the mundane world behind and enter the realm of the gods. Aoshima is roughly circular, a few kilometres in diameter, and covered with a dense growth of palms. These were identified as 'biro palms' on an information board, but are actually a variety called *Livistona chinensis* whose seeds were, most likely, carried north from the Ryukyu Islands on warm ocean currents many thousands of years ago and endemic here ever since. They flourish especially well in the wet micro-climate of the island.

The shrine, which you enter from the south about a quarter of the way around the island, is known for its *en musubi* — the power to initiate, bring together or bind people into relationships. 'En' (fate, connection, chance) is a concept which deserves an essay of its own; 'musubi' means to bind. It must work. While Mayu paid her respects at the altar, I watched a beautiful young woman in a wheelchair reading aloud in the rain from one of the scrolls you can buy (donation only) with your fortune inscribed upon it. Her girlfriend, also young and beautiful, held an umbrella over both of them. When the girl reading reached the end of her recitation, they looked at each other and smiled with such joy that it lit up the whole gloomy afternoon.

The shrine at Aoshima is connected with the story of two brothers, Hoderi and Hoori, the sons of Ninigi, the grandson of Amaterasu, and the man who brought rice cultivation to Japan. Their mother was Sakuya-hime, the Blossom Princess, whose portrait we had seen on the wall of Max's kominka in Kikuchi. Hoderi was a fisherman and possessed a magic hook, given to him by his father, with which he could catch any fish in the sea. His younger brother Hoori was a hunter who could bring down any animal in the forest with his magic bow and arrows. Hoderi was jealous of Hoori, however, because he could hunt in any weather, whereas Hoderi could not go fishing when the sea was rough. He proposed that the two swap their professions, their tools, and their luck; Hoori agreed.

Hoderi turned out to be a poor huntsman and Hoori an indifferent fisherman; furthermore, he lost Hoderi's magic hook somewhere beneath the waves. Hoderi was furious and would not be placated, not even when Hoori broke up his own sword and made five hundred replacement hooks from the pieces. Hoori had no choice but to go down under the waters of the ocean to look for his brother's hook. There he met Owatatsumi, the Dragon Lord of the Kingdom under the Sea and his daughter Toyotama. He and Toyotama fell in love and got married. It was at Aoshima that Hoori came ashore with his bride; hence its reputation for en musubi.

Owatatsumi also helped Hoori search for the missing fishhook, which they found caught in the throat of a sea-bream. When Hoori, who was homesick, returned with Toyotoma to land, he brought with him the magic hook and also two jewels Owatatsumi had given him. One raised the tide and the other lowered it. Hoderi, still angry, attacked his brother as soon as he saw him, whereupon Hoori used the first jewel to raise the waters, so that Hoderi began to drown. Hoderi pleaded for his life, Hoori relented, and with the second jewel made the waters recede. In gratitude Hoderi vowed that he and his descendants would serve his brother and his children in perpetuity; they became the Hayato, the soldiers who guard the emperor's palace. Hoderi remains a god of fisherman and of the bounty of the sea; while the son of Hoori and Toyotama, Ugayafukiaezu, fathered Jimmu, the first Emperor, with Toyotama's sister, his aunt Tamayori.

This tale of the hunter and the fisherman reminded me of two stone age toolkits exhibited in the museum at Saito. One belonged to fisher folk, the other to those who lived by hunting; they were distinct from each other for thousands of years before rice cultivation arrived, with the Yayoi, early in the first millennium

BCE. Whether they represented two different peoples, or were two different technologies used by the same people, wasn't clear; but the father of the brothers, Ninigi, who brought the rice, does sound like an avatar of the Yayoi; and his 'sons' like moieties of the indigenous people coming to terms with the new economic paradigm that agriculture established.

It is also the case that in the old chronicles Hayato people and Kumaso people are mentioned as semi-legendary occupants of Japan before, during, and after the arrival of the Yayoi. Some scholars believe the Kumaso ('bear people') were Austronesian speakers; while it has been suggested, less plausibly, that the Hayato ('falcon people') were Austronesians too. Both peoples (if they were not two expressions of the same culture) lived in Kyushu and both had a history of violent opposition to the Yayoi before their eventual assimilation, submission or destruction. It's perhaps fanciful to associate the falcon people with the sea and the bear people with the land; but it isn't inconceivable that they might have had such affiliations. If so, the Hayato and the Kumaso could also stand behind the story of Hoderi and Hoori.

Sun Messe and the Cave of Milk

It was a fine clear day as we headed south down the same avenue of palms we'd driven in the rain the day before. We passed the turn off to Aoshima and continued on until we saw an Easter Island statue, a Mo'ai, standing somnolent and grim in the brown grass on the right hand side of the road: the gateway to a theme park called Sun Messe Nichinan. The road wound up towards an extraordinary pink building at the top of the hill, which included an observatory, a museum and a tower with a Peace Bell — which is illuminated by the sun's rays at the summer solstice. These rays also pass over the central figure on a platform of seven Mo'ai figures set up below the pink building and above the sea, facing inland.

The sound of Polynesian chants echoed from above, recordings I think. They sounded both incongruous and deeply familiar: hearing te reo Māori, or rather one of its close cousins, so far from home made me nostalgic for something I could not quite remember. Families picnicked on the grass in front of the Mo'ai and a group of uniformed school children, mostly boys, shrieking with happiness, played amongst the giant statues, all of which had small piles of coins left as offerings in front of them. As I stood in the shade of a palm tree watching the children play, a little girl about five years old came and stood before me, looking solemnly up as if I might have been a Mo'ai myself.

The park opened in 1996. Sometime previous to that, a Japanese company spent three years helping restore fifteen toppled Mo'ai on Rapanui / Easter Island; permission for these replicas to be made was given as a gesture of thanks by ranking elders on the island. They are sculpted out of Fukushima tuff, the closest local stone to the material used on Rapanui, and represent a specific formation called Ahu Akivi. On most of the platforms on Rapanui the Mo'ai face inwards, away from the sea, looking over the villages of the people whose ancestors and protectors they are; Ahu Akivi, however, it is said, faces the sea. Nor is it, as most other platforms are, on the coast, but inland. Ahu Akivi is also precisely aligned, so that the Mo'ai face the sunset at the spring equinox.

The originator of Sun Messe was an eccentric who conceived the park as a contribution to world peace. The inward-looking, solstice-aligned statues are, to his mind, projecting the ancient wisdom of Rapanui across the Pacific Ocean into Japan. Perhaps for this reason the place has become a shrine in its own right. Each of the seven figures represents one of a set of desirable attributes or attainments and people pray to them in the hope that those attainments and attributes might come into being, for themselves or for humankind. They are: good health, true love, peace on earth, a happy marriage, luck with money, success in work, and high academic achievement.

Their significance on Rapanui is different. Legend has it that a priest in the service of Hotu Matua, the first *ariki mau* (high chief) of the island, had a dream in which Hotu Matua's soul flew across the ocean and saw Rapanui, uninhabited, below him. The priest then sent scouts out to try to locate this dream island. Seven of them found the place and stayed there, awaiting the arrival of Hotu Matua; it is these seven who are commemorated at Ahu Akivi and at Sun Messe. At Ahu Akivi the Moa'ai are more or less the same size but at Sun Messe there is some variation between them. I don't know what, if any, significance these variations may have. Nor do I know why the statues at Sun Messe lack the red topknots the Rapanui ones have or would once have had.

The date of Rapanui's settlement is disputed. It might be as early as 400 CE or as late as 1200 CE. The settlers are said to have come from the lost land of Hiva, which is almost certainly the group now known as the Marquesas, still called the Hivas in some old chronicles. Ahu Akiva wasn't built until much later, in the sixteenth and seventeenth centuries, so its alleged commemorative function, if indeed true, comes long after the fact. It is also not certain that the platform and its Mo'ai were actually intended to face the sea. More likely, their alignment is tutelary with respect to the village they once overlooked. Ahu Akiva was built by, and in the territory of, the Miru, at the time the highest ranking clan on Rapanui.

I don't usually like theme parks but I loved Sun Messe. It was a hot sunny day, the views out over the blue Pacific were immense, the people who had come there that day seemed joyful, indeed exuberant, as people at shrines in Japan so often do. Worship is not usually performed in a state of solemnity, though there may be solemn moments devoted to prayer or thanks-giving. We fell in with a group of four twenty-something girls, and exchanged phones with them so that they could photograph us and we them, in front of and in amongst the Mo'ai. Even the statues seemed companionable, and not in the least regretful that their putative island home was nearly 14,000 kilometres away. Perhaps they were avatars of peace after all.

The turn off to the shrine at Udo-Jingu is a few kilometres past Sun Messe, leading on to a small peninsula, resembling Aoshima to the north. Here thick vegetation grew, including some fine examples of cycads, tree-sized, with many thick and branching trunks and glossy green-gold fronds. We parked next to the ruins of a building, a kiosk or a restaurant, climbed some metal stairs, walked through a long dark tunnel along which the cold north wind blew, then up and down a series of stone steps in which you could see how, over the years, the tread of the feet of countless pilgrims had worn away the stones. Udu-Jingu is old; people have been coming here for more than a thousand years.

Newlywed couples, seeking good fortune, would travel together, wearing traditional dress, including straw sandals, along the shore then climb the 715 steps to Udo-Jingu. It is said that a Buddhist nun carried the stones to make these stairs, one by one, on her head up from the beach. The shrine is on the northern side of the peninsular, perched high above the ocean and reached by a cliff path. It looked out over sea-washed, extravagantly shaped rock formations, volcanic in origin. They resembled, to my mind, the gnarled outcrops over which the robed and mitred bishops clamber in the Bunuel / Dali film, *L'Age D'Or*.

The shrine stands at the mouth of the cave in which Toyotama gave birth to Ugayafukiaezu, the father of the first of the imperial line. Hoori was making Toyotama a birthing shelter out of cormorant feathers when she went into labour. She knew that, in the process of giving birth, she would revert to her ancestral shape and, not wanting Hoori to see her like that, retreated into this cave and asked him not to watch. Of course he looked, saw her transform into a dragon and was repulsed. She fled below the sea and they never saw each other again. Their son, however, survived, suckling upon fluid expressed from two breast-shaped rocks at the back of the cave. Later Toyotama sent her sister Tamayori to foster the child. Later still, he married her, even though she was both his aunt and his foster-mother. They became the parents of Jimmu, the first Emperor.

At the back of the cave there were indeed two breast-shaped protuberances in the moist, dripping darkness and they did give forth a cloudy liquid. They were lit by the light of a single red lantern and looked both monstrous and companionable. I would have liked to have tasted the milky secretion but did not want to cause offence. There were other pilgrims passing by and each one would pause and pray and then clap twice over the breast-shaped rocks; so I left whatever it was unsampled. Water, probably, with minerals held in cloudy suspension.

The shrine itself, massive, crimson, built of wood, had some external panels carrying enigmatic paintings, the pigment of which had decayed and peeled, leaving behind imagery that was all the more evocative for its inscrutability. One was, I think, a tree growing before the waves of the sea and reaching towards a range of distant mountains; but when I looked at the photograph I took of it, what I thought was its trunk could just as easily have been the thick, dappled grey skin of some long-necked sea creature — Toyotama in her dragon shape perhaps.

From a stall in front of the shrine, for ¥200, you could buy five *undama*, small clay tokens like flattened marbles, which you threw one by one towards a rope marking out a circular pool on top of a sea-side boulder below. Men threw with their left hand, women with their right; if one of your clay tokens came to rest inside the rope circle, that meant good luck. All of mine missed; one of Mayu's knocked some other person's token into the circle. 'I've given my good luck to someone else,' she said, and laughed. On the way out we saw the four young women from Sun Messe again.

Kagoshima

The next morning, when I went to stand up, I couldn't. My left knee had locked and to straighten it was extremely painful. I felt like I might fall over, which would have caused a degree of chaos in our tiny room. We were in a business hotel called the Lexton on the fringes of the red light district of Kagoshima. The city was built on the shores of a bay which is the rim of another massive caldera, formed after a blow-out-and-cave-in eruption of the Aira volcano 22,000 years ago. It was overlooked by the perpetually steaming volcano Sakurajima. The name means island of cherry blossoms and refers to the way, during its frequent eruptions, a multitude of incandescent red lights climb into the sky then fall like petals into the sea.

The knee had been bothering me ever since I'd felt a muscle at the back of it tear when we were walking up the steps to the dance performance at the shrine in Takachiho a few days previously. I'd been managing it without too much trouble and without having to modify our (largely improvised) schedule too drastically, though there were places I could not go, for instance the ornate pink palace on top of the hill at Sun Messe. This was different. This was serious. For about a quarter of an hour I stretched, limped around the room, massaged the muscles behind my knee and swore, until I felt strong enough to go for the walk we'd planned to nearby Francis Xavier Park.

The park was a dusty rectangle of bare earth with an ornate archway at one end and a bust of the saint (head and shoulders only) on a plinth, with two clipped conifers behind. The saint's helpers were memorialised nearby, three Japanese who appeared, bizarrely, under their Portuguese baptismal names. They were smaller and lower than he, perhaps because in real life that would have been the case; perhaps because, in the light of eternity, they are of less significance than the Basque hidalgo turned Jesuit missionary. His father had been seneschal of a castle in Navarre. Opposite was a large, ugly, modern Christian cathedral, made of concrete, steel and glass, where a wedding was in progress. Women in bright dresses, men in dark suits, passed up and down the staircase and into and out of the church.

There was another white marble statue of Francis Xavier there, full bodied, with his arm flung out in a characteristic pose. I remember seeing one like it in Malacca, on top of a hill overlooking the town, before the ruin of a church which had lost its roof and become a refuge for homeless people. That statue had lost its outflung arm and I wondered then if the saint had too? Not exactly. Xavier once claimed to have performed so many baptisms he could no longer raise his right arm. After the saint's death that arm, which turned out to be incorruptible, became a holy relic and is still, on occasion, taken out on tours of catholic dioceses. Xavier, however, remained one of the two armed men of the world until his death, aged forty-six, from fever, in 1552, on Changchun Island off the coast of China.

One of the three helpers, Anjiro (sometimes Yajiro), baptised in Goa under the name Paulo de Santa Fé, is accounted the first Japanese Christian. His story is a curious one. He came from a Kagoshima samurai family and, in circumstances which remain unclear, killed a man and went on the run to avoid the consequences. He sought refuge on board a Portuguese trading vessel in Kagoshima Bay, the captain of which, Alvaro Vas, offered him a position in the crew. Anjiro accepted but when the time came to leave, boarded the wrong ship and ended up on another one whose captain, Jorge Álvares, was a personal friend of Francis Xavier. Álvares took him to Malacca and introduced him to Xavier. Anjiro arrived towards the end of 1547 and met the saint-to-be in December of that year. He was thirty-six years old; Xavier was forty-one.

Álvares had already given Xavier positive reports of Japan; his arrival with a Portuguese-speaking national must have seemed providential. Anjiro had learned enough of the language on board ship to tell Xavier about his home country, which he did in extravagant terms, while Xavier began to teach his acolyte the rudiments of Christian doctrine. They went to Goa, where Anjiro was baptised into the church and studied Portuguese at St Paul's College. When Xavier set out for Japan, in April, 1549, Anjiro went with him as his interpreter.

Two other Japanese Christians were included in the entourage of seven, one of them Anjiro's servant. The rest of the party was made up of two more Jesuit priests and their servants, a Chinese and a Mlabri from Siam. Xavier went first to Malacca where, pragmatically, and in the absence of any other option, he chartered a Chinese pirate ship for the voyage to Japan. They left on Midsummers Day, visited Canton, and were moored off Kagoshima by the fifteenth of August, 1549. Initially, at least, the daimyo of the Satsuma clan, Shimazu Takahisa, was prepared, for the purpose of encouraging commerce, to tolerate these new people and allowed them to proselytise.

This seems to have been, in part, because of a misunderstanding perpetrated, wittingly or not, by Anjiro. He was not a scholarly man and could not, for instance, read Chinese, as all educated Japanese at that time could. He had been raised a Shingon Buddhist and in his translations called the Christian God Dainichi, Great Sun, a Japanese term for the Buddha. Because of this, and because the Jesuit party had come from India, many believed they were preaching a new kind of Buddhism. It was some time before Xavier realised what had happened; he was appalled when he did.

He spent the best part of a year in Kagoshima, living with Anjiro's family then, when things became difficult, moved to Hirado on the north-west coast of Kyushu. By this time Shimazu Takahisa had ceased to tolerate Christians and become their sworn enemy, furious because the majority of Portuguese merchants, rather than using Kagoshima, had decided they preferred to trade in and out of Hirado. Trade was always an inducement for daimyo to entertain missionaries, whom they thought of, not erroneously, as facilitators. Hirado was an ancient port out of which trade with Korea and China to the west had proceeded for centuries; whereas Kagoshima looked south to the Ryukyus, Taiwan and the Philippines.

From Hirado, Xavier set out for Kyoto, where he hoped to convert the emperor, his shogun, and through them the entire population of Japan. He travelled via Yamaguchi, on the southern tip of Honshu, where he was well received, but found, in Kyoto, that the only way he could have an audience with Emperor Go-Nara was by paying a large sum of money, which he either did not have or would not give. This was still the period of Sengoku jidai (1467-1568), the country at war, and the capital was in disorder. Xavier returned to Yamaguchi where, having understood what Dainichi meant, proclaimed in the streets of the town that the word for God was, always had been, and always would be, Deus, and that Dainichi was a demon. This did not endear him to the Bonzes, the Buddhist clergy, who from this time forth opposed the Jesuits.

In Kyoto, Xavier also learned that the Japanese were unimpressed by the Christian virtues of piety, humility and poverty, and changed his approach. He went next to Bungo, near Oita, on the east coast of Kyushu, where a Portuguese ship had arrived and where the local daimyo had asked to see him. Xavier arrived for the audience richly dressed in cassock, surplice and stole, and attended by thirty gentlemen and their servants; all likewise wearing their finery. They proceeded bearing cushions carrying treasures, including a portrait of the Madonna and a pair of velvet slippers. Xavier gave the daimyo letters and presents: a Spanish guitar, a watch, and other things from Goa which had been meant for the emperor. He was offered in return an old Buddhist building to use as a church and allowed to continue the work of conversion.

After just over two years in Japan, towards the end of 1551, Xavier returned to Goa. He had personally baptised about seven hundred and fifty people (that right arm!) and left behind a few thousand Christians in small congregations at Yamaguchi, Hirado and Bungo. Some scholars believe he avoided Kagoshima on his way south, because of the continuing hostility of Shimazu Takahisa, who was already executing converts. Anjiro was still there, however, tending to a small mission at Ichiki. It did not thrive and within a year or two of Xavier's departure, Anjiro was himself driven out of town. He went back to sea as a pirate, a *wako*, and died in a raid off the coast of China. Perhaps for this reason the Jesuits did not admit him into their pantheon of martyrs. He remains an enigma. A murderer before his decade as a Christian, a pirate afterwards, he was perhaps an opportunist, albeit a talented one, before anything else.

Xavier's early observations of Japanese culture noted that, whatever their status, most people were poor; that they were abstemious eaters but enthusiastic drinkers. They abhorred theft and anyone caught stealing was hunted down and killed. Rank was obsessively observed. No matter what their material condition might be, those of higher rank were always given both precedence and respect. These qualities are still found among many Japanese today. The Portuguese were less impressed by other aspects of the culture, and often remarked upon the habit the locals had of taking a hot bath every day, something they, who rarely bathed more than once a week, if then, accounted unhealthy. Xavier didn't comment on their personal hygiene but did say that the Japanese were the most civilized people he had yet encountered in the east and thus the ones most likely to receive the Word of God. Another Portuguese observer remarked, apropos of the piratical wako, but with a wider application, that the Japanese were 'lambs at home but wolves abroad.'

Even though it was just a few blocks away, we caught a cab to the Meiji Restoration Museum down by the Kotsuke River. It was one of those places organised around the great man (and, as an afterthought, the great woman) view of history. Banners on either hand were hung in a hallway leading to the main display room. Each included a portrait and brief biography of a significant actor in the drama. Probably because of their long history of contact with Europeans, and their consequent enthusiastic embrace of modernization, many of the drivers of the restoration came from Kyushu and particularly from the Satsuma domain, still ruled over today, as it was in Xavier's time, by the Shimazu family. These lords of southern Kyushu nurtured grievances dating back to the redistribution of wealth, power and land at the founding of the Tokugawa shogunate more than two hundred and fifty years before. They had long memories and played a long game.

The greatest of the Satsuma heroes was Saigo Takamori, a samurai who rose to power through force of character and native ability. For complex reasons — they had gone further than he thought they should in the destruction of the old ways — he ended up in rebellion against the Meiji government he had helped to install and died, along with most of his followers, in the Battle of Shiroyama, near Kagoshima, in 1877. Saigo was a big man; there was a life-sized statue of him in the museum. He has been mythologised: he survived and fled to Russia; or travelled to Mars, from which he will return in the form of a comet. At one of the ryokan we ate fish cakes for breakfast which had his image printed upon them. A kind of holy communion, I suppose.

I wasn't really interested in great men; I was hoping to find out more about the arrival of the Japanese sweet potato in the archipelago. It is usually known as the *satsuma imo* (potato from Satsuma) because the Shimazu clan of Satsuma were the first to grow and promote it as a food. In a curious coincidence, the delicious, yellow-fleshed, purple-skinned satsuma imo resembles, in both taste and appearance, the most popular New Zealand variety of kumara these days, the Owairaka red. Yet they seem to have arrived at their respective destinations down wholly different paths.

The first kumara came into the Pacific from South America, probably coastal Ecuador or northern Peru, to the Marquesas, and then travelled via Tahiti and the Cook Islands to Aotearoa early in the last millennium. The two other kinds of sweet potato found in South East Asia today were introduced by the Spanish and the Portuguese, respectively. The so-called *camote* lineage, from Mesoamerica, was brought about 1500 CE by Spanish galleons sailing between Mexico and Manila; while the *batata* lineage from the Caribbean came, via Europe, into South East Asia with Portuguese traders around about the same time. The Japanese sweet potato, a camote, made its way from the Spanish Philippines to Fujian in China, then across the sea to the Ryukyu Islands and thence into southern Kyushu. There, for generations, the Shimazu clan, centred on Kagoshima Castle, were responsible for its cultivation.

The Shimazu invaded the Ryukyus in 1609, early in the Edo period, and the island group remained a vassal state of theirs until annexed by the Meiji government into the Okinawa Prefecture in 1879. Perhaps, I thought, the advent of the sweet potato in Kyushu followed the Shimazu conquest. The myth of origin, however, credits a sailor named Riemon who, in 1705, returned from a voyage to Ryukyu bringing with him a new kind of food. People in southern Kyushu sometimes struggled because of poor rice harvests due to the warmer climate, rugged geography, volcanic soil, and numerous typhoons. This new crop, however, flourished in these conditions. The locals called it *kara imo*, or potato from China, as did the people of Ryukyu.

The success of sweet potato cultivation became known throughout the island, and eventually to the central government in Edo. One of the men responsible for popularizing it was the agronomist Aoki Kunyo, who always referred to it as satsuma imo. The volcanic soil of the gardens of Kagoshima prefecture are still the most prolific producers of the tuber. As for Riemon, who was not a samurai and so lacked a family name, he was given one, Maeda, and upon his death deified and enshrined at Tokko Shrine, informally called Kara imo Shrine, in Yamakawa. It wasn't really surprising that there was nothing about him among the accounts of great men in the Meiji Restoration Museum.

We walked back to the hotel but my knee was no better for the exercise. At a drug store along the way, I bought a pressure bandage and a packet of Voltaren plasters; the bandage helped, the plasters not so much. We ate that evening at the counter of a tiny restaurant around the corner in the red light district, while on the television Japan played Korea in the World Series baseball; the first of a number of matches we saw in eating houses in Kyushu. Then I limped back, on Mayu's arm, past the touts outside the girly clubs, the revellers and the lonesome wanderers, the couples all dressed up with somewhere to go, to the Lexton.

There was a gleaming black baby grand player piano in the corner of the lobby which, without anyone at the keys, gave forth ghostly music at all hours. There was also a kitsch display of artefacts, including a wooden boat, purporting to belong to the Ainu of Hokkaido, and the figure of a man, bigger than Saigo Takamori, dressed in bear skins. I spent a restless night trying to find a way of lying in bed that did not exacerbate the pain in my knee. I was starting to wonder if I would ever walk properly again.

Tokkotai

Next morning it was clear I wouldn't be able to get around without a stick. Mayu asked hotel reception for directions and they pointed us to a shop downtown, in an old-fashioned, open-walled, glass-roofed arcade between a big department store and a city hospital. I waited in the milky, antiquated light falling from above while she went on a reconnaissance. It was a Sunday morning and a few people were going quietly about their business. I saw a little girl riding a two-wheeled, polka-dotted wooden hobby horse down the arcade. Kagoshima, too, was fire-bombed, eight times between the eighteenth of March and the sixth of August 1945, causing thousands of deaths and thousands more injuries. These arcades, so spacious and so elegant, either survived the conflagration or were built afterwards.

The shop, a small boutique full of walking sticks of many different kinds, wasn't far away and there I bought, for ¥16,000, a splendid iridescent purple titanium stick made by Sinano, the ski manufacturers. It's adjustable and has a horizontal handle with a moulded rubber clasp. It also has a hard black plastic ferrule and a woven strap to go around your wrist, should you need it. It will probably last me the rest of my days. At first, I tried to use it in my left hand, on the same side as the gammy knee, but the woman who sold it to me indicated it was better utilised on the right. So it proved. She was in her fifties perhaps, friendly and kind. I said to her, 'You've saved my life.' She was very moved by this and stood outside her shop for a long time, watching us walk away.

We drove further south down the Satsuma Peninsula, turning inland to visit Chiran where, it is said, the best green tea in Japan is grown. It was a neat, well-ordered town on gently sloping land amid lush green hills. There was a ruined castle and the so-called Special Attack Peace Museum, where we didn't go. We did, however, visit a street of samurai houses which have been restored and conserved. There were seven of them and they had been impeccably maintained, with ornate gardens behind their severely clipped camellia hedges and their old wooden gates, most of which were closed on this particular day. In medieval Japan, samurai constituted a pool of warriors which a daimyo in his castle could call upon if and when he needed them. There were, of course, many more of them than the seven whose houses remained. The closer you lived to the castle, the higher your status.

Most of these houses were still inhabited. We only went into the yard of one. It was not lived in and open for viewing, although you could not go inside. We saw bare floors, bare walls; great wooden shelves with large ceramic storage jars upon them; a square, open hearth with a suspended hook from which a cooking pot hung; the altar at the back of the main room with framed family portraits leaning against the wall above; the god shelf with ancestor figures and the miniature, votive houses; the tatami mats and the *shoji* screens. The primary feeling was of a way of life of great austerity and discipline, which soft moderns, like us, would have found intensely uncomfortable.

Along the main street of the town, a stream had been confined to a small canal which ran parallel to the road, and where, in open ponds or beneath iron grills, multi-coloured carp lived. When I stood before one of the pools, all of the fish swam towards me and broke the surface of the water, opening their O-like mouths as if to say: 'Feed me! Feed me!' There were small antique water wheels set up at intervals along these miniature canals, not for any practical purpose, just to turn and gather ornamental beards of green weed. I saw some young boys intently examining the carp, who would become their exemplars when Boy's Day came around on the fifth of May, during Golden Week, and households flew their aspirational carp banners in the spring air.

Further down the road we visited a museum, in a small wooden two storey building which had once been the restaurant of a ryokan, whose accommodation wing was still extant behind, though not used for that purpose anymore. The museum commemorated those tokkotai who had stayed or eaten there in the days and nights before their final, fatal mission. 'Tokkotai' is an abbreviation of *tokubetsu kogeki tai* or special attack unit; they are commonly known in the west as kamikaze pilots. The proprietor, a woman called Torihama Tome, now long deceased, had played a maternal role for these doomed young men, who had all been told the last thing they'd see before they died would be their mother's face. There were many photos of Tome, and of her two daughters, and a section upstairs devoted to her afterlife, as it were, including her wheelchair and her walking stick (which I examined with interest).

Most of the land-based kamikaze missions were flown out of airfields on southern Kyushu (they also flew out of Okinawa and Taiwan) and there was one of these in the Chiran area. Various items of memorabilia were collected in the display cases. Two small grey pebbles, utterly insignificant, turned out to be the last things one of the pilots had seen before boarding his plane; he had picked them up and asked that they be sent to his mother. Another story told of two friends who had flown together on their last mission; one, because of bad weather, was forced to turn back. His friend told him that after he died, he would return as a firefly, and, sure enough, that night, a firefly had flown in the window of the room of the pilot who'd turned back. His fate was melancholy in the extreme. He had not been able to bear the shame of failure and, after various visits to his and his friend's families, he 'disappeared' — presumably a suicide.

You weren't supposed to take photos but I did take one picture of the tattered shoji screens drawn against the light from the street. When I look at it, it brings that place back to mind, tiny, full of faded and sometimes inscrutable memorabilia, in which at one point involuntary tears sprang to my eyes. Why, exactly, I could not say. Perhaps just because these pilots were so very young, some only seventeen years old and, contrary to popular understanding, often conscripts rather than fanatics who volunteered to sacrifice themselves for their country and their emperor. They were also commonly injected with amphetamine before taking off on their fatal mission. I wondered if the restaurant and ryokan might in fact have been a brothel set up especially for those about to die. We saw no sign of this but the possibility remains. There were certainly ryokans where married pilots could spend their last night on earth in the arms of their wives.

Our hotel at Ibusuki had a view, past a bank of solar panels, of the flat pale blue sea of the lower reaches of Kagoshima Bay. Here, while Mayu went to a nearby beach to have a hot sand bath, I consulted Doctor Google and discovered I had most likely torn my popliteus, a triangular muscle behind the knee.

> Despite its small size, the popliteus is a major stabilizing muscle of the knee. The popliteus is involved in both the closed chain phase and open-chain phase of the gait cycle. During the closed chain phase, which is when the foot is in contact with the ground, the muscle externally rotates the femur on the tibia. In the open-chain or swing phase of the limb, the popliteus acts to internally rotate the tibia on the femur.

No wonder I was having so much trouble walking. A torn popliteus is a common sports injury; sprinters and downhill skiers are particularly susceptible, and the cure is what I was already practicing. Rest, massage, artificial stabilisation, continued gentle activity, assisted walking. Whether because I now knew what it was, or because of the pressure bandage and the stick, the onsen and the hot baths, it was already improving. That thick swollen triangle behind my knee was becoming less swollen by the day. Along with the pain, the fear that my mobility might be permanently affected also began to recede. I started thinking I might be going to be alright after all.

That night there was a thunder storm out at sea. Lightning turned the windows white before they went black again. Silver rain slanted through the air. When it cleared, I saw fireflies tracing random, amber arcs upon the air. It was impossible not to think of the spirits of dead pilots returning to trouble, howsoever briefly, the living.

Nagasakibana Misaki

Not far from the hotel was a sign pointing off the road to another tokkotai memorial. It was a small shrine among trees on a knoll above the sea and commemorated navy pilots who had flown their sea-planes on suicide missions. They had taken off from the flat waters of the bay we could see glinting through the trees. The Japanese military had no air force; all their flyers were either members of the navy or the army. At the shrine, in the grass to one side, an upended propeller from a piston-engine aeroplane, like a mutant spider, had one of its three bent blades stuck into the soil. Next to that was a *kannon*, a goddess of mercy, in white marble with bunches of flowers laid before her. On the information board, below a blurry photograph of a sea-plane, I saw the skull of a small lizard which had crawled inside the glass case and died there.

We were heading for Nagasakibana Misaki, the cape at the tip of the Satsuma Peninsula. It isn't quite the southern-most point of Kyushu; Osumi Peninsula on the other side of Kagoshima Bay extends twenty kilometres further south. From the promontory, with its tiny lighthouse, we could see the pale blue outlines of islands further south. A map named the more distant ones and gave their distance away in kilometres. One was called Iwo Jima (Sulphur Island) but it wasn't *that* Iwo Jima. The Ryukyu Islands, of which Okinawa is the largest and best known, began down there, and the chain goes almost as far as the northern tip of Taiwan. This was another possible path for the sweet potato, not appropriated during military conquest, but island hopping peacefully north, in the hands of traders and fisherman, like Maeda Riemon, until it reached the mainland.

From Nagasakibana there were spectacular views of the near perfect cone of Mount Kaimon, about a thousand feet high and last active a thousand years ago. You can climb it in a few hours, taking a spiral path that winds around the mountain, but that was not an option for us today. We retraced out steps. In a low, open, wooden enclosure, reposed a white marble figure with a white marble bag slung over its shoulder and a bamboo fishing pole in one hand. Its other hand was held out in blessing over a sculpture of a turtle made from reddish stone. The enclosure was brim-full of white sea shells, left there as offerings. This was Urashima Taro and the story about him featured Toyotama, known here as Miss Otohime and sometimes depicted as a goldfish mermaid — another incarnation of the dragon woman who married Hoori.

Urashima, a fisherman, rescued a turtle, which was being tormented by some kids, and released it. The grateful turtle took him on its back down to Ryugu Palace under the sea. There Urashima fell in love with Otohime and she with him. However, after some happy years together, Urashima decided he wanted to return home. Otohime could not persuade him to stay, so she gave him, as a parting gift, a *tamatebako*, a jewelled box which, she said, contained the most important thing in the world. He was not to open it; if he did, they would never see each other again. When he reached home he discovered, like Rip Van Winkle, that many years had passed since he left and all those who knew and loved him had died. In his loneliness, unable to restrain his curiosity, he did open the box. He turned instantly into an old man and realised, inter alia, that the most important thing in the world is the span of your own life.

The information board upon which I read this version of the story went on to give some detail about the turtles at Nagasakibana. They still come ashore here to lay their eggs on sandy beaches, and the young turtles still hatch and flap down to the water and swim away into the ocean. Local fisherman call them 'the guardians of the sea' and treat any they catch in their seine nets with great solicitude, giving them saké to drink before setting them free again. The shrine at Nagasakibana, called the Ryugu Shrine, overlooks that pit full of shells where Urashima blesses the red turtle; because of its connection to his romance with Otohime, people go there to wish for a happy marriage, well-being for their family, and safety in voyages upon the sea.

At the souvenir shop you could buy satsuma imo slow baked in their jackets. They also offered free cups of green tea and a large variety of carved wooden goods, most of them extremely ugly, for sale. Among them were some actual carapaces of sea turtles. That didn't sit too well with the fishermen's alleged solicitude. There was a distinct Pacific theme noticeable among the other goods on offer, which included Hawaiian shirts. We used some of our coupons to buy a set of wooden chopstick pillows, *hashi-makura*, with designs upon them which could have come from Samoa or Tonga. Loggerhead turtles, so-called because, with their big heads and strong jaws, they can crush sea urchins and clam shells, do in fact cross the Pacific Ocean, from Japan to Mexico, on their migrations.

On the way back from the cape we had seen a monument set up beside the path to a poet, Shinohara Hosaku (1905-1936). He was born in Kagoshima, became a teacher on Okinawa, and died young, aged just thirty. A brain tumour perhaps. Or tuberculosis. Or both. Three of his *haiku* — or rather, since they lacked seasonal words, *muki* — were inscribed, vertically, side by side, on a rectangular stone. They read (in loose translation):

> There is still a mast | for voyaging through heaven | 's sky full of stars

> Sailing over seas | lungs become suffused with | the cool and the blue

> If you spend many days | on the ocean's blue waters | sea and sky become one

Mt Kaimon had the same near perfect profile from the other side. We drove around it on our way to Sea Horse House, a ramshackle building made out of drift wood, built above, and partially upon, a rocky shore. As soon as we walked up the rickety steps to the room with the aquariums, the proprietor, a woman, was at our elbow, pointing into one of the tanks.

'See,' she said. 'See! Babies!' They were tiny, mere threads of life, little strands of DNA. She'd left a magnifying glass next to the tank with which you could see them more distinctly. Beside another tank was a small crusty pile of the dead; not for sale. Everything in there, including the mobiles, the wall decorations, and the handmade souvenirs, related somehow to sea horses. The souvenirs were rough-hewn and unappealing; although SHH called itself a café, there was nothing to eat and only a few soft drinks available from a machine. We bought some postcards.

Outside, bizarre and complex plumbing was built across the rocks to supply water to the tanks inside; and in a series of dank, shallow pools, sea anemones and scarlet starfish with indeterminate numbers of arms were living. The concrete pillars supporting the building had scallop shells stuck to them with glue and secured by lengths of white cord wrapped round and round the poles. A small red shrine, homemade like everything else, was adorned with reliefs of white sea horses; in the centre, her hands clasped in prayer, was the figure of a woman. She wore a yellow jacket with a blue sash and had a fish carved onto her breast. I think this was another version of Miss Otohime, or Toyotama, the goddess of the sea. You could dive beneath the waves, find her, marry her and bring her back, but she would always belong to the ocean.

The Bansei Tokko Peace Museum in Minamisatsuma was something completely different: a brutalist concrete mausoleum dedicated to the 201 tokkotai from the nearby Bansei Air Base who died in the last year of the war. There were photographs and biographical details of each of these young men. I selected one at random and re-photographed him but I did not keep the picture. He had glossy black hair, downy unshaven cheeks and soft brown eyes; Mayu said later he looked like he might have been Ainu. He was clearly very young, if not the youngest there. That was a seventeen-year-old who was shown, with half a dozen others, in the centre of a group shot, holding a puppy that looked as stupid and innocent as they did. The museum was the brain child of Naemura Hichiro, a flight instructor at Bansei in 1945, and thus one of those who taught these young men how to die.

It was a macabre place. The first thing you saw when you walked in was a Mitsubishi Zero, huge, war-damaged, in a pit of sand in the middle of the floor. Apparently, it had been pulled out of the sea. Nothing was said about who its pilot had been or what had happened to him: ditched? drowned? shot down? There were many other, much smaller, model aircraft scattered throughout the museum, as if in a boy's bedroom. When I was ten or eleven, I used to buy kitset aircraft which I would assemble, paint and decorate. They were all models from World War II and most of them were fighter planes. I had a Zero along with a Spitfire, a Hurricane, a Messerschmidt 109 and a Focke-Wulf 190. The real life Zero was more sinister than I imagined them to be and could not have been anything else but a machine made for killing. Or for being killed. It was hard to know which were being memorialised here: the killers or the killed. Tokkotai, of course, were both.

Hidden Christians

We stayed that night in an old ryokan at a place called Fukiage Onsen, up a narrow valley with a boisterous river running through it. There were no lifts; as at Takachiho, I had to haul myself up a steep wooden staircase, clinging to the bannisters, clutching my stick, to the upper floor where our rooms were. We had three: one for sleeping, one for relaxing, one for eating — it was there, in a dining room decorated with panels painted in glowing greens, muted reds, and soft blacks on an ochre ground, that we were served fishcakes with the image of **Saigo Takamori** upon them. There were two seascapes, which alternated around the walls. One showed the profile of a rocky coast, with small promontories where pine trees grew; behind the largest, the roof of a shrine could be glimpsed. The other, in reverse profile, showed a similar coastal scene, this time with a small boat out on the water. In the background, a pale view of hills. They were generic and undistinguished but, in their faded glamour, very beautiful.

We had a private bath in a room downstairs, a rectangular stone pool set in damp, mossy ground, just the right size for two. Next to it was an open kitchen with elegant tile work on the benches. People who come here for their health bring their own rice and cook their meals on wood stoves or open charcoal fires. Such long stays were once popular, not just with the invalid and the unwell, but with itinerant writers too. All over Japan you find ryokan with onsen where some well-known writer came to live and wrote one or other of his (they were usually men) notable works. Often such works include a dalliance with a local woman, along with the heartbreak of parting when the sojourn is over. Or the love affair ends in a fatality for one or other party, usually the woman.

We went, next morning, via a car ferry, to the island of Amakusa, where we stopped for lunch at a fishing village called Sakitsu, clinging to the side of a rocky coast above the luminous blue green waters of Yokaku Bay. There have been Christians at Sakitsu since the 1560s when Luis de Almeida, a Portuguese doctor, surgeon and hospitaller, a good man, first proselytised amongst the locals. Persecution was rare, or at least intermittent, for the remaining decades of the sixteenth century, but became increasingly common once the Tokugawa shogunate established itself early in the seventeenth. After the Jesuits were expelled for good in 1614, many of those who were unable to go into exile, or unwilling to renounce their faith, went underground and worshipped in secret. These were the Hidden Christians.

By the 1620s active persecution, including some inventive and extremely cruel forms of torture, was commonplace. They including the slashing of the flesh and the pouring of scalding water from hot springs into the wounds; the *mino-odori*, the mino dance, in which the victim would be dressed in their straw raincoat, their hands tied behind their back, and then the raincoat set on fire; and *ana-tsurushi*, in which a body was wrapped in a cocoon and the unfortunate person suspended from a gallows upside down in a pit full of excrement. A cut would be made in the forehead to relieve pressure on the brain; and one arm left free to signal submission, when and if it was desired. Not many could resist this particular form of torture, and in time it replaced burning alive and crucifixion as the preferred method of executing *Kirishitan*.

Somewhat later, in 1629, in Nagasaki, the practice of *fumi-e*, or stepping on a picture, was inaugurated. The picture would be an image of Christ or the Virgin, usually cast in bronze but sometimes made of painted stone or printed from a woodblock. In Nagasaki and in other cities which were known haunts of Christians, the icons were taken yearly from house to house and the residents, whoever they were or pretended to be, were required to trample upon them. In smaller places like Sakitsu, people went annually to the headman's house, and, in a public ceremony, before the whole village, trampled upon the icon there. Japanese Christians, who were exclusively Catholic and thus knew about confession, evolved a form of prayer which absolved them of any wrong-doing before or after they had trampled upon the icon; otherwise, Christianity probably wouldn't have survived.

The Tokugawa didn't stop executing Christians until the beginning of the nineteenth century and the ban on their worship wasn't lifted until early in the Meiji period, in 1873. Everybody, including themselves, was surprised by how many Hidden Christians there turned out to be: about 30,000 (there are now 1.26 million). The first church at Sakitsu was built fifteen years later, in 1888, over a Shinto shrine at the base of the cliffs on the landward side of the settlement. In the 1930s it was removed to its current location in the centre of the village and renovated after a design by architect Tetsukawa Yosuke. The old church was wooden; the new one was built partly of concrete, partly of wood, apparently because supplies of concrete ran out during the reconstruction.

This enterprise took place under the auspices of a French priest, Father Augustin Halbout, who funded both the relocation and the renovation, and also purchased the plot of land upon which the new church stands. He must have had a sense of humour: the land he bought belonged formerly to the village headman and the altar was built over the very place where the villagers had once been forced to trample upon the icons of their faith. The church precinct was spotless, as if the very stones had been scrubbed. The church itself, a miniature in the gothic style, had a grey concrete façade picked out in white and a steeple covered in knobby protuberances. Beautifully tended gardens, featuring glossy, healthy-looking cycads and fantastically coloured *habotan*, the Japanese ornamental cabbage, flourished either side of the door.

The floors inside, unusually, were covered in tatami mats, except for the surrounds of the altar and the path to it, which were carpeted in red. The altar was ornate, golden, with a moulded Christ in a scarlet gown high up on the wall behind. Small, dark, grim, brown paintings of the fourteen stations of the cross hung around the walls, their effect somewhat ameliorated by the lovely, restrained, stained glass windows, made from clear panels in plain colours, through which limpid afternoon light fell. We saw another larger church later that day, also built by the French, which featured equally beautiful glass and an equally grotesque set of the stations of the cross

In a tiny museum opposite the church the story of the miracle of the Hidden Christians was set out on wall texts and there were icons and artefacts which had survived along with them: a medallion with a Christ figure upon it, together with the sliding panel in a wooden house post behind which it had been concealed; a picture of a priest who resembled a Japanese kami more than he did a Christian prelate; an abalone shell bearing the image of the Virgin. People here were, and are, especially fond of Christ the fisherman and still perform annual ceremonies asking him to ensure a rich haul. In fact, as in other parts of western Kyushu, their forms of worship combine aspects of all three main religions in Japan: Buddhism, Shintoism and Christianity.

One of their ceremonies was described in detail in a wall text:

> *Sawagi*, the New Year decoration, consisting of *usu* (a huge bowl made of pine), three pieces of *kine* (wooden hammer), *shime-nawa* (twisted straw rope), and some vegetable are prepared before New Year. It used to be displayed on the dirt floor of each house. Food offered to Christ is put inside the *usu* and three pieces of *kine* representing the cross are put on it. A hanging *shime-nawa* is a decoration for Shintoism while the *usu* and *kine* are for *Kakure Kirishitan*. After completing the decoration, people bow twice, clap their hands twice, and bow again (a form of Shinto prayer). Making *sawagi* is a custom for families who have *Kakure Kirishitan* ancestry.

Sakitsu was a busy trading port during the Edo period. Later it became a site of literary pilgrimage and there was a famous ryokan, now demolished, called the Montsukiya Inn, which you came to by boat. There was a picture of the old building on a bulletin board and you could still see the stone steps leading up to the landing place, rising mysteriously out of the waters of Yokaku Bay. The writers who came here were all active in the first half of the twentieth century and included Shiba Ryotaro, the historical novelist; the poet Noguchi Ujo; playwright Kikuchi Kan; and feminist author Hayashi Fumiko. The shadows of fish hawks, like their ghosts, fled across the wooden pier. Their high piping cries hung in the air. Stray cats, many of them without tails or with only half a tail, waited for fishing boats to return with their catches.

Boyokaku

The hotel at Boyokaku stood on a narrow strip of land between the cliffs of Amakusa and the waters of the East China Sea. It was built in the 1930s at the mouth of a small river on the western coast of the island with views out over the ocean and was famous for its sunsets; there was a viewing platform. Emperors have stayed here. To the south was a bridge and, if you drove up that way, you found an antique town built on both sides of the river. Opposite, probably on reclaimed land, stood a large flat concrete wharf sheltered by a breakwater, behind which a dozen fishing boats were moored. The whole time we were there a group of men were picking over a huge fishing net laid out on the concrete, repairing the rents and tears in it.

When we arrived, in the afternoon, having driven from Fukiage Onsen via Sakitsu and then along the coast road, a uniformed hotel employee, grinning from ear to ear, gave me to understand I had not parked the car correctly: it was sitting slightly awry between two parallel white lines on the gravelly pavement. After I made several failed attempts to remedy this grievous error he offered, with great good humour, to do the job for me. I was tired and didn't really mind, so I let him. He made an excellent job of it and there the car sat, splendidly exact between the lines, in the otherwise empty, alarmingly pot-holed carpark. Then he carried our baggage into reception.

The décor had a Portuguese theme. There was a letter from the Portuguese consul, and a Japanese translation of it, on a sign out the front, and when you came into the lobby from the carpark, a large mat sat on the floor with the red outline of the map of Portugal upon it. There were some indifferent *azulejo*, blue and white tiles, here and there, and some of the stained glass, much better, was also Portuguese in inspiration. The basement onsen had magnificent panels along one wall and two narrow windows, like clerestory windows, over the main pool. Two streams of very hot water cascaded from a great height and there I stood, letting it fall heavily upon my shoulders, which were stiff from driving and from clutching my stick too tightly while limping along.

The lobby featured some pieces of abstract art which, although modest in size, suggested an acquaintance with the work of Mark Rothko. Nearby, in a glass case, stood a stuffed albino boar. There was a story about that. At a time of drought and famine, during the Pacific War, it turned up at the hotel, starving, and the wife of the owner had taken pity on it and fed it scraps from the kitchen. The boar formed an unshakeable attachment to her and visited every day thereafter for treats and caresses. When it died, she was desolated and insisted upon having it preserved and set up as a display in the hotel. Though moth-eaten and a bit dishevelled, it retained a certain gravitas.

In the afternoon we went for a drive up the coast to where a small circular promontory, Tomioka Peninsula, extended out to sea. There was said to be the ruin of a castle upon it. On the way we passed a coal fired power station with a port for unloading the fuel, conveyor belts to feed the furnaces and two squarish towers in which the coal was burned. From a distance it looked pristine, a white enigma on the skyline, but as you got closer you could see the rust, the decay, the industrial stains and the grime. We had passed the shadowy gates to a nuclear power station on the road the day before. Banks of solar panels were quite common, occurring in the most surprising places, some of them quite small, some enormous. Now and again, we saw the turbines of wind farms turning spectrally on the brow of a distant hill.

Tomioka Castle, however, proved elusive. The peninsular was forested and mazed with narrow, twisting roads and as we drove along, we would see, looming out of the green, white-painted, grey-tiled towers which might once have been part of a castle complex or replicas of such buildings. One of these was a visitor's centre but, because it was Wednesday, it was closed. In another part of the forest, we found some massive stone walls sloping upwards towards parapets with loopholes in them. An information board told us there were at least three layers of stone on the wall before us because when a castle was renovated, the original walls would simply be covered over with new stones, new mortar. The last of the layers, it said, had been constructed during the Christian rebellion in 1637-8 when the castle had been several times, without success, attacked by the rebels.

The Shimabara Rebellion actually began on Amakusa, where it was soon suppressed, after which the survivors crossed the water and joined their comrades on the Shimabara Peninsula. It was seen by the Edo *bakufu* ('tent government') of the Tokugawa shogunate as a religious revolt, but it was also economic. The farmers of Amakusa and Shimabara were being taxed to within an inch of their lives — as Charles Boxer put it, 'all they had left was their eyes to weep with.' Those who could not pay were tortured, or their wives and daughters were. The revolt began when a father killed the men who were torturing his daughter and the whole of his village rose up in support of him. And then the country followed.

Most of those who revolted were Christians who had publicly abjured their faith, either under torture or out of concern for their survival, but they had not abandoned it. They were, after all, living in the heartland of the Jesuit mission, where their seminary had been, and their printing press, and where they used to retreat during the worst of the persecutions in Nagasaki. That there was a religious dimension to the revolt is undeniable. As early as 1614, when the ban on the Jesuits came into force, a prophecy had begun to circulate, allegedly a revelation granted to a Japanese priest who had gone into exile:

When five years have passed five times
all the dead trees shall bloom
crimson clouds shall shine brightly in the western sky
and a boy of divine power will appear.

In 1637 the cherry trees flowered, unseasonably, in autumn. The winter was exceptionally dry, with red clouds in the sky at sunset. The marvellous boy was Masuda Shiro Tokisada, AKA Amakusa Shiro, just eighteen, the son of a samurai, who was elected commander of the rebels. However, the real power seems to have been with a small group of *ronin*, masterless samurai, who managed to recruit several hundred of their fellows from the ranks of those who had once served the Christian daimyo of southern and western Kyushu. The Tokugawa regime had a great fear of ronin, of whom there were many thousands, some engaged in criminal enterprises, others working as mercenaries and some, indeed, as these ones were, plotting to overthrow the bakufu.

The Christian forces, inexplicably, declined to take Nagasaki, which was undefended, when they probably could have, and gathered instead in an old castle at Hara on the east coast of Shimabara, which they re-fortified in anticipation of a siege by government forces, which indeed ensued. Two assaults failed, during which the Christian forces fought rather better than the government soldiers. They also captured, after annihilating two samurai columns, guns and ammunition. These they added to the scythes, sickles and improvised spears most of them were armed with. Ronin were desperate men, outlaws of a kind; upon the death of their daimyo they had declined to commit *seppuku*, as they were supposed to do, and so assumed the status of dead men walking. Or else they had simply fled the service of a living lord and turned renegade.

The Tokugawa enlisted the Dutch to their cause and some Dutch ships did shell Hara Castle: '426 rough cannon salvos both from land and sea.' This intervention was extremely unpopular in Europe, when people there heard about it, but it pleased the Tokugawa, as the Dutch, who were of course Protestants, had calculated that it would. It was estimated that 15,000 Christian soldiers gathered in Hara. Including women and children, a total of perhaps 37,000 people had taken refuge there. Their problem, and their ultimate downfall, was logistical: the paucity of supplies of food and the impossibility of re-provisioning the castle. The defenders nevertheless fought to the bitter end, using iron cauldrons and cooking pots as weapons of last resort.

When Hara Castle fell in April 1638, all those within — men, women and children — were massacred. There was, reputedly, just one survivor. He was Yamada Emosaku, an ex-Jesuit *dojuku* (layman) painter who had apostatized some years earlier and was an unwilling participant in the revolt. He had been discovered communicating with the enemy, probably by means of *ninja* warriors who infiltrated the castle and was in the dungeons, awaiting execution, when the castle was stormed. The three-month long siege cost the besiegers 13,000 men out of a force of perhaps 100,000. Heavy losses. Amakusa Shiro was taken alive, executed, and his head displayed on a pole in Nagasaki.

Shimabara and Amakusa were almost depopulated; people had to be brought in from the Goto Islands offshore to work the fields and the fishing boats. The dead at Hara are not, however, considered martyrs by the Catholic church, because they had taken up arms and because their motives were economic as much as religious. There were other consequences. The government received such a fright that it called off a proposed invasion of the Philippines, apparently because, after the siege of Hara Castle, it no longer had the confidence that the 10,000 men it planned to send south could take the garrison town of Manila. Further Japanese geographical expansion had to wait until the Meiji Era.

The rebellion also marked the effective end of the Portuguese trade from Macao to Nagasaki, which had flourished for nearly ninety years and continued even after the expulsion of the Jesuits in 1614. Trade could no longer continue in the face of Japanese suspicions that the merchants and the Jesuits were colluding, not just in the trade of silks for silver, and in other commodities, but in a deeper design: to infiltrate the land with missionaries as a preparation for an armed takeover of the state. This was a method the Spanish had in fact used in the Philippines and in south and central America. Yet it was never a modus operandi of the Portuguese who were in this respect as pragmatic as the Dutch.

We abandoned the search for the fugitive castle and drove further down the maze of little roads until we reached the sea. Above a small cove, some farmers, a man and two women, were bringing home baskets of *fuki*, butterburs, they had picked in the hills. We could see a grove of orange trees fruiting lusciously behind their house; next to it was a flourishing vegetable garden. The three farmers looked incuriously at us and went on with their work. I walked out onto a rocky beach and, from amongst the tide wrack, picked up a smooth, yellow stone to use as a paperweight.

That night we ate in a tiny restaurant in town. While the old man cooked for us, his wife, whose mind was wandering, asked Mayu the same questions over and over again, mostly about who I was and where I came from; while another World Series baseball game played on the TV in the corner. When, after the meal, the old woman insisted upon helping me on with my jacket, I felt her soft breath on my cheek. I thought about this when I fell ill in Nagasaki a day or so later. All night, already feverish, I was troubled by the image of the palm tree out the window of our hotel room, buffeted by incessant northerlies coming down past Korea into the East China Sea and rattling its fronds like knives. Stars glittered in the sky beyond, cold and brilliant as minds planning a war.

Towards Nagasaki

There was a public swimming pool, using thermal water 'out of the ground', nearby, so we went there to do some laps. We had been in and out of water many times during the trip but hadn't done much actual exercise apart from walking; or, in my case, lately, limping. The pool was built on the top of a low hill, looking out over flat cropped fields to the sea. Children were taking lessons inside and various aged souls gathered in the foyer awaiting the official 10.30 am opening for their turn to swim. The woman at the desk explained everything to me in meticulous detail, including how to work the shower in the men's changing room (she came in to show me) and the way to mop the floor if I happened to splash any water upon it.

Inevitably, I ended up using the wrong shower — the one in the changing room was for *after* your swim while the one just inside the entrance to the pool was for *before* — as a couple of amiable old fellows made clear to me; but when I showed them my skin and hair were wet they decided not to insist I shower again using the correct fount. Once they ascertained that I was going to be swimming freestyle, they told me which lane to use, and off I went in the warm, slightly cloudy water. Mayu came into the same lane with me and we swam companionably back and forth together for half an hour or so, doing our requisite number of lengths. Afterwards one of the old men asked how old I was? I told him. He turned out, much to his delight, to be a decade older than I am. These active, fit and cheerful old people were a joy to be around.

We drove on through fields of potatoes, their dark green leaves and bright white flowers resplendent against the black earth, on our way to the second ferry, which took us off Amakusa Island and on to the Shimabara Peninsula, which consisted essentially of the land surrounding another huge, active volcano, Unzen-dake. We could see it glowering and steaming across the water from the ferry terminal. There was a statue of Amakusa Shiro as a young man on a plinth outside the terminal building; he looked more like a Boddhisatva than a Christian. At the edge of the carpark, a pale green tanker truck was parked, with its engine running, in front of a line of dark green cypress trees. The driver was asleep at the wheel.

We disembarked at Kuchinotsu, a significant port in the days of the Portuguese and the Dutch; there was a set of old European buildings, now restored as a folk museum, on a small promontory to the left as we came into the harbour. It was linked to the rest of the city by a bridge with a single, splendid red arch. Subsequently, in the nineteenth century, Kuchinotsu had become a busy coal port and a place where young women stowed away on freighters in order to go to other lands, including Australia, where many of them ended up working as prostitutes. Mayu had been here before, researching her theatre piece *You've Mistaken Me for a Butterfly* (2017).

A collaboration with composer / musician Narushima Terumi, she described the work as 'a performative poem reflecting on Okin, a Japanese woman who was caught up in a court case in 1898, when two white men were accused of sexually assaulting her. The events took place near Butterfly, an outback mining town in Western Australia.' Okin had been working at a laundry in the town when she was assaulted; 'laundry' in those days often meant brothel. The case, unusually, had gone to trial; there were transcripts, which Mayu used in her work. Okin wasn't a victim, however, she was a survivor who went on to better things. I remember Mayu telling me once, in exasperation, that what people never understood about Okin is that she wasn't a butterfly, she was a moth. She meant they didn't get the fairly obvious reference in the title to *Madame Butterfly*.

Some of these young women were sold by their families, who might or might not have known what their ultimate fate was to be. They were treated as indentured labourers and had to re-pay their sponsors the price they had been bought for as well as the cost of their passage before being able to earn any money for themselves, hence the frequent recourse to prostitution. Of course, the ships' captains usually knew what was happening; one of the strategies the traffickers used to smuggle the women aboard was, on the night before a ship was due to sail, to light fires on the hills behind the town to divert the attention of local officials; while they were thus distracted the captives embarked.

Kuchinotsu was a sleepy place; the main port was now further up the east coast of the peninsula towards the ruins of Hara Castle. We went the other way, along the west coast road. It was an uneventful drive, first beside the sea, then inland, then via a freeway, into the city of Nagasaki. I did not expect that it would resemble Wellington, New Zealand: built on hills around a deep harbour with steep streets running upwards from narrow coastal flats or reclaimed land. Our hotel, Setre Glover's House Nagasaki (AKA the Glover) was perched high up on a hill on the southern side of the harbour at Ishibashi, the old International Settlement, near Glover Garden, Dutch Slope and the Oura Church. You could see industrial and port facilities across the water and the city lights glimmering at the head of the bay. A cruise ship like a giant floating hotel was anchored below.

Weekend in Nagasaki

The Glover billed itself as a European style hotel but I think what the proprietors really meant was English; even though the eponymous Thomas Glover, of whom more later, was actually a Scotsman. In our suite there were several pieces of massive, varnished wooden furniture with no discernible purpose, including an empty cabinet on the top of which stood a bowl of fruit; both bowl and fruit were made, in one indivisible whole, of painted plaster. It was as light as the cabinet was heavy. There were three rooms which, although small, gave onto one another in a way that was elegant and accommodating and made the apartment feel much larger than it was.

In the lobby downstairs you could help yourself to free drinks — beer, wine, and highball (pre-mixed whisky and soda) — as well as make tea and coffee, toast, and some kind of local sweet which I never tried. A small Nagasaki-themed library included several photography books. Here I first learned about Felice Beato, the Italian British commercial photographer who worked in Japan from 1863 until 1884. His staged shots of seppuku and of executions are extraordinary; his documentary work is even better. He had a brother, Antonio Beato, also a photographer, who took the famous shot of thirty-seven samurai in front of the Sphinx in Egypt in 1864.

Next door was a building site and in the morning I watched while the assembled workers, about thirty of them, at 8.00 am sharp, gathered outside and went through a program of Tai Chi like exercises under the instruction of some *sensei* I could not see. It was beguiling watching these fellows in boots, overalls, vis-po vests and hard hats going through the motions — without enthusiasm, but dutifully, calmly, perhaps resignedly. They then resumed the hard labour of construction on a site that was just a ledge on a cliff that plummeted towards the harbour below.

Mioko, Mayu's sister, was joining us from Tokyo for the weekend so after lunch we drove out to the airport to pick her up. It turned cold and rainy during the afternoon and by evening was really wintery. We took a taxi to Chinatown for dinner. As we drove through the wet streets, a song came on the radio and the driver started singing along: 'You're the only one I ever loved / I believed you when you said you loved me too / it's another rainy night in Nagasaki'. Then he laughed.

'It doesn't rain that much here,' he said.

We looked it up later: 'Nagasaki Wa Kyo Mo Ame Datta' was sung by Maekawa Kiyoshi, the front man and vocalist for Uchiyamada Hiroshi and the Cool Five, a *kayokyoku* (pop music) group formed in 1967. A doo-wop influenced number with a catchy chorus, it was a huge hit in 1969. It's one of those tunes that mixes evocative beauty and melodramatic absurdity in about equal measure.

Afterwards, back at the hotel, we broached a bottle of saké we'd bought from the maker in Kikuchi and carried with us since. Five Daughters, he'd told us, was brewed and bottled without the use of preservatives and so had to be drunk immediately or else kept on ice, which we hadn't really done although we'd tried. It was delicious and after a few glasses the sisters, as they are wont to do, got a bit hilarious. There's a Nagasaki delicacy called Castella (*Kasutera*), Portuguese sponge cake, and they remembered an old TV ad for it, with a jingle based on a tune by Offenbach and featuring five furry figures, cats or foxes, doing the can-can. At the end of the jingle, they are revealed to be marionettes. Mayu and Mioko danced the dance and sang the song and then fell about laughing.

Thomas Glover, the man after whom the hotel, and the nearby Glover Garden, were named, came as a very young man from Fraserburgh north of Aberdeen to Shanghai, where he worked for Jardine, Matheson and Co., notorious for their involvement in opium trafficking but also traders in silk, tea, cotton and other commodities. In 1859, aged just twenty-one, Glover was sent to Nagasaki as their agent. He soon went into business on his own account and, in partnership with an Englishman, Francis Groom, made a fortune exporting tea, camphor, timber and other local products, and importing steamships, machinery and industrial goods. He diversified into coal and, as a good Scot, into ship-building too. He also enriched himself in the arms trade, selling weapons and ammunition, as well as gun boats, to the Kyushu daimyos who brought down the Tokugawa bakufu during the Meiji Restoration. He then acted as a de facto advisor to the renegades on matters of effective political strategy and sound business practice.

Ironically, the peace after the Restoration bankrupted him, and he moved to Tokyo in the early 1870s in an ultimately successful attempt to restore his fortunes. He visited Nagasaki often thereafter but never returned to live. He had a son and a daughter, by two different women, and lived with the mother of his daughter as his common law wife until her death in 1899, after which he expressed a wish to be buried next to her when he himself died — which he was, in 1911. A fluent speaker of Japanese, from his early years in Nagasaki, Glover established himself in the community as a respected and influential figure. Businesses he was involved with have lasted until today. They include the corporation that became Mitsubishi, and the brewery that makes Kirin Beer.

Glover's house is extant in the gardens named after him; a museum now, of the sparse and unconvincing kind. After going there, we had afternoon tea in a café opposite, reputedly the first European style restaurant in Japan. Jayuti was opened by Kusano Jokichi in 1863; he had learned how to cook while working for the Dutch on Dejima Island, their dedicated base in the harbour. When Jokichi died in 1886, Jayuti closed and the building was sold to the Nagasaki District Court, which used it as a reception room. In 1974 it was dismantled then reassembled in Glover Garden. It featured some lovely stained glass and an elaborate Dutch method of making coffee via the expression of cold water through the grounds, over a twenty-four-hour period, using an array of complex and beautiful glass vessels. Mayu and Mioko ate kasutera with their tea. I had a fruit tart.

Nagasaki (long cape) is not an old city by Japanese standards. It was still an obscure fishing village when, in the second half of the sixteenth century, the Christianised Kyushu daimyo together with the Portuguese chose it as their harbour of choice to host the China trade. It was to replace Hirado which, although more ancient, had a smaller and more exposed harbour. The local daimyo, Omura Sumitada, in 1569 issued a permit for the establishment of a port with the express purpose of receiving Portuguese ships. It was set up in 1571 under the supervision of Jesuit missionary Gaspar Vilela and Portuguese Captain-Major Tristão Vaz de Veiga, working closely with Omura.

Because of the depredations of the wako (who were not exclusively Japanese pirates but made up of renegades of many nations), Ming Dynasty China refused to trade directly with Japan; but they didn't mind using the Portuguese, from their base in Macao, as intermediaries. Nor did the Kyushu daimyo who, however sincere their Christianity might have been, were still very much aware of the commercial advantages it gave them in dealing with the Portuguese. The same, from a different point of view, might be said of the Jesuits themselves, with respect to both the Japanese ruling classes and the Portuguese merchant adventurers — that is, when it came to using commerce to facilitate their missionary endeavours.

On account of continuing civil strife at the tail end of the Sengoku jidai, the century of wars, Omura and the Jesuit Alessandro Valignano, an Italian, decided to hand administrative and military control of Nagasaki over to the Society of Jesus, turning the city, albeit briefly, into a Jesuit colony. By 1587, however, Toyotomi Hideoshi's effort to unify the country had reached as far south as Kyushu and he placed the city of Nagasaki and its trade under his direct control, while at the same time ordering the expulsion of all missionaries. The expulsion order wasn't enforced, however, and the Jesuits continued to practice business as usual (both God's and Mammon's). Nagasaki remained a largely Christian city, while direct control of the port was retained by the government.

By then the mendicant orders, mostly via the Philippines, had also begun proselyting in Japan; much to the chagrin of the Jesuits. In the wake of the wreck of the *San Felipe*, a Spanish galleon, off the Pacific coast of Shikoku in 1596, Japanese authorities decided, on the basis of some intemperate boasting by the Spanish pilot of the ship, that the Franciscan missionaries were the vanguard of a planned Iberian invasion of Japan. (The Portuguese and Spanish monarchies were united at the time.) Hideyoshi, in retaliation, and as a warning, ordered the crucifixion of twenty-six Christians in Nagasaki. They were mostly Spanish Franciscans and their converts, with one unlucky Japanese Jesuit included apparently by mistake.

Portuguese traders were not really affected, however, and nor were the Jesuits; Christian Nagasaki continued to thrive. The Tokogawa shogunate which, from 1603, continued to administer the city from Edo, also maintained a policy of de-facto toleration, at least until after the final defeat of the Toyotomi, their great rivals, in the siege and burning of Osaka Castle. Then, in 1614, Christianity was officially banned and all missionaries ordered to leave Japan. The persecutions that followed were violent and extreme. The trade with Macao, and therefore China, continued but there were now English and Dutch merchants as rivals to the Portuguese.

The Tokugawa several times investigated the possibility of opening up a relationship with the Spanish in Manila, and at one stage, as mentioned, intended to invade the Philippines. From 1609 the Dutch were allowed to trade into and out of the port of Hirado, to the north of Nagasaki; the English voluntarily withdrew from their uneconomic Japan trade in 1623. The failed Shimabara Rebellion of 1637-8 ended the Portuguese trade for good, after which the closed country policy, *Sakoku*, endured for more than two centuries. The word Shimabara had come to signify the connection between Christianity and disloyalty to the state; the rebellion convinced the Tokugawa that foreign influences were more trouble than they were worth; with just one exception.

In 1641, after the expulsion of the Portuguese, Dejima, the fan-shaped artificial island built in Nagasaki harbour, which had served as their trading post, was given over to the Dutch, who were allowed to continue to trade there on condition that they did not proselytise. The Dutch, ever practical, agreed. The island was so small there was room upon it for only about twenty people to live; a single causeway connected it to the mainland and there was always an armed guard at the city end. Nevertheless, the Dutch were permitted, or rather required, to process to Edo (Tokyo) for an audience with the shogun once a year between 1660 and 1790; and thereafter once every four years.

One of the consequences of this arrangement was that, for more than two centuries, Dutch was the language of diplomacy in Japan. When the English returned, in the mid-nineteenth century, they recruited diplomats who were already fluent in Dutch. Nor was there a protestant church in Japan until 1872, at Yokohama, and then it was Presbyterian — of the reformed, American variety. The Dutch connection is also why Nagasaki became a centre for learning. In 1720 the ban on Dutch books was lifted and Japanese scholars came from all over the archipelago to study European art and science. Subsequently, the city became the major centre of *rangaku*, or Dutch Learning. Japanese purchased and translated scientific and medical texts from the Dutch, obtained Western curiosities and manufactures (clocks, surgical instruments, celestial and terrestrial globes, maps and seeds), and were given demonstrations of Western innovations, including the flight of a hot air balloon. In 1813 a Dutch ship came into port with an elephant on board.

Photography, too, came to Japan via Nagasaki; the first camera arrived in 1848 and the first known photograph by a Japanese was taken in 1857. Then, in 1862, photographer Ueno Hikoma opened his studio. The city was also much photographed by foreigners; Felice Beato was preceded, in 1859, by Swiss photographer Pierre Joseph Rossier, who taught Ueno Hikoma, and by a telegrapher in the German navy, August Sachtler, who arrived with the Prussian Expedition to East Asia in 1861. When the Americans dropped a plutonium bomb on Nagasaki on August 9, 1945, they probably didn't realise (or didn't care) that they were obliterating the most Christian, and the most Western, city in Japan.

We had a discussion that night over the remains of the saké: whether or not to visit Ground Zero the next day. Mayu had been there before; Mioko didn't want to go. She argued that for her there were better reasons to remember her first visit to Nagasaki than a bomb dropped upon it by the Americans seventy years ago, before she was born, in a war she did not know or care very much about. In a way I agreed with her: Nagasaki was an elegant, sophisticated and cosmopolitan city, easy and graceful, wearing its past as lightly as it could. On the other hand, I felt a dull anger that it had been bombed at all, in the arbitrary, indeed cynical way it was, especially when I ran across parties of loud, crass and garrulous American sight-seers from the cruise ship anchored in the bay below our hotel.

Nagasaki wasn't the original target and it wasn't a major military site either, despite the presence of a Mitsubishi ship-building yard: the US military, having tested their uranium based device on Hiroshima, wanted to see what a plutonium bomb would do. The original target was Kokura, on the northern tip of Kyushu; but there was cloud over the Shimonoseki Straits that morning so the planes headed to Nagasaki instead. Like Hiroshima, Kokura had not been firebombed so that it remained a pristine target for the new weapons to show their capabilities. Nagasaki had been hit four or five times before but the city was difficult to locate at night using radar and none of the conventional bombing raids had caused much damage. A few weeks earlier, it had not even been on the list of potential targets; it was only when the ancient capital of Kyoto, which had also not yet been bombed, was taken off the hit list that Nagasaki came into contention. Such are the vagaries of war.

In the end, Mayu and I decided to visit the memorials on Sunday morning before returning to the hotel to collect Mioko and take her with us to Sasebo for lunch; from there she could catch a bus to the airport and a return flight to Tokyo. We drove to the site, parked the car and took a series of elevators up to Peace Park. At the top of the last one was the Peace Fountain. A man and a woman were standing before it, side by side, with their hands clasped in prayer. They both had their eyes squeezed shut; but the man's were not closed tight enough to stop the tears rolling down his cheeks.

Beyond the fountain was a wide flat area with sculptures, ruins and places you could sit and contemplate what happened here. As we walked along, for no particular reason, I found myself in tears as well. We were crossing the site of a prison, the nearest public building to the point of impact: you could still see the lines of the foundations of its stone walls in the grass. How unlucky is that: to be in jail when they drop an atomic bomb on you? Those imprisoned were mostly foreign workers from the occupied territories, many of them Korean, Chinese or Taiwanese, who had somehow transgressed Japanese law and been locked up.

The centre piece of the park was a huge figurative sculpture with one arm outstretched and the other pointing to the heavens. It seemed outré to me; but then none of the sculpture (and there is a lot of it) looked right. On the other hand, this inadequacy, if that's what it is, does not seem to require any explanation. What work of art, sculptural or otherwise, could be equal to what happened here? I liked the images of cranes, however, both graphic and sculptural; they even featured in the stained glass windows of the ablution block. Cranes are associated with Nagasaki because the long, narrow harbour is thought to resemble the bird in flight.

Traditionally cranes are believed to live for a thousand years; they also have the power to grant wishes and answer prayers. This is where the practice of *senbazuru* comes from: the folding of a thousand origami cranes to make a single wish come true. It was revived in the 1950s by Sasaki Sadako, a little girl irradiated, aged three, in the bombing of Hiroshima. She folded more than 1,450 cranes in the hope that her illness might thereby be cured. It wasn't. She died of leukemia, aged twelve, in 1956.

Ground Zero was on flat land in a separate, adjoining park. A simple black obelisk marked the spot and there were children running around it, chasing each other and laughing in the sunshine. In another place you could look down, through glass, at the actual rubble left on the ground by the blast. It reminded me of the dirt floor of the sexton's shed at the cemetery in Greytown where my father is buried. Another public building destroyed that day was Urakami Cathedral: the largest, most sophisticated and most beautiful church in East Asia. During the Occupation, the Americans feared the ruins of the cathedral might become, like the Genbaku Dome in Hiroshima, a memorial to their war crimes and insisted they be demolished; some of the masonry survived and has been reconstituted and placed near the obelisk, with a statue of the ubiquitous Francis Xavier on top.

The bomb didn't fall on the Mitsubishi shipyards, its target, but exploded in the air about four kilometres up the valley where the surrounding hills shielded the rest of the city from the worst of the blast. Nevertheless, windows were shattered and rooves torn off buildings in Ishibashi, ten kilometres away, where we were staying. There wasn't a firestorm afterwards either, as there was at Hiroshima, although there were many smaller fires. Oddly enough, the only reference to the catastrophe I encountered elsewhere in the city was in the caption of a bad painting of the Twenty-six Martyrs of Nagasaki, which I saw at the Oura Church in Ishibashi. It said it was 'damaged by the atomic bomb.'

I suppose some things are better forgotten; however hard that might be, remembering may be harder. Mayu and Mioko's mother, Yoshie, born 1934, like so many other Japanese children, endured desperate suffering during the Pacific War, including starvation, separation from family, deaths of loved ones, and a pervasive sense of impending, actual or already accomplished doom. She is a forgetter rather than a rememberer; by which I mean, while she does in fact remember, she would prefer to forget. No wonder the GNA is as high as it is. For some, the war never ended.

In Sasebo we had lunch in an Italian restaurant then saw Mioko off on the bus to the airport. Sasebo was the main launching point for the United Nations and United States armed forces fighting the Korean War. Tons of ammunition, fuel, tanks, trucks and supplies flowed through the port during those years; thousands of troops embarked or disembarked. Here too the dead came back. There's still an American naval base, one of fifteen extant in Japan; and Sasebo is also the home port of the Japanese Maritime Self-Defence Forces. We could see the sinister gun-metal-grey American ships, with their round communication domes, moored further up the harbour, and the tiny little white patrol boats of the JMDF nearer at hand.

At a village to the north of Sasebo, Mayu wanted to do some more filming. It was for an hour-long show plus some videos to accompany a recording of eight songs by her friend Odamura Satsuki, a Koto player from Sydney; the village, Sazacho, is where Satsuki comes from. It was a fine afternoon in a quiet little town built on the banks of a river not far from Sazaura Bay. Mayu filmed the primary school and the junior high school where Satsuki studied; a Shinto shrine and a Buddhist temple near where she lived; the house where she grew up; and the river that flows out to the sea. Then we drove on north towards the ancient port of Hirado.

Kawachi

Hirado, the port where the Dutch concession was first granted, is on another island, also called Hirado, which you reach by crossing a splendidly engineered fire-engine red bridge. We by-passed the harbour and drove instead down the east coast to our hotel, the Yukai Resort Ranpu. It was vast, modern, about a dozen floors tall and almost as wide as the bay. There were views of the sea and collections of mostly Dutch, or Dutch inspired, paintings, objets d'art, pottery, artefacts, some very fine, in the foyer; and some beautiful glass and tile work elsewhere in the building.

I was still nursing the cold I picked up in Nagasaki — or else from the old woman at the restaurant at Boyokaku — but it wasn't too bad. The sun was streaming through the window, our room was large and generous, the onsen hot, varied and convivial. I saw two young men, identical twins, big as Sumo wrestlers, gravely descending the stairs to the dining hall, which resembled those you find on a cruise ships. It was a buffet and smoke from the beef, pork and chicken which people cooked on small braziers at their own tables hung in the air and clung to your clothes, making them smell of charred meat and burnt fat. There were lots of children and young people. Some kids were playing croquet on the lawn outside our room.

From there we could see a line of monuments on the other side of the road, looking out to sea. A tall standing stone, no doubt with an inscription upon it, flanked by two smaller stones; a rectangular tablet, almost certainly inscribed as well; a life-sized white marble statue of a gowned figure, probably a kannon the goddess of mercy. Perhaps, I thought, they had something to do with the Dutch. The shrine, however, which we visited the next morning, commemorated someone else entirely: the warrior hero Zheng Chenggong AKA Koxinga, called Teiseiko in Japan, who is more or less unknown in the West but famous throughout East Asia.

He was born here at Kawachi in 1624, the son of a Chinese merchant, Zheng Zilong, and a Japanese woman, Tagawa Matsu, who was from a samurai family. On the rectangular tablet there was indeed a short biography of him, in Chinese characters, composed in 1852 by Confucian scholar, Hayama Gaiken, on the orders of Matsura Hiromu, the 35th daimyo of Hirado, who was 'concerned that he would be forgotten about.' The patina upon the stone was very beautiful but it was so encrusted with lichen the characters were unreadable — except perhaps by treating them like braille and tracing them with your fingertips.

Zheng Chenggong was raised by his mother until, aged seven, he was summoned by his father to Fujian in China. Aged fourteen, he became a successful candidate in the Chinese Imperial Examinations. In 1641 he married the niece of a high official and, in 1644, while studying at the Imperial University, met the scholar, historian and poet Qian Qianyi and became his protégé and student. In 1644, the Ming capital of Peking fell to the Manchu armies from the north, the emperor hanged himself from a tree in the palace gardens, and the Ming forces retreated to Nanjing, then further south to Fuzhou. Subsequently Zheng Zhilong and his family became supporters of the Prince of Tang, installed in 1645 on the throne of the Southern Ming.

Around this time Tagawa Matsu rejoined her husband and her son in mainland China; whereupon all three of them became implicated, in different ways, in the complex diplomatic manoeuvrings between the Ming and the Manchu. This culminated in Zheng Zhilong's surrender to the enemy in exchange for certain benefits, Tagawa Matsu's suicide to avoid capture by Manchu forces and Zheng Chenggong's appointment in his father's stead as military leader of the Southern Ming forces. This was when he was given the title Koxinga (Lord of the Imperial Surname) and, in 1646, led the army against the Qing Dynasty founded by the Manchus.

The war between Ming and Qing lasted another decade before the Ming were defeated. Koxinga then turned his attention to Dutch Formosa and, in 1661, invaded the island. Taiwanese aboriginal tribes, many of them still head hunters, were offered an amnesty if they allied themselves with Koxinga's Chinese army. They were restive under the Dutch, who had imposed compulsory religious education upon them, and celebrated their freedom by burning their prayer books and beheading any of their oppressors that they could get their hands on. On the first of February 1662, the Governor of Formosa surrendered Fort Zeelandia to Koxinga and the island was his.

His conquest was, in part, an attempt to find a base for Ming forces from which they might, at some point, retake the mainland: just as Chiang Kai-shek would do three hundred years later, in a territorial division which has still not been resolved. Koxinga sponsored migration of Han Chinese to Taiwan; taught farming techniques, including rice cultivation, to indigenous farmers, giving them oxen and tools; and distributed tobacco to the crowds who met and welcomed him when he visited their villages in triumph following his victory. And he founded a dynasty.

After Taiwan, Koxinga turned his attention to the Philippines, where he again sought the support of indigenous people in a war to free them from their European colonisers. Early in 1662, his forces raided coastal towns on Luzon and he sent his chief advisor, an Italian friar called Vittorio Riccio, to Manila to demand tribute, threatening to expel the Spanish if his demands were not met. The Spanish did not comply; instead, they reinforced their garrisons in anticipation of a full scale assault. However, the planned attack, which might well have succeeded, never took place. Koxinga died suddenly from malaria in June, 1662. He was just thirty-seven years old.

His early death might also have been a consequence of his alleged syphilis; or from apoplexy during one of his frequent rages, which led some to suggest he was mentally ill. He left many descendants and the dynasty he founded on Taiwan, the Kingdom of Tungning, lasted twenty more years before the Qing finally assumed control of the island. Koxinga was as much a warlord as a servant of the Ming Dynasty or anyone else. As such, his legacy is complex: he is remembered differently in Japan, in China, and in Taiwan, though in all three places he is accounted a hero.

He was honoured as a divinity in parts of coastal China, especially Fujian, and still is worshipped by overseas Chinese in South East Asia. In Taiwan he is a national hero, with temples, schools, universities and other public facilities named after him. Japan treats him as a native son and during their fifty-year occupation of Taiwan (1895-1945), emphasized his maternal link to their country. In the Peoples Republic of China, he is 'Conqueror of Taiwan, Great Rebel-Quelling General', a military hero who brought the island within the Han Chinese polity where, they say, it still belongs and to which it will one day return.

A graceful, curving breakwater, comma-shaped, sheltered the beach from the wide bay beyond. After looking at the shrine to Koxinga, with its tall palms growing behind, we walked out along the curve of the comma. At its further end, hammered into a block of sandstone, was a pin with a steel ring attached; tied within the ring were frayed fragments of black heavy duty marine rope, as if some ghost ship had been moored here once but had now sailed away. Just a few hundred metres to the west was the rock to which Tagawa Matsu clung as she was giving birth to Koxinga. It was silhouetted black against a line of green trees.

Our room looked south and we could see parts of mainland Kyushu on the other shore, as well as the opening of a passage to the East China Sea. We were there for two nights. Mostly we just hung at the hotel. It was cold, with a wind from the north, and we'd done enough sight-seeing for now. During the day, small steamers sailed back and forth along the reach of the strait, going to and from Hirado; in the evening, fishing boats anchored across the mouth of the bay, setting their nets against the night tide's turning. Their lights, mirrored in the dark water, resembled cathedrals in which, I imagined, drowned Dutchmen muttered imprecations against ghosts of boisterous wako.

Towards Fukuoka

After checking out of the hotel we drove into the old port at Hirado. The Dutch weren't allowed to trade from here for very long, only about thirty years, from 1609 to 1641, before they were removed, en masse, to Nagasaki. The town was small and old, built along narrow curving streets which followed the line of the waterfront. Long before the Portuguese or the Dutch came, this was the principal Japanese port for voyages to and from Korea and China; both green tea and Zen Buddhism entered Japan through Hirado. There was a huge castle, recently restored, on the other side of the water, the seat of the Matsura clan. We didn't go there; nor to the pale green St. Francis Xavier Memorial Church we could see on a hill overlooking the town.

We went instead to Okawachiyama, the Village of Hidden Kilns, in the mountains behind Arita. Everything connected with Okawachi, and with the famous Nabeshima ware made there, is mysterious, as if the secrecy that originally surrounded the village still persists. The chronology is variable or confused and the sequence of events remains uncertain. Towards the end of the sixteenth century, it seems, probably during Toyotomi Hideyoshi's attempt to invade Korea in 1592, Japanese forces abducted a number of skilled Korean artisans, brought them to the town of Arita and set them to making pottery. The Ming Dynasty was in strife, and supplies of ceramics from mainland China disrupted; hence the Japanese plan to make their own.

In 1604 one of these Korean potters, a man called Risanpei (Lee Cham-Pyung) recognised deposits of kaolin (China clay), so crucial for the making of fine porcelain, in the cliffs near Arita and began to experiment with it. It took him until 1616 to learn how to make ceramics from it. He then returned to Korea, recruited more potters and bought them across the sea to Japan. Subsequently, the Nabeshima clan, the Lords of Saga, kidnapped thirteen of these Korean potters and relocated them and their workshops to the newly built village of Okawachi. Kilns were built specially for them to use and the village's location kept, as far as possible, secret. There were mountains on three sides and just one road in. On this road a guard house was set up to monitor the movements of people in or out and to prevent any leakage of information.

The finest pottery made at Okawachi, the Nabeshima ware, went exclusively to the tables of the wealthy and the powerful — the Imperial Court, the shoguns, other feudal lords — as prestige gifts. As custom made offerings they did not need to be profitable, just of high quality. The Nabeshima paid the potters themselves and gave them samurai status, thus allowing them the use of family names. The distribution of their work was managed by a special government office and strict rules remained in place, including the restrictions upon who could enter and leave the village. The designs drew upon Japanese rather than Chinese traditions, especially motifs derived from textiles, and were characterised by a free use of empty space.

Animal and plant motifs were popular and a design showing three patterned jars a particular feature. Often tableware was produced in sets of five, with a high foot, in imitation of the dishes made of lacquered wood which were traditionally used on the tables of the rich. The anonymity of the potters was a feature of both Nabeshima ware and of Okawachi ware in general. This anonymity continued after death. A strange pyramid-shaped monument, made of shattered pieces of porcelain, has been built as a memorial to the Korean potters and their heirs; while the 880 graves surrounding it in the local cemetery are all unmarked.

It was raining as we left the highway and drove up a narrow winding road into the hills, crossing over a bridge decorated with large porcelain vessels and blue and white murals made from square tiles, to reach the village. On that misty morning it seemed an occulted place. The steep paved roads disappeared into the hills where the foliage on huge stands of bamboo shifted in the wind like kelp under water. Tall, square, brick chimneys smoked above black tiled roofs. The paving stones were dark, slippery, and wet, and all the restaurants were closed. There were about thirty workshops still operating, each with a shopfront; we visited several of these, and made some modest purchases, buying only pieces we would actually use and passing over those too heavy to carry or too expensive to risk breaking in transit.

Tokyo Bound

Fukuoka is a big city, the fourth biggest in Japan. We were flying out of there the next day. I dropped Mayu and our bags outside the hotel and went to park the car in the basement. Coming out into the busy Friday afternoon streets, I became disoriented: where was the hotel? I didn't know. It seemed to have disappeared. I didn't panic. The strange thing about being lost, I thought, is that you do not know how much time will pass before you find yourself again. It wasn't very long: I realised I'd inadvertently caught the lift from the underground carpark to a mall / department store that adjoined the hotel, back-tracked, and found my way to reception.

They were already looking for me. The tall thin fellow who had taken our luggage from the car came gliding across the floor, flapping his hands, in equal parts consternation and relief. A search party would have been sent out next. On each of the pillows of the twin beds in our room, delicately placed, was an origami crane. And in the slot outside, an English language newspaper, the *Japan News*: the first newspaper we'd seen in a month. Therein I learned that the percentage of people in Japan with antibodies to Covid is around 42% and the figures are skewed overwhelmingly towards the young. Of all the major cities, Fukuoka had the highest rate of infection, about fifty percent.

All told, as of March 2023, there had been over 33 million confirmed cases of Covid-19 in Japan — out of a population of 224 million — and 74,000 + deaths. The first case was identified on the sixteenth of January, 2020, in a resident of Kanagawa Prefecture who had just returned from Wuhan in China. The first death followed a month later, on the fourteenth of February. A second outbreak occurred in mid-March, 2020, introduced by travellers and returnees from Europe and the United States. By then, cases caused by the Wuhan variety were diminishing and those attributed to viruses with a European provenance, increasing. Mass vaccination began a year later, on the seventeenth of February, 2021; 96.4 million people received at least one jab and 86.9 million were fully vaccinated. Ten days later, on the twenty-seventh of February, all elementary, junior high, and senior high schools were closed and an indefinite State of Emergency declared in Tokyo and the prefectures of Kanagawa, Saitama, Chiba, Osaka, Hyogo and Fukuoka. On the sixteenth of April the State of Emergency was extended to cover the whole country.

Japan's death rate per capita from coronavirus, despite its aging population, was one of the lowest in the developed world. The prompt, efficient and relatively strict government response was one factor; a milder prevalent strain of the virus another; cultural habits such as bowing etiquette, a commitment to bodily cleanliness, and tendency follow the rules, a third. It's also been suggested that Japanese people possess a 'protective genetic trace' and that enhanced immunity was conferred upon them by the BCG tuberculosis vaccine, which is compulsory for all infants during their first year of life, and usually administered, in a single dose, when they are between five and eight months old. Apparently deaths from pneumonia in Japan also fell as a result of infection control measures people took. This happened in other parts of the world too, where rates of influenza, the common cold and other transmissible viral diseases declined.

Another article reported, in tones of muted irritation, that since the mandate upon wearing masks has been dropped in Hong Kong, hardly anyone has dispensed with them. This was funny because exactly the same thing happened in Japan. Since the fourteenth of March, 2023, you no longer had to wear a mask in public; yet almost everybody still did. People even wore them when they were driving alone in their cars. It was the tail end of the pandemic but I took a test anyway, because of my cold, and because Mayu's mother is well into her eighties and shouldn't be exposed to Covid. It came back negative. My injured knee was feeling much better too.

The next morning we went for a swim in the hotel pool and then took a hot bath before checking out. We filled the Note up with gas and returned it to the depot. The shuttle driver who took us to the airport, a cheerful fellow, was replaying a radio broadcast of the previous night's baseball game, the World Series Final, in which the Japanese had beaten the United States. We had been following the national team's progress, intermittently, since Miyazaki. We'd seen them play the Czechs, the Danes, the Italians and the Koreans but not, alas, the Americans. The flight took off north and east, and the land below was soon lost beneath the clouds. It was melancholy leaving: so that was Kyushu. Or those parts of it we were lucky enough to see.

Island of Silver & Gold

Sado | June | 2023

Beyond Ogi

As soon as I learned that Highway 18, which runs through Shinanomachi, was one of the routes down which gold and silver was transported from Sado to Edo during the Tokugawa shogunate, I wanted to visit the island. Once Yoshie, Mayu's mother, after an extended stay at her *besso*, returned to Tokyo, we had the opportunity and decided to go. Mayu booked ferry tickets to and fro, and three nights in a resort hotel on the west coast of the island; and one rainy morning in June we set off in the car for Joetsu to rendezvous with the 1.50 pm sailing. Sado is about a hundred kilometres north-west of Joetsu's port, Naoetsu, in the Sea of Japan; the boat trip takes two and a half hours, so we could expect to arrive there a bit after 4.00 pm. Our vessel was a blinding white, sturdy, diesel-powered roll-on roll-off ferry, rumbling contentedly at its moorings at the terminal.

The terminal itself was a utilitarian building from the 1960s set amongst huge, stark concrete carparks, almost deserted this Wednesday afternoon. We secured our tickets, but not before a couple of men in uniform had inspected the documents in the glove box of the car to confirm that we did indeed own it. It was a 2013 Toyota Vitz ('one lady owner') I bought for the ridiculous sum of ¥200,000 — just over 2,000 Australian Dollars. We walked up a nearby street, looking for a place to eat, but all the restaurants were closed. There was a noodle shop at the terminal, however, and we ate there; the food was excellent. Then we boarded, parking the Vitz with half a dozen other vehicles in the almost empty hold of the ferry and joining a busload of Japanese Hawaiians on some kind of jaunt as fellow passengers up top.

Naoetsu Port is set between immensely long breakwaters reaching far out into the sea. As we sailed between them, on flat wharves to the north, a claw crane was lifting load after load of scrap metal into the hold of a tramp steamer registered in Freetown, Sierra Leone and going, most likely, to China, if it was not heading to Korea or to another domestic port in Japan. There were piles of scrap everywhere and other steamers, moored at more distant berths, were taking on similar loads. The Japanese are world experts at sorting scrap metal for material that can be used again; but these glittering piles, like dragons' hoards from legend, seemed not to have undergone any ordering yet. On the tip of the longest breakwater I have ever seen was a trim red lighthouse shaped like a rocket; then we were out on the open ocean.

About an hour later, from the viewing platform on the top deck, I could see a pale blue line of land ahead. Sado Island consists of two parallel mountain ranges, both inclining north-east, with a flat plain between them. The Osado range on the seaward side, just over a thousand metres tall at its highest point, is more rugged; the landward Kosado range is lower and gentler, with orange trees and tea plantations growing on its fertile slopes. In between the two, the Kuninaka Plain is drained by the Kono River flowing into Mano Bay in the south-west. In the north-east lies Lake Kamo, once fresh water but now, after an opening was made to the sea, a brackish lagoon in which oysters are cultivated. The flat lands of the plain are extensively farmed, mainly growing rice. Sado City is here, and Ryotsu Port, where the ferries from Niigata dock. We were, however, heading for the port of Ogi, on the east coast, near the southern tip of the Kosado range.

There was another breakwater at the entrance to the harbour, zig-zagging out into the water, with a white lighthouse at its tip. As the ferry rumbled past, its engines decelerating, I saw a fisherman in black cast his line into the water; he and his rod looked tiny beside the lighthouse which had seemed, until then, diminutive itself. Ogi is the port from which the gold was shipped to the mainland in the Edo period, but it is much older than that. Sado has been inhabited for at least 10,000 years, since the Jomon period; the Yayoi and the Kofun were here as well. The island became a place of exile early in the historical period and those who were deemed troublesome or undesirable were sent here from the mainland; this had the effect of exporting elements of the imperial culture to this remote place where, inadvertently, they flourished.

We didn't linger in Ogi. We drove out of town and south down the coast a few kilometres to the village of Shukunegi, a port since medieval times, which became prosperous during the gold years, and a place where *kitamaebune* (ships trading between Edo, Osaka and the northern ports) called. It was also a centre of traditional ship-building, with a dozen families engaged in the trade until modernization following the Meiji Restoration made them redundant. The village was built at the head of small cove. We came down the hill and pulled into a carpark on a flat wharf opposite, where a man and a woman were in the process of pulling a small, circular boat, a *taraibune*, like a wooden bath tub, out of the water.

The man, who was older, wearing a blue shirt, a black cap, and a raffish look, apologised, unnecessarily, explaining that the demonstration was over for the day; had we arrived earlier, we could have gone for a ride in the taraibune ourselves. The taraibune ('tub boat') is peculiar to Sado, and was probably invented here at Shukunegi. As the man in the blue shirt explained, following an earthquake a couple of hundred years ago, which raised up the land, they were an innovative design which turned out to be useful for navigating between rocky outcrops in search of seaweed (*wakame*) and shellfish, especially *sazae*, the horned turban, which I had eaten at Oita.

The woman, aged about thirty, formally dressed in a dark blue top over white trousers, and a yellow straw hat, climbed back down into the taraibune, cast off its mooring and, using the single oar, held upright, showed us how manoeuvrable it was. It was late afternoon. The setting sun cast silver light upon sea and the reflection of the green headland to the north wavered in the clear water of the bay. I watched a sea-slug, whitish-yellow, about a foot long, with two questing horns, grazing the rocky bottom near where the stream ran out. Then we crossed over the road to the village itself, where various residents were parking their cars after returning home from the day's activities.

Shukunegi, which consists of about a hundred closely packed houses, was built around a canal in a small, oval shaped valley; it looks, from above, as if cupped in the hand of a benevolent god. Narrow, paved laneways run between the houses and alongside the canal. The houses, which are all different shapes and sizes, were mostly built using recycled ships' timbers and the wood had been stained the same black I'd noticed on a tobacco shop in Naoetsu: Black Japan, so-called, is a bituminous solvent used to stain lighter timber to a dark, almost black, colour, often over coated with shellac to give a gloss finish. It has preservative and anti-corrosive properties, resembles what we used to call creosote, and weathers from ebony to various attractive shades of black and brown; colours can range from gold to amber to silver grey.

I felt like an intruder as we walked down the laneways between the houses, even though Shukunegi is an established tourist destination and there were signs identifying the cinema, the meeting hall and other attractions, including the open houses where you can go inside for a look: also closed this Wednesday afternoon. We took photos at the famous triangle corner where there was a sign upon which the character for salt had been inscribed. Further on, towards the back of the village, I wandered into a shrine which turned out to contain the Shoko temple. It was founded in 1349 as the first school on Sado devoted to Pure Land Buddhism and the Amida Buddha, the recitation of whose name may accomplish beatitude, not after the death of the body but in this life.

Shoko-ji also enshrines Benzaiten, one of the Seven Fortunate Gods, mistress of all that flows: water, music, arts, love, wisdom, wealth, fortune. Here she is worshipped as goddess of the sea, who protects against shipwreck; she is usually shown with a *biwa*, the Japanese lute. The grave of Shibata Shuzo is here too. He was a Shukunegi native, the son of a fisherman who became a doctor, later a geographer, and drew an elaborate map of the world. I didn't see the grave. In fact, I didn't enter the temple precinct, I just looked in from the outside, through the square, open wooden gate. There was an unusual *Jizo* with a child, seen from behind, clinging to its chest, three small figures lined up at its feet and flowers laid on the plinth beneath. It was most likely a guardian of unborn or stillborn children. The shrine was a quiet and shadowy place, full of presences which seemed both ancient and benign, and after being there for a while I did not feel so much like an intruder in Shukunegi.

Late afternoon was turning to evening as we drove over the range and around the shores of Mano Bay. The streets of the towns of Yawata and Sawata were lined with houses, temples, barns and other buildings all that same shade of matt or glossy black; their roofs were of tiles made of local clay, which bakes to a handsome dark reddish colour, making the houses seem like those of another land than the one we had just come from. As with other old towns in Japan, the local architecture had been meticulously preserved and yet was serviced with the most modern utilities, while the residents drove immaculate, up to date vehicles. The tide was low and we could see many silvery racks for the cultivation of oysters gleaming in the bay, before the road rose up into the southern reaches of the Osado Range and then took us, through a tunnel, to the other side.

Aikawa looks over the western sea towards Korea. The Azuma Resort Hotel was further south down the coast, on a promontory which claimed to be the most westerly point of the island and therefore 'closest to the setting sun'. Our room had tatami mats on the floor, gold paper covering the wall panelling and on the screen doors that closed off the bedrooms and the balcony, views to the west and the south, and its own private onsen. You could recline on the blue stones, looking over the hotel lawn, at the end of which was a white swing, untenanted, with its own illumination, swinging back and forth and turning ghostly as night came on and the sea darkened to black.

The Ruins of Aikawa

The next morning we drove back around the seashore into the town of Aikawa then turned right and climbed a narrow, twisting road leading between lushly vegetated slopes up a steep hill. Every now and then an extraordinary image would appear on the skyline: a mountain peak which was split down the middle, as if cloven in two by the blow of some cosmic axe. Doyu no Wareto is not a natural feature, however, but man-made, the result of open cut gold and silver mining (from the summit of the peak down) in the early seventeenth century. The V-shaped crack is thirty metres wide and seventy-four metres deep. Here was the mother lode, the Doyu vein, about ten metres broad. After it had been exhausted, most mining took place underground. Some of the tunnels had been preserved and it was into one of these that we were going to go.

The origins of mining on Sado are ancient. Gold ornaments sometimes turn up in Kofun tombs; surface deposits of gold and silver were known in the Heian period (794-1185). The precious metals were used to gild altars and statues of the Buddha before becoming indices of private wealth. The twelfth century compilation *Konjaku Monogatari* (Anthology of Tales from the Past) includes the advice: 'Go to Noto to dig iron, go to Sado for gold.'

Zipangu, the Isle of Gold recorded by Marco Polo, was almost certainly Japan, and may have been a garbled account of Sado. The mines of Sado were a source of the wealth of the Honma clan; when they were defeated, in 1589, by the Uesugi clan, the bounty passed into their hands; a few years later, in 1603, the Tokugawa came to power and took the mines for their own.

There had just been a major find. In 1601, prospectors looking for silver at the Tsurushi Mine, co-terminus with Aikawa, uncovered a new, hitherto unsuspected, vein. As soon as they had defeated their rivals the Toyotomi at the Battle of Sekigahara, the Tokugawa took executive control of the whole island of Sado and began to investigate the new discovery. Okubo Nagayasu was appointed as *bugyo* (magistrate) to govern both the mine and the island itself. Okubo was an experienced administrator who had previously been in charge of silver mines at Sagami, south of Edo, and, after leaving Sado, moved on to administer mines at Izu, south of Sagami; in all three places he expanded production. At its peak, in the first half of the 1600s, the mine at Aikawa was producing 400 kilograms of gold and forty tons of silver per year.

Okubo Nagasayu's skills were in accounting and logistics, and in those areas he made a significant contribution to the military successes of the Tokugawa. On Sado, his influence went beyond the maximization of mining revenues; he had been a Noh actor in his youth and remained devoted to the form. As Lord of Sado he brought with him actors, masks, costumes, and scripts, and was responsible for a resurgence in the practice of the theatre on the island which continues to this day. Curiously enough, after his death in 1613, 'evidence of misconduct was found'. His fief was confiscated and all of his seven sons were ordered to commit suicide. You wonder what this 'misconduct' might have been: one source suggests misappropriation of public funds, not by himself but by his unfortunate sons. I found out later the real reason for this calamity.

The mine continued operations for 388 years until in 1989, its ores exhausted, it closed. By then it had yielded seventy-eight tons of gold and 2,230 tons of silver. Remarkably, up until the Meiji Restoration, it was worked entirely by manual labour; and was yet able to deliver gold of a purity — 99.54% — greater than that produced by mechanical and chemical means in comparable operations in Europe and America at the time. In the early years it was particularly lucrative and it was gold and silver from Sado which underpinned the economy of Japan in the early years of the Tokugawa shogunate and ensured its economic viability. The cost of this prosperity was borne in the bodies of the miners; at its peak, the model village built on the slopes below the mines was home to five thousand workers and their families.

We parked the car and at the ticket office bought entry to the Sohdayu Tunnel Course, which takes you down one of the old shafts from the Tokugawa era. It was dark and cold and, although the ground was dry underfoot, the walls were dripping; it seemed incredible that these relatively spacious tunnels had been hewn from the rock by hand tools alone. In the early stages there were maps and information boards on the walls; lower down, in side tunnels which were presumably part of the original mine, life-sized mannequins, some of them mechanically animated robots, had been placed in such a way as to show how the work was done.

These figures inside three-dimensional dioramas seemed improbable at first but became more believable the lower down we went. I was reminded of those forms of Japanese theatre in which human actors approximate the movement or the stillness of puppets, and those in which puppets are the main actors and humans their aides and attendants. On one occasion, while looking at a mannequin representing one of the *mushukunin*, homeless people forcibly brought in to work the mines, the figure, head-down, somnolent, apparently washing gold from a wooden pan using a bucket on a rope, suddenly raised up his head and looked me directly in the eyes.

There were scribes recording data with brushes on wooden panels; supervisors monitoring the output and assayers grading the ore; miners with chisels held between the pincers of a pair of pliers to spare their hands; simulacra of the oil lights which were the only means of illumination; groups of men eating their lunches of rice and vegetables; ventilation shafts; *tanuki* tunnels, which were exploratory and could only be entered, like dogs, by a man on all fours; and many ingenious ways of removing water from the diggings, including examples of the screw pump invented by Archimedes.

Underground water was the main hazard and it became more hazardous the longer the mining went on and the deeper the tunnels were dug; sometimes they extended out under the bed of the sea. The quartz rock that bore the veins of precious metal was so hard that collapses were uncommon and the tunnels did not usually need bolstering with timber supports. However the hardness of the rock took its toll on the tools: an iron chisel lasted just two days before it had to be sent up and sharpened again.

The most elaborate and impressive of these dioramas was the last. In a cavern hollowed out of the rock, a priest in golden robes and a conical hat, sitting on a high platform, flanked by four musicians with flutes and drums, chanted a sonorous prayer which played, to the sound of clinking chisels, through hidden speakers. On the floor below, two miners examined silver-black, gold-bearing veins in the rock while a third sat before one of the wooden trays used for assessing samples; two more, their backs to us, one sitting and one standing, looked over an elaborate set of sacrificial offerings laid out on a cloth spread upon the ground.

This was a staged version of a ritual performed every year, its purpose to implore the gods to lead the miners to veins of softer ore where the gold and silver were to be found. The eerie sound of the chanting, with its percussive and musical accompaniment, the repetitive movements of the robots in the stark white light, which you saw through an opening, like a proscenium, in the black rock, had the effect of animating the underground into something rich and strange. Somehow the display conjured the illusion, brief though it was, that these mechanical actors were actually human.

We came out into the light of day, crossed over a bridge, and on the other side entered a museum. It was devoted almost exclusively to the techniques and processes of mining and the tools with which it was done: understandable, perhaps, since both practices and implements are now obsolete; and the achievement of pulling forty odd tons of pure gold out of the ground using such primitive means was undoubtedly impressive. At the same time, it seemed as dull as the work itself must have been, and scarcely graspable in an imaginative sense. A display of a rock face containing actual ore was more interesting: you could see the tiny specks of gold within the black and silver that was the predominant colour of the veins. Most of the gold came from pulverizing the ore to recover these specks. Nuggets were so rare as to be almost unknown.

Another display consisted of a three-dimensional map of the ore bodies as they had once existed, visualized without the mass of rock that once surrounded them. These ore bodies, made of a kind of translucent plastic, grey-white in colour, were beautiful, ethereal. They looked like underground clouds, like lungs or wings, like billowing fungi. An information card noted that the eight large veins of gold stretched three kilometres east to west, 600 metres north to south and to a depth of 800 metres. About 400 kilometres of tunnels, including ventilation shafts, had been excavated in the quest to recover this ore. Curiously enough, this was the same length as the road to Edo, where most of the gold had been transported.

There was also a model of the village, its rows of identical houses clustered on the slopes below the Magistrate's Office, really a kind of palace, on the crest of the hill. I was looking for some actual gold, and there it was, next to the translucent ore bodies, in a small display case containing just two coins: a *koban*, oval, the size of a child's hand, beaten thin, delicately inscribed. Next to that, smaller, thicker, and more heavily inscribed, was a rectangular *ichiban*. Four ichiban made one koban; one koban, in turn, was worth three *koku* of rice. A koku was enough rice to feed a single person for a year and the standard measure of the wealth of an estate in the Edo period. When Okubo Nagasayu's fief was confiscated in 1613 it was worth 30,000 koku.

Another display featured what appeared to be a gold bar, rectangular, gleaming, with an aperture in the perspex case through which you could reach to lay your hand upon it. If you could lift the ingot up and withdraw it through the aperture without dropping it, some unspecified reward (not a gold bar) would be yours. It was so heavy I couldn't even get it off the base it sat upon, but a young man, stronger or perhaps more motivated than I was, did manage to pick it up. Alas, he was unable to hold onto it for long enough, or in such a way, as to manoeuvre it through the gap and so claim his reward. I congratulated him upon getting thus far. He laughed ruefully and shrugged his shoulders. As I left the room, he was having another go.

Outside the museum was a hand-turned Archimedean screw pump which recycled coloured plastic beads in lieu of water and a stall where you could buy ice-cream sprinkled with gold flakes. I asked the young woman serving if it was real gold. She giggled and said that it was. While I was licking my gold encrusted ice-cream, I looked at a line of graves opposite, set against a low earthen bank upon which shrubs and ferns grew. These were tombs memorializing mushukunin who had, after their deaths, been given Buddhist names to place beside their common names, which were inscribed, along with their birthplaces and, if known, their ages, on their gravestones.

During its peak period, from 1615 to 1645, mine workers were paid handsomely and the surrounding towns became prosperous. Later, however, extraction became increasingly difficult, mainly because of the inflow of water from natural springs and the infiltration of sea water. People no longer came voluntarily to work in the mines and the shogunate began using forced labour, including convicted criminals, to work them. Conditions for these men were extremely harsh; they were used for the most dangerous tasks, particularly the heavy labour involved in dewatering the tunnels.

Later in the Edo period, about 2,000 mushukunin, homeless people who were unregistered and of no fixed address, were rounded up by military police off the streets of Edo, Osaka and Nagasaki (all, like Sado, directly administered by the bakufu) and forced to come here and work as drainage labourers. Most died young. Their tombs were imposing, moss-covered, sombre; some had yellow and white flowers placed in vases before them. I kept thinking of the robot who had so unexpectedly looked up and fixed me with his black, resigned and soulful eyes.

We went back down the mountain and found ourselves in a traditional village which resembled a hillside version of Shukunegi. Up the far end of the narrow, steep, main street, lined with houses stained with the many shades of Black Japan, was an abandoned detention centre. I parked the car next to an ancient watch house with a drink vending machine installed, incongruously, inside it. A line of artefacts, all labelled, lay in the grass next to it, overgrown with wild strawberries: the roof peak of a house, with the *kawara*, tiles, made from the local clay; several misshapen grinding stones, worn down by the sharpening of chisels; a stone pot with a stone lid, to be filled with water in which a fire from a brazier could be extinguished; a wide, oblong, shallow, stone sink of traditional design, used for washing up in domestic kitchens.

The main gates faced the road. They were of rusty, white-painted iron and they were locked; but there was smaller gate within which was open and a notice inviting interested parties to enter. The detention centre was a remand facility where those who had been accused of a crime but not yet convicted were held; in Japan, then and now, an accusation of wrong-doing is almost always tantamount to a conviction. This place was a twentieth century ruin. Built before the war, it had ceased operation as recently as 1972, cleared out and then left as it was, with the addition of information labels telling you what each room had been used for.

On the right as you came through the double glass front doors were two tiny rooms, side by side, about the same size, one empty, the other with a wooden bench, at chest height, dividing it in half and a chair on either side. The first was where visitors waited to be called, the second, with the barrier, where the visit took place, with visitor and visited sitting opposite each other with the bench between them. Visits were closely monitored and strictly timed, just half an hour long. Past these grim and poignant spaces were the more generously proportioned administration areas. These rooms were all empty apart from one which contained a dusty, three-legged, leather upholstered swivel chair in one corner, and a heavy metal safe with a pale green door in the other. It was massive, baleful, inscrutable, like a prop for a horror movie: what might it have contained?

The grief and sadness of the place was palpable, the air full of the cries of lost souls; but, strangely, the prison wing, which stretched away to the right of the admin area, was less forbidding. Here were facilities for bathing, cooking (inmates prepared their own food) and exercise. Individual cells, numbered 1–10, were tiny, the size of three tatami mats. Each had a straw covering on the floor for sleeping, mostly still in situ but much decayed; a hole in the floor for a toilet; and a tap and a sink for washing. They had a single barred window and a viewing aperture, also barred, in the door. Down below, at floor level, was a wooden opening through which, presumably, food and drink could be passed to those condemned to solitary confinement.

In one of these cells someone had scratched their name in Roman capitals on the whitewash and then scribbled a signature beneath it. In another there was a mechanical trolley with a wooden seat upon it, so that a disabled or incapacitated, perhaps bound, person could be wheeled under the shower to bathe. One of the cells, number nine, marginally bigger, was for women with children. The exercise yard was reached by double glass doors like those at the entrance. It was an L-shaped space, quite large, overgrown with grass, weeds and wildflowers, and closed on three sides by plastered stone walls twice the height of a man; these were covered with creepers. I walked up and down a few times, trying to imagine what it might have been like to have been locked up here with your likely fate either further incarceration in a larger prison or else execution.

Towards the bottom of the village, opposite a large, modern administration block, was a building described as 'The Ruins of Sado Bugyosho (the Office of the Magistrate)'. Whatever else it might have been, it was not a ruin. Rather, the *bugyosho* was the immaculately restored government facility from which the magistrate, the bugyo, who administered both mines and island, had ruled. The wooden building had burned down five times since it was established in 1603 to house the first magistrate, Okubo Nagasayu. This was a replica, built in the year 2000 'based on excavated evidence and drawings from 1859.' The exterior was made of plain grey planks which gave it an aura as stern and unyielding as the colonial headquarters of a military occupation, which, in fact, it was.

Here were the government offices dealing with public administration, judicial procedures and the gold and silver mining; the bugyo's official residence, a veritable palace, which had not been rebuilt, stood behind. To one side, below the ground and behind a moat, was the vault where the gold and silver were kept; on the other, also down a level, was a large rectangular building, the *seriba,* or factory, in which the ore had been pulverized and the gold and silver smelted, cast, and minted. Inside the bugyosho, belying that grey exterior, the rooms were lined with golden wood and floored with tatami mats. The better class of people walked upon tatami, while those of lesser importance walked on wooden or on earthen floors. In some of the rooms, for instance the elegant and capacious reception hall (still used for official functions) at the heart of the building, the decorative nail head covers, *kugikakushi,* were made of gilt bronze, not copper, iron, or wood as they would have been in less prestigious rooms.

Off the corridor, running down the right-hand side of the reception hall, were the archives, the libraries and the offices where the scribes, clerks, and accountants had worked. To the rear were the kitchens and toilets, with upright urinals in the style still used today and old fashioned floor lavatories for those who needed or wanted to squat. Instead of porcelain, however, they were made of wood gone dark with age and moisture. Identical facilities were installed diagonally opposite, on the other corner of the building. Also on that side were the *shirasu* (courts of white sand) where audiences were granted and justice dispensed.

The bugyo, who was both inquisitor and prosecutor, sat in state above those he was to examine; they wore sandals and waited on straw mats below, in a pit covered with chipped white stones. From there they made their pleas or asked their favours. The smaller and meaner of these two rooms was the one where criminals were arraigned; the accused entered from outside, through a low wooden door, and presumably exited the same way once their doom had been pronounced. Meanwhile, those petitioners who had been granted a more formal audience had their own entrance inside the building and a dressing room where they could prepare themselves for the fateful encounter.

Most of the rooms in the building were bare of furniture and exhibits. In one, however, there was a glass case containing a large oval lead plate upon which the gold, already beaten thin to make kobun, was stamped, leaving behind the imprint of enigmatic hieroglyphs on the soft grey surface. Another, much longer, glass case held a painted scroll which pictured the progress of the gold from the mines up above, through the various stages of refinement it underwent, to the transports which took it to the port, culminating in a picture of a boat, in heavy seas, working its way towards the mainland. More than a hundred of these painted scrolls survive. They are the documentary basis for what has been re-constructed into exhibits in the two museums: the one we had seen up above, the other in the seriba, the adjoining factory in which the 'beneficiation' or separation of metal from ore was accomplished.

Here another scroll, meticulously detailed, showed men using the tools and techniques with which this work was done. It was first crushed with hammers and the residue sieved; the sieved particles were ground further under millstones. This gravel was then panned before being sluiced through cotton. These processes were repeated many times until every particle of the precious metals had been retrieved. After that, the gold and silver was smelted, cast and minted. The technology used in these mechanical processes had also been re-constructed in the museum, using models, so that you had both the illustration and the actuality before you; the art and the work, perhaps. I found this museum as dazzling and as inscrutable as the one up the hill.

Below the bugyosho, at Kitazawa, on flat, park-like land either side of the river running down from the mountains, stood a set of veritable and spectacular ruins dating back to the early twentieth century. In 1869, after the Meiji Restoration, the new government took over management of the mine and, with the help of Western engineers, inaugurated the processes of industrializing production. In 1889 the mine became the property of the Ministry of the Imperial Household; seven years later, in 1896, that ministry sold it to Mitsubishi Goshi Kaisha, the forerunner of the Mitsubishi Corporation.

The next half century saw production levels exceed those attained during the first lucrative years of extraction under the Tokugawa, when the veins of ore were pristine and, relatively speaking, accessible. Using imported machinery and modern mining techniques, by 1940 the Aikawa mine was yielding 1,500 kilos of gold and twenty-five tons of silver annually. The war disrupted production even though forced labour from Korea was brought in to do the bulk of the work. The mine never really recovered and large-scale operations had ceased by 1952, before it closed for good in 1989.

These then were the ruins of that industrialization. The most spectacular was a vast, decayed, terraced structure, overgrown with ivy, which resembled the flank of a Meso-American temple. It was the remains of the Flotation Plant, built in the late 1930s as part of the so-called 'war-time increase in production plan'. This was where, using chemicals and oils dissolved in water, the precious metals were separated out from their ore bodies, a process accomplished by altering the surfaces of mineral particles to a hydrophobic or hydrophilic condition — that is, so that they either repelled or were attracted by water. Harvesting then followed. Flotation requires huge amounts of energy. This one had its own power station, now another museum, built next to it. At its peak it was able to process over 50,000 tons of ore per month.

On the other side of the river was a circular concrete structure, a tank, built into the side of a hill. Its flat roof was supported by a number of slender columns, dark, arched shapes visible in the shadowy depths beneath. This was the Thickener, where solids in suspension were persuaded to settle, under the influence of gravity, to form a thick pulp. This pulp, and the clear liquid on top of it, could then be removed and the grains of gold isolated and retrieved. Like flotation, thickening, also known as sedimentation, has affinities with the old methods of panning and sluicing for gold; both techniques were used to extract remaining precious metals from ore which had already been subjected to those more primitive and laborious processes.

The third ruin was the back wall of what had once been a factory for casting, using wooden moulds, iron and steel machine components. It looked like a narrow bridge without roads leading to or from it. All three of these structures possessed an enigmatic grandeur that was unaccountable in terms of the mundane details of how they operated and what they did. They seemed more like the relics of a lost civilization than did the mines up above, the bugyosho, or even the detention centre; perhaps because they did in fact anticipate the coming state of our doomed industrial complexes. We live surrounded by future ruins; here they were, eerily, already present.

On the Kuninaka Plain

Beneath soft grey skies, in desultory morning rain, we drove north along the flat plain of Kuninaka between two mountain ranges, rugged Osado on the left, gentler Kosado on the right. We were going to Ryotsu Port to see the festival at Ebisu, held at the Suwa

Shrine in June every year in honour of the tutelary god of the area, a deity no-one seemed able to tell us anything about, not even its name. The shrine was in a pocket of residential houses behind the junction of two main roads, decorated with lanterns, next to a pre-school where children in coloured hats were being marshalled on the long veranda at the front of the classrooms. A small group of people stood around outside the main building; from within, the sound of chanting, clapping and some muffled drumming could be heard.

We sheltered under an unwalled roof standing over a stone basin into which the purifying water ran, with two black ladles for making libations. There were a couple of older fellows also waiting there. One of them, who got around with a ski pole and a furled umbrella as walking sticks, was a photographer; the other, portly, wearing a tweed jacket, his journalist partner. They were covering the event for the local newspaper. The journalist went around the side of the shrine to investigate and came back a few minutes later to report that the ornate gold carriage, the centre piece of the procession, remained in its shed. Evidently there was still some concern that the skies might, literally, rain on the parade.

Various other people acting in an official capacity came and went from the shrine to a small, functional complex off to the right, which looked like an admin block. Everybody else just stood around. No-one seemed too concerned, not even when a party of pre-schoolers, about two dozen strong, wearing the different coloured hats which told you their age and year, came with their teachers and carers up the drive to join us. These children were very polite; the elder ones bowed gravely and said '*konnichiwa*' as they passed us by. The younger ones, wide-eyed, just looked. They too milled around for a while and then trooped back to the pre-school.

It must have been about half an hour before a subtle increase in activity in and around the shrine suggested a decision had been made. The drumming and chanting had ceased some time before; now the doors opened and three young girls dressed as princesses, and the three young princes who were their escorts, appeared. They were gorgeous and shy; the girls wearing pink diaphanous dresses and veils, the boys in dark suits. Then several men disappeared around the side of the shrine and came back, not too long after, pushing and pulling the carriage. It wasn't very large, squarish, a wooden cart on inflated rubber wheels bearing an elaborately carved golden casket with red accoutrements. It had black lacquered handles front and back where, in former times, it would have been carried, like a litter, on men's shoulders.

Everyone gathered around. The children in their red, yellow and blue caps had returned; there was another group of kids, younger than the princes and princesses, dressed in grey robes with yellow scarves if they were boys, and blue kimono with pink jackets if they were girls. From somewhere, but I don't know where, a tall figure in green trousers and a pink embroidered jacket, carrying an ornate staff and wearing a mask with a long nose beneath a platinum blond wig, appeared. This was Sarutahiko, the herald god, leader of earthly kami, who would guide the procession which was slowly and cheerfully organising itself around him. He was, perhaps, originally a monkey god. His long-nosed mask, called a *tengumen*, is said to bring good fortune and protect those who wear it from malign influences. This fellow was genial and companionable and keen to be photographed alongside anyone, including me.

While everything else was being marshalled behind him, he waited at the gate outside the shrine until, at a signal, with help, he began to put on a pair of high-heeled wooden sandals, really mini-stilts. He had a male attendant, with a small folding stool, upon which Sarutahiko sat while the sandals were fitted to his feet, already encased in white cotton socks, before teetering uncertainly upright. This attendant, I noted, with his stool, accompanied him on the procession and was always nearby if he needed a helping hand or a sit down.

I joined several men gathered around watching this interesting process unfold. From their jokes and jibes, it became clear that this role was taken in turn and some of these men had done it themselves, without mishap, in earlier years. Our Sarutahiko, who was a first-timer, assured everyone he would be fine, even though the hair of his platinum blond wig kept falling over the eyeholes of his mask, making him look like an exotic, distracted version of Andy Warhol. Just before he set off, a serious young woman in overalls came out of the crowd and brushed it back for him; but as soon as he started down the road, forward it fell over his eyes again.

Apart from the golden cart, the other vehicles in the procession were a wagon bearing the three princes and princesses and another, larger one in which the younger children sat. All three were pulled along by hand. There were about a dozen standard bearers, mostly middle-aged men, with their poles and flags flying. Two other men had wooden boxes slung around their necks; these they shook up and down, making the coins within jingle-jangle to encourage people to add their own contribution to the store of donations. Finally, there was a small Chinese-style lion, with one dancer, a young man, as its head and another, smaller and less expert, as its tail. This lion wove in and out of the procession; at one point I saw it in the playground of the pre-school, frightening the little children, who squealed and ran away and then came back for more.

The rain, which had never been heavy, stopped. The procession, at once orderly and chaotic, set off, heading north to the junction with one of the major roads. Marshalls negotiated traffic, which included heavy trucks and buses. Drums beat and coin boxes jingled and the small children in their cart sang beautifully and in unison. It was going to be a long day. The parade would go on through the afternoon, visiting many different parts of the city before the festivities continued into the night, when there would be dancing in the streets. We accompanied it only to the corner where we had parked the car outside a house which turned out to belong to the head priest of the shrine.

There we were joined by a middle-aged woman who was, she said, the head priest's wife; and, she added, a concert pianist. I looked at her hands. They were compact, muscular, capable and strong. Mayu asked her who the tutelary god of the shrine was; but she would only say, as others had said, that it was the god of the shrine of Ebisu. Perhaps we were being obtuse. Ebisu, as well as the name of the shrine and of the locality where it was situated, is one of the Seven Fortunate Gods. He is usually depicted as a fat, happy, laughing man with a red sea bream in one hand and a fishing rod in the other; it must have been him. He is the god of fishermen and he keeps the seas fertile and clean.

We chatted to her for a few more minutes then said our goodbyes and went on our way, turning right into the street where the procession had turned left; we could still see its raggedy line of poles and standards in the distance and hear the distant beat of the drums. As we drove down the main drag, a block from the sea, I looked to the left and saw a bridge adorned with bronze mermaids and other mythological figures. I think it was spanning the channel where the former freshwater Lake Kamo, now brackish, had been opened up to the ocean.

We drove down the eastern shore of the lake, heading south onto the Kunikaki Plain; to the west the dark green hills of the Osado Range were reflected in still, silver waters. Soon the country opened out into rice fields disposed in rectangles between raised and grassed earthen banks on either side of the road. The electric green shoots on the young plants were about a month old now and seemed bigger and more advanced than those growing in Shinanomachi. Sometimes we saw grey herons or white egrets; on several occasions I mistook the raised, curved shape of a water outlet for a wading bird because I knew there were crested ibis, *toki*, living wild around here, having been released from a nearby facility where a breeding program had been in progress since the last decades of last century. It was there, to Tokinomori Park, that we were going.

We turned off to the right and drove through more rice paddies until the road lifted and climbed and we found the entrance, among pine trees, to the park. Crested ibis nest in pine or chestnut trees overlooking rice fields, where they feed upon small fish, frogs, crustaceans and insects. It seems likely that, since the Yayoi period began 3,000 years ago, they have co-evolved alongside rice cultivations all over the archipelago. For a long time, they were revered; then they weren't. Their status as pests, which led to a steep decline in numbers, is relatively recent.

Early in the Tokugawa period, in 1639, records show that one hundred pairs of ibis were released along the river Oyabe, on the mainland to the south, to provide feathers for arrows. Some think the population on Sado descended from these pairs. The chronicles of the Tokugawa also include detailed descriptions of the hunting of ibis using falcons, an elite sport reserved for aristocrats during the shogunate.

By the 1700s, however, they were being seen as a problem. A report in 1737 notes that the magistrate's office at Hachinohe, in the north of Honshu, had received reports of 'several instances of toki ruining rice crops.' The magistrate ordered that rifles be provided to people in three affected villages, with instructions 'that no birds other than toki may be shot.' There are songs recorded from the Niigata Prefecture, which includes Sado, called '*tori oi uta*' or bird-chasing songs. They were sung by children to drive birds away from the fields. One of these, from Ojiya, includes the words: 'Ora ga itchi nikui tori wa / do to sangi to ko-suzume / otte tamae ta no kami' — the three birds I hate the most / the toki, the heron and the sparrow / spirit of the paddies, drive them away.

Their steep decline in numbers following the Meiji Restoration was the result of several additional factors. After the invention of the Murata rifle in 1880, and the granting of gun and hunting licences to ordinary folk, ibis were shot and killed in their thousands. They had several uses; their down, valued for its softness, was used in quilts; while their wing and tail feathers were made into dusters popular in silkworm factories, and used as decorations on Buddhist altars. Meanwhile their crests were exported to Europe to ornament ladies' hats. Even the meat, while not accounted tasty, was boiled to make a bloody soup thought to have medicinal properties, good for anaemia and for 'female chills'. From the 1950s, the increased use of pesticides in the rice fields had a major impact upon their food supplies and, most likely, on their own health as well.

Crested ibis, which used to range across East Asia, from Siberia to Korea, China, and Taiwan, survived on Sado after they went extinct in the rest of Japan. In 1981, the five remaining wild birds on the island were captured and brought to Tokinomori for use in a breeding program which, however, failed. It was only when a relict population (just eleven birds) was discovered in Shaanxi, China that successful captive breeding began. Here on Sado, using birds imported from China, they were able, in 2008, to release ten ibis bred in captivity into the wild. In 2012, the first wild chicks were born; in 2016, the first birds born from parents who were themselves born wild, fledged. There are now thought to be about 400 wild crested ibis on Sado, and some pairs have returned of their own accord to the main island of Honshu.

The facility was more like a zoo than I expected. As well as the one breeding cage we were allowed to see (through glass and at such a distance the birds were just silhouettes behind wire netting), there were enclosures where pairs of other kinds of ibises were kept: two scarlet ibises, a brilliantly coloured variety native to tropical South America and the Caribbean; and half a dozen black-headed ibises, widespread in south and south-east Asia. Neither of these is a threatened species and their presence here seemed anomalous. I suppose if you know how to breed one kind of ibis, you can breed other varieties as well, but why? So people come and see them I guess. We all photographed the scarlet ibis.

The Observation Gallery was closed but we were able to go to the Toki Rapport Plaza where, from upstairs, through binoculars, 'ibises can be observed close-up living in a semi-natural environment.' There were four of them, a parental pair and two half grown youngsters, all standing on a wooden platform where one of their characteristically messy, twiggy, shit-spattered nests had been assembled. Both parents wore their grey breeding costume, achieved by daubing a black secretion from a facial gland over their plumage. The male bird stood motionless and in profile the whole time I watched; he looked depressed. The female was being harassed by one of her young, continually importuned to regurgitate food into its wide-open beak. The other one, perhaps a male, seemed as depressed as his father.

When they are not in breeding mode, crested ibis are large white birds with bright red faces, red legs, and a red tip to their curved beak; in flight the undersides of their wing feathers, especially when lit up by the sun, are a spectacular orange-pink colour, called *toki-iro* in Japanese and much prized; it has entered the official palette. The crest itself, a gathering of dense, spiky white plumes at the nape of the neck, is dishevelled yet somehow heraldic when upraised. The black beady eyes in amongst the scarlet skin of the heads of the adults make them appear to be more than a little mad.

The enormous effort that has been made to preserve these birds is at least partly because of their central, indeed emblematic, position in Japanese culture. Toki are mentioned in the early chronicle, the *Nihon Shoki*, a history of the nation compiled in 720 CE. The term also appears in names on imperial tombs, written with characters which translate to mean 'peach-flower bird' — referring to the colour of the underside of its wings during flight. Another ancient work, the *Engishiki*, a book of laws and rituals compiled in 927 CE, stipulates that the legendary Sugari no Ontachi, the sacred sword at the Ise Grand Shrine, dedicated to Amaterasu the sun goddess, must have two crested iris feathers adorning its hilt when it is used in ceremonies.

These ceremonies include the periodic rebuilding of the two main structures in the inner sanctum of the Ise Shrine, an event known as the Shikinen Sengu, which is supposed to take place every twenty years. The practice began in 690 under the Empress Jito and has continued for 1300 years, apart from a century-long hiatus during the Sengoku jidai, the period of warring states. At this time it is customary to renew all the sacred treasures of the shrine, of which the Sugari no Ontachi is one of the most important. There was consternation during the sixty-first re-building in 1993 when no wild crested ibis feathers could be found to adorn the hilt of the sacred sword. A collector supplied the missing quills from his own store. This was the year the bird was officially declared endangered.

At Tokinomori Park we were told to look out for ibis feathers, which are considered lucky, but we did not find any. Nor did we see any ibis in the wild, although there was a moment when I spotted, in a gully off one of the paths, the silhouette of a bird in the long grass; it turned out to be a stone replica. Driving away between the rice paddies, however, we came across a pair of green pheasants, Japan's national bird. The male is about twice the size of the black and brown speckled female. He had a scarlet head, a pale green crest, blue iridescent neck feathers, a dark green breast, pale green wings fading to brown scallops and a long, barred, pinkish-grey tail: a magnificent sight as he shepherded his mate along one of the grassy, humped banks between the paddy fields.

That evening we went to Shoho temple in Izumi to see a Noh play. Shoho-ji was established in 1324 to honour the ancestors of the Honma clan, the feudal lords of Izumi. It was also the place of exile of Zeami Motokiyo, the son of Kan'ami Kiyotsugu, a pioneer of Noh theatre, and a Noh actor, writer and theoretician in his own right. Zeami was sent here from Kyoto in 1434, for complex reasons, towards the end of a long and successful career, and wrote a diaristic account of his exile on the island. His seating stone remains at Shoho-ji. The play we were to see was one of his compositions and afterwards we were invited to view one of the temple's treasures: the ritual mask Beshimi, made late in the Kamakura period (1185-1333) and brought here by Zeami, who is said to have used it in rain dances.

Izumi Village was off the main drag not far from Sado City. A succession of empty lots along the narrow road had been designated as parking areas; they were interspersed with residential houses, farm buildings and vegetable gardens. It was early evening and the sky above the Osado Range was turning Prussian blue, pricked with silver stars, as we found a spot to park and, in the gathering crowd, made our way to a side entrance to the temple. It was lit by paper lanterns; out the front, stalls were selling various things, including Noh masks and large bottles of saké. We secured our tickets, were given a program each, and a fan, then joined the hundred or so others waiting to be admitted to the temple where the night's entertainment would take place.

The audience sat on small fold-out backed, armed but legless chairs set up on stepped wooden tiers on two sides of the open stage. Our seats were in the last row, with an oblique view of the performing area; an open sliding window behind wafted cool air over us and up above were two large objects like bales suspended from the roof — baskets for transporting temple accoutrements. Monks with tapers lit the lamps disposed at floor level around the stage and along the aisles. It was going to be a candle light performance. An elaborate ceremony ensued, entirely inscrutable, involving half a dozen monks, traversing to and fro, bowing and scraping, exchanging ritual objects with each other and then placing them on an altar, and much else besides. They were cleansing the space, making it sacred for the events which would follow.

The first of these was a talk by a local author from Niigata who had written a book about Zeami. Fujisawa Shu won Japan's premier literary award, the Akutagawa Prize, in 1998 for his novella *Buenosu Airesu gozen reiji* (*Midnight in Buenos Aires*; referring not to the Argentine capital but to a hotel in Niigata City). He is now a professor at Hosei University. He was about 60, soft-voiced, with a cultivated manner, who spoke for about half an hour. Much of what he said concerned the historical background of the play we were about to see, particularly its roots in the national epic, *Heike Monogatori* (before 1330), which describes the late twelfth century Genpei War between the Minamoto and Taira clans for control of Japan. He also spoke about Zeami himself, giving an account of his exile on Sado which, Fujisawa said, he actually enjoyed because of the generosity of the local people and the relative freedom he had after the constricted, highly formalised and factionalised life he had led in Kyoto.

After a short interval, during which we went outside and ate sandwiches, the performances began. A man played the biwa, the Japanese lute, on a darkened stage and sang a song to its accompaniment. Biwa are plucked, not strummed; they have a high, piercing plaintive sound with notes that often seem about to fracture and sometimes do. *The Tale of the Heike* was traditionally recited by storytellers playing the biwa, the way Homer's epics were chanted to the music of the lyre. Before they became instruments used in epic recital, biwa were commonly played by blind monks as a musical accompaniment to their readings of scriptural texts; perhaps that was why this man performed in the dark. He only did one number; then the Noh play, *Tsunemasa*, began.

First the choir took its place in the stalls to the right of the stage; there were ten of them and, unusually, they were all women. Then the three musicians filed in from the left, from the mirror room, through the curtain, along the bridge and past the pine to take their places, sitting at the rear of the stage: two drummers and a flute player. The stage attendants, men in black, appeared from behind the rear curtains and also sat. The wooden stage was bare and raised just a few centimetres above the level of the temple floor. There was no set apart from a fold-out stool an attendant brought on for the first of the two actors to use. He was Gyokei, an historical figure, pre-dating by centuries *The Tale of the Heike*, here to be understood as the generic figure of a monk.

The set-up was simple and the play, which took about forty-five minutes, effectively without a plot. Gyokei has come to lay the famous biwa, Seizan, which Tsunemasa, a gifted musician, played in his youth, on an altar and then to spend the night in prayer, performing a *kagen-ko*, a service in mourning for the dead warrior's soul. Tsunemasa died in the battle of Ichi no Tani at Suma west of Kobe during the Genpei War. It was a catastrophic defeat for his clan, the Taira. While Gyokei is engaged in his devotions, Tsunemasa's ghost, played by the *shite* or lead actor, appears and the rest of the performance unfolds in dialogue between the monk, the ghost, the choir, and the musicians.

Noh is sung poetry, with minimal (though significant) movement and little direct action: the modern stricture, show don't tell, has no place here. It is a highly wrought, stylised form, perhaps most akin to opera among Western genre; like opera it is intensely emotional, but its intensity comes from restraint, not extravagance.

The words, mostly expository, were sometimes spoken by one or other of the principal actors and sometimes taken up by the choir. The musicians, especially the two drummers, were an integral part of the proceedings. One of them, the shoulder drummer, with his strange, yelping cries and wild other-worldly demeanour, was a star of the show. These drum calls, *kakegoe*, are used to help adjust the timing and drive the rhythm. They sounded like the ancient, inarticulate cries of spectres or revenants.

The two principals were gorgeously costumed, Tsunemasa in particular. He was masked, while Gyokei was not. Every person on stage in a Noh play carries a fan; Tsunemasa's was large, red, and ornately patterned. Its movements, sometimes sweeping and emphatic, sometimes tentative, were intrinsic to his performance. He also carried the single prop, a sword which, at the climax of his performance, he pulled from its scabbard and cast aside in impassioned rejection of the warrior code which led to his untimely death. Sometimes Tsunemasa would run several steps across the stage in one direction or another, like someone who wishes to escape the prison of his days, or rather, in this case, of his death. These movements, which were always somehow thwarted, were wonderfully expressive. So was his gesture when he cast aside the sword. I did not understand a word of what anyone said yet the play had such emotional clarity I did not ever once feel that I did not know what was going on.

Later I found an English text online. The translation was awkward and strange but also powerful. Here are Tsunemasa's first words:

> The voices of the wind sweeping in the deadwoods sound like rain in sunshine. Moonlight illuminating the desert looks like frost on a summer night. I, like the rain and dewdrops, appearing and disappearing, cannot find safe

refuge. But I am here temporarily under the sod. Myself like a dew comes back to this world. How vain the tie made by delusion is.

His last words, as he leaves the stage and returns to the underworld, are spoken by the choir:

The waves of the scarlet blood return as roaring flames. It is shameful to see myself rumbling the pain of burning myself in flames. I tried not to be seen by anyone. I would like to extinguish the light. This silly me, like a moth flying into the flame, jumping into the fire.

It is perhaps unnecessary to add that there was no biwa on stage, just as there was no altar for the instrument to be laid upon; the ghost, fully visible to us in the audience at all times, was referred to on stage as a phantom, effectively invisible to the other protagonist, the musicians, the attendants and the choir. All they hear is his voice and, sometimes, catch 'a glimpse of a shadow shimmering like a heat haze.' When the living actor left the stage, it was as if a visitant had faded back into the nether world from which it had come and I felt as if we had indeed been in the presence of a ghost which the play, while never attempting to conjure an illusion of any kind, had somehow brought before us. I am quite sure this feeling was shared by everyone else in the audience and probably by the actors and musicians too. It was a magnificently haunted performance.

After the show we lined up to view the Beshima mask Zeami brought with him into exile. It was in a box lying on a cushion covered in silver cloth embroidered with flower motifs and made of unpainted wood which was a dark purple-black colour with light reddish patches where the surface had worn. Its brow was wrinkled, its eyebrows heavy and louring, its eye sockets set so deep they could hardly be seen above a bulbous nose with wide round nostrils. The square chin had been carved from a separate piece of wood and attached to the upper part of the mask; the thin line of the mouth was closed tight shut. That is in fact what beshima means (clenched mouth) and is the characteristic feature of this kind of mask. It is used by actors playing demons, ogres, thieves and the like, and the closed mouth signifies that the considerable power it possesses is kept under strict control. It is also thought that, if the Beshima did open its mouth, the effect would be comic, not tragic. In other words, it would laugh.

The Beshima pre-dated classical Noh masks, which look neutral but are in fact artefacts of great subtlety. Udaka Michishige, a mask maker, writes:

> The narrative is divided into a first and second half: in the first half the actor's movements place emphasis on the right side of the mask and in the second on the left. Because the Shite in the first half is a wandering spirit unable to rest in peace, the right side features an eye which looks downward; the cheek is gaunt, and the corner of the mouth downturned, as if to express the state of limbo. In the second half of the play the character's soul is cleansed by the offering of a memorial service, resulting in a calmer countenance. A left eye which gazes upward, a fuller cheek, and a corner of the mouth curving upward. Thus the right and left sides of the mouth are as different as yin and yang, and though the difference might be subtle in design terms, it is essential to keep in mind when making a mask.

Noh (the word means skill or talent) originated in a fusion of aspects of a number of different theatrical forms. These included *dengaku*, derived from agricultural work songs and dances; *ennen*, performances staged for their own entertainment by monks at large monasteries at the conclusion of religious festivals; *okina* or old man plays, which have a relationship with Shinto ritual dances like those we'd seen on Kyushu; *matsubayashi*, rhythmic songs and dances popular among from the warrior classes; and others, including temple ceremonies designed to attract good luck or avert bad. Most scholars, however, consider the primary source of Noh to have been the popular theatre called *sarugaku* (monkey music), ultimately Chinese in origin, which used acrobatics, juggling and pantomime in a way reminiscent of modern day circuses.

In Japan, the comic sketches characteristic of sarugaku predominated, at least initially: *toben*, dialogues based on word play; *ranbu*, improvised dances; and short sketches using several actors performing to music of the kind that high ranking courtesans used when entertaining clients. By the fourteenth century, words, gestures, musical arrangements and programs had become standardised and a guild system, called *za*, had been initiated, one which continues in Noh schools to this day. The comic interludes in a typical program of Noh plays, called *kyogen*, also came out of sarugaku. However, sources for Noh are eclectic and complex and include lyric verse as practiced in *renga*, group composition, and other aspects of the classic literary tradition, many of them Chinese in origin.

Why did Zeami bring this mask, out of all those he might have chosen, to Sado? I don't know, but it may have been because it had a connection with his father, Kan'ami Kiyotsugu, from whom he learned his trade and from whose practice he derived, ultimately, his own kind of theatre; which differed from his father's robust, conflict based drama, with opposing, sometimes clashing, points of view. Zeami's style of performance was more introspective, a psychological examination of particular states of mind, including remorse, regret, guilt, fear and, especially, too great an attachment to worldly emotions leading to painful existence after death in a kind of limbo. A change in aristocratic taste seems to have been a factor in this evolution.

Since their rediscovery early in the twentieth century, Zeami's writings have been influential among Noh scholars — to the extent that his particular type of theatre is now thought by many to have been the predominant form historically, as well as the template for much of the Noh theatre practised today. However, while the second point may be conceded, the first is unlikely. It is the survival of his plays, and the rediscovery of his theoretical writings, which has given him that prominence, not his actual historical significance. He seems, like Shakespeare among the Elizabethan and Jacobean dramatists, to have been one of many in a vibrant, complex theatrical scene which included other practitioners and other styles. The various Noh troupes competed with each other informally, and also on formal occasions such as religious festivals.

Zeami was born in 1363 near Nara, the old Imperial capital in Yamoto, the eldest son of Kan'ami, who was the shite of a sarugaku troupe of actors called the Yuzaki Theatre Company. His mother is sometimes said to have been the daughter of a priest or a military official but it is possible that she too came from a theatrical background. Kan'ami founded his theatre group in the provinces but moved to Nara when they came under the protection of Kofuku-ji, one of the main Buddhist temples. When Zeami was about twelve years old, the Yuzaki Company began making regular trips to the capital in Kyoto to give performances there; and at one of these they were seen, fatefully, by the third shogun of the Muromachi bakufu, Ashikaga Yoshimitsu, who was just seventeen years of age at the time.

Zeami was said to have been performing the role of *shishi*, a lion, when he was noticed by the shogun, who became enamoured of the boy and, inter alia, a patron of his father's troupe. Yoshimitsu regularly invited Kan'ami to perform at court. Under his influence, the troupe began to focus more on the entertainment value of their performances than on the magical aspects favoured by the temple; but it was entertainment of the more refined sort preferred by aristocratic audiences. Yoshimitsu sometimes took Zeami with him as his companion to public events, where he could be seen drinking from the same cup as the shogun. During this period Zeami also received an education of a kind which was unusual, to say the least, for an actor.

As well as being a favourite of the shogun, Zeami was on intimate terms with the court poet, Nijo Yoshimoto, and with another eminent figure, the monk, Sonshoin Keiben, sometime superintendent of the Todai temple in Nara. These two were old men who both seem to have become infatuated with the beautiful young actor. The poet even gave him a name, Fujiwaka, Young Wisteria, which contained part of his own clan name, Fujiwara. From Yoshimoto, Zeami learned about poetry, philosophy, and how to write *kokinshu*, a form of *waka*, and *renga*, linked verse, of which Yoshimoto was an acknowledged master. The nature of his relationship with the old priest, and the benefits Zeami might have received from him, are more obscure but they were surely educative as well.

If the young shogun's infatuation with the boy from the provinces was controversial, it would only have been for class reasons. Shirasu Masako notes in her book about him that 'pederasty was neither unusual in Zeami's time nor considered unhealthy.' It was not considered sexual degeneracy but an expression of the attachment between master and apprentice (*chigo*). 'Japanese,' she writes, 'did not seek feminine beauty in boys but celebrated them as symbols of youth and beauty, and sought the ideal of maleness within them.' Zeami, in his writings, shows an appreciation of his debt to Yoshimitsu but he is not particularly boastful of his relationship with the shogun which, anyway, did not continue past his teens.

In 1385, Zeami's father, aged fifty, died suddenly en route to Suruga, in present-day Shizuoka prefecture, where Yuzaki were due to perform. Zeami, who was just twenty at the time, succeeded him as leader and manager of what is hereinafter known as the Kanze troupe. He became the shite, both stage director and main actor, and began to arrange and improve his father's repertory of plays, as well as writing and adapting, from various sources, new ones of his own. As a playwright he was methodical, beginning with a theme, determining a structure, and finally writing the lyrics and the music. When he produced his treatise *Fushi Kaden, The Book of the Flower*, a manual for Noh actors which is still used today, he said he had taken it down in dictation from his father. He, in turn, dictated it to one of his sons.

The *Heike Monogatari*, as mentioned, was a source for many of his plays. He also brought ancient Chinese and Japanese poetry into his theatre, mixing classical poetics with popular dance, drama, and music, thus broadening and popularizing the tradition. It's likely that his knowledge of such poetries was second hand, however, coming to him through Yoshimoto's teaching rather than his own reading of original texts, which were probably not available to him. There is some evidence that his reputation, in the years immediately following his death, was as a playwright rather than an actor or a theatre manager. Or, indeed, a favourite of shoguns. Again, there are analogies with Shakespeare.

Zeami was registered at a Zen temple and a friend of Zen priest, Kiyo Hoshu, with whom he held many 'laughing discussions'; in later life he became a lay monk. Key theoretical concepts in his writings, like the importance of *no action* and the centrality of the mysterious power called *yugen*, have a relationship with Zen Buddhism.

> Dancing and singing, movements on the stage, and the different types of miming are all acts performed by the body. Moments of *no action* occur in between — if it is obvious, it becomes an act and it is no longer *no action*. The actions before and after an interval of *no action* must be linked by entering a state of mindlessness in which the actor conceals even from himself his own intent.

Yugen, meanwhile, 'is attained when all different kinds of visual and aural expression are beautiful.' It is not a moral or an ethical quality; there is a yugen of ugliness, a yugen of demons.

Zeami's early patron, Yoshimitsu, was a significant figure, calling himself the King of Japan, a claim echoed in the annals Ming Dynasty China. As well as a patron of the arts, he was a diplomat, a soldier and an administrator who was able to subdue the wako, the Japanese pirates, during his term in office. For his retirement he built Kinkaku-ji, the golden pavilion, now a Zen temple on the shores of a small lake in Kyoto. While he once invited Zeami to perform in 1399 before the 100th Emperor, Go-Komatsu, Yoshimitsu's patronage of the young actor did not continue into adulthood. His favourite performer in later years was a rival, Inuo, who practiced a broader kind of sarugaku than the more refined, more literary, form of the Kanze troupe's Noh.

When Yoshimitsu died in 1408, the new shogun, his eldest son Ashikaga Yoshimochi, preferred yet another actor and another kind of theatre, the dengaku influenced work practised by Zeami's contemporary, Zoami. Dengaku was based upon work songs, rice planting and harvest festival dances, which had been incorporated into Noh Plays. Zoami was a colleague and a friend of Zeami; his position as the new shogun's favourite actor wasn't necessarily a problem for him. Zeami was by then well-known, with access to a number of other patrons among the wealthy and the aristocratic. He continued working and, in the years between 1408 and his official retirement in 1424, wrote a number of plays, poems and treatises.

His real problems began after the accession of the sixth shogun, Ashikaga Yoshinori, a man of unpredictable and violent temper who, because he was Yoshimitsu's third son, had initially been passed over and sent away to live as a monk in a monastery. His predecessor, the fifth shogun and second son, the callow and dissipated Ashikaga Yoshikazu, died young, and, in 1429, Yoshinori was chosen (by lot) to succeed him and summoned back to court. Zeami soon found himself in trouble with Yoshinori. The problem seems to have been with succession which, in Za troupes, was usually hereditary.

Zeami had previously nominated his nephew, On'ami, his younger brother's son, as the next leader of the Kanze troupe but, in the year Yoshinori came to power, changed his mind and offered the position to his own son, Motomasa, who had since come of age. Yoshinori had, however, in the meantime, made On'ami his favourite, because he specialised in the type of demon plays the shogun was fond of watching. After Motomasa's sudden death in 1432 (he was probably poisoned), Yoshinori, ignoring precedent, selected On'ami as the next head of the Kanze. Also in 1432, Zeami's other son, Motoyoshi, probably anticipating trouble, retired from acting and became a priest instead.

Zeami also had a daughter, married to a Noh actor called Konparu Zenchiku. One version of the cause of Zeami's exile to Sado was his opposition to On'ami's appointment as the new head of the Kanze troupe and his consequent refusal to hand over his writings, including his scripts and his treatises, to his nephew. The fact that most if not all of these texts ended up in the possession of his son-in-law Konparu tends to support this interpretation, but there are several other theories, including the suggestion that Zeami was aligned with Yoshinori's political enemies and that he supported an imperial restoration. But Yoshinori was unpredictable. He might have exiled Zeami on a whim.

Zeami was seventy-two when, in 1434, he was sent to Sado. In 1436 he published a stoic, not disenchanted, first person account of his exile. His later years are obscure. Some think he died on the island; if so, you would expect there to be a tomb, or at least a memorial, extant, but there is not. It is far more likely that, after Yoshinori was assassinated in 1441 — stabbed, appropriately enough, while watching a Noh play at the house of one of his subordinates — Zeami was pardoned and returned to Kyoto. He died in 1443 and is buried alongside his wife, who outlived him, in Yamoto.

His plays make up the largest group of Noh works still performed today. His treatises, however, were private documents passing on the secrets of his particular form of Noh to his heirs and successors. For centuries they remained unknown outside the troupe until, in 1908, a manuscript copy turned up in a second hand bookstore in Tokyo. Since then they have been studied, edited, and published in various Japanese editions; the first full compilation came out in 1940 and an English edition of the major works in 1984. As for his school, it was continued by Konparu Zenchiku's grandson, Konparu Zenpo, whose lineal descendants, more than five hundred years later, remain at the head of what is still called the Konparu School of Noh.

Zeami (1363-1443) was a younger contemporary of English poet Geoffrey Chaucer (1340-1400). The magistrate Okubo Nagasayu's time on Sado early in the seventeenth century, during which he revived and augmented the Noh tradition Zeami founded on the island, coincided with the years during which William Shakespeare was writing his great tragedies and his late romances.

Zeami's own life, and especially the period leading up to his exile, reads like the plot of a Jacobean drama, albeit without the bloody ending characteristic of that genre. But Zeami was not the first to be exiled to Sado and nor was he the last; the roll call of his predecessors and successors is a long and fascinating one. I found a partial list of them in a scholarly book on the poet Matsuo Basho. They included a soldier, an emperor, a monk, a philosopher — and a woman who perhaps never existed.

The soldier, Mongaku Shonin (1139-1203), under the instructions of the 77th emperor, Go-Shirakawa, encouraged Minamoto Yoritomo, the first Kamakura shogun, to begin the Minamoto clan's war against the Taira clan. The conflict is commemorated in *The Tale of the Heike* and led to the defeat of the Taira and the extinction of their clan. Shonin was exiled after the death of both emperor and shogun and died on the island of Tsushima in the Korea Strait. He is a semi-legendary figure, a reckless, uneducated man of action who revered the *Tengu*, the long-nosed, bird-winged, monkey-man forest demons whom we had seen impersonated at the festival at Ebisu.

The emperor, Juntoku (1197-1242), the 84th, was exiled to Sado in 1220 after becoming involved in an attempt to overthrow the Kamakura shogunate and restore the imperial line to real power in the land. He spent the rest of his life on the island and is buried there. Juntoku was a poet and his lament for the decayed imperial house reads, in loose translation:

> Hundreds of paving stones
> the palace's ancient eaves
> remember the climbing ferns
> there isn't much left
> of the old days now.

The monk was the fanatical and incendiary Nicheren (1222-1282), founder of one of the major schools of Japanese Buddhism which, with a block of seats in the parliament, remains a force in electoral politics today. The son of a fisherman, Nicheren claimed to have read every single one of the Buddhist scriptures and concluded that *The Lotus Sutra* was the only true guide for the age of calamity in which he found himself living. He made such a nuisance of himself that he was exiled three times before going into seclusion on Mount Minobu, ending his days there as a writer and a teacher.

As for the philosopher, he was the neo-Confucian Hino Suketomo (1290-1332), close advisor to the 96th emperor, Go-daigo, who also attempted to re-institute direct imperial rule. Some of the plotting took place during what were ostensibly literary gatherings, not the first time, nor the last, that such scheming took place under the aegis of poetry. After the discovery of the plot in late 1324, Suketomo was arrested and sent into exile on Sado. Seven years later, in 1331, when another anti-shogunate plot surfaced, even though he was still in exile, he was again implicated and this time sentenced to death. He was executed by decapitation in May 1332.

The fifth and last exile was Tamaki, a figure from folklore, whose story became, in the 1950s, the basis of Mizoguchi Kenji's classic film *Sansho Dayu*. She was the wife of a virtuous governor of the Heian period, banished by his corrupt feudal lord to a remote province. Tamaki and their two children, a boy Zushio and a girl Anju, set out to find him, but along the way all three were captured and sold into slavery, the children to a manorial estate with a brutal overseer called Sansho, the mother into prostitution on Sado Island. Here, after many vicissitudes, she was discovered, having gone blind, by her loyal son Zushio, who restored both her sight and her honour. We visited the spring whose healing waters gave back her vision.

This list of exiles appears in *Traces of Dreams* by Shirane Haruo, and is included there because of Basho's famous haiku, written during the journey down the coast of Honshu opposite the island. The haiku reads:

araumi ya | Sado ni yokotau | amanogawa
rough seas | over Sado lies | the Milky Way

It is considered by many to encapsulate in its seventeen syllables both the grandeur of Sado Island lying there in the turbulent ocean under the river of heaven and its sadness as a place of exile and servitude.

Ogi Again

Every night at the hotel, after dinner was over, there would be folk dancing in the foyer. Five woman dancers in blue kimono, yellow straw hats, white socks and thonged sandals would process out of the gift shop and, to recorded music, slowly circle the floor, making intricate movements with their hands and feet. Their hats, called *okesa kasa*, were remarkable: made out of a woven circle of straw folded in half, they were worn with the edge of the V-shape uppermost and tilted in such a way, high at the back and low at the front, so as to entirely obscure the faces of the dancers. Each one must have been able to see only the back of the one in front and the floor beneath her feet. All the women were tiny; the eldest of them, according to Mayu, was the most skilled in her movements and also the most sexy, but I did not know which one she was.

This kind of dance, called Sado Okesa, is derived ultimately from harvest songs from Kyushu called Haiyabushi. Sung originally by *geisha*, they were introduced to Sado by sailors coming into the port at Ogi. They were performed at parties and then used as musical accompaniment for dances at Obon Festivals, when the spirits of the dead are welcomed home. Later still, the songs were sung, and the dances danced, at official functions at the gold mine. Blue and white kimono were traditionally worn for such dances, as was the straw hat covering the dancers' faces and obscuring their peripheral vision. This was apparently because commoners were not allowed to look at the magistrate and the other high officials, which may indeed have been the case. The music was melancholy and the dances stately, elegant and restrained.

On the morning of our last day on the island we checked out early and retraced our route of four days before, up the mountain, through the tunnel, down the other side and along the streets of the black towns bordering Mano Bay, and so over the Osado range to the sea. At the terminal in Ogi, waiting to board the ferry, I saw a statue of a woman dancing the Sado Okesa, cast in some kind of blue metal, unpainted, wearing the kimono, the sandals and the hat, one leg raised, one hand, the right, held out flat and palm down, the other, the left, with the palm raised. Most public sculpture is uninteresting because of the lifelessness of the figures; this one was uncannily present, as if the sculptor had somehow arrested the movements of the dancer as she danced. Even more intriguing, although she had a face under her hat, that face could not be seen.

The voyage back, as such voyages often do, seemed much shorter than the voyage out, as if the mainland were calling us home from our brief and inconsequential exile. In no time at all we were passing the red rocket shaped light house at the tip of that immensely long pier and sailing past the large warehouse I had noticed on the way out, with its curved corrugated iron roof red with rust and the blue and white snow-capped peaks of the Japanese Alps beyond. The glittering piles of scrap metal on the wharves seemed undiminished, a resource that would never be exhausted.

One of the restaurants, which had been closed the Wednesday before, was now open for business so we ate there. It was a place where sailors, waterfront workers and local residents came for large servings of plain, good food, with a choice of either Japanese or Chinese cuisine. A hearty, white-haired old man, obviously a regular, stopped in mock consternation when he saw us. 'You are attracting an international clientele now,' he boomed to the proprietor, a woman, before sitting down to a vast plate of fried noodles. Afterwards we drove back up into the hills, returning to our small house in the midst of the green summer forest on the slopes of Kurohime.

Eight Days in the Oku

Tohoku | July | 2023

Basho and Sora

We were going to spend two weeks at Togatta Onsen in the town of Zao in Miyagi prefecture. It was an artist's residency Mayu applied for successfully while we were still in Australia. The position came with a live-in studio (actually a converted fish shop) for which we would be paying ¥2,500 per night — about $25.00. We'd known about the gig for a while but it still seemed to come around very quickly. No sooner were we back from Sado than it was time to start preparing for the journey to Zao — a road trip of about five hundred kilometres each way. We were going to do it in the Vitz.

There were, it turned out, several possible routes we could take. I had been reading *Oku no Hosomichi*, Matsuo Basho's account of his 1689 journey to Tohoku, the northern part of Honshu, alongside *Traces of Dreams* and realised we could, on the way to the residency, intersect at various points with the route Basho and his companion Kawai Sora had taken. Once I suggested this to Mayu we were both seized by enthusiasm for the idea and decided to leave early so we could explore those places where the poets had been in a bit more detail. With her usual efficiency she began to prepare an itinerary; while I attempted to put some order into my understanding of who Basho was and what he had accomplished.

I did not have a clear idea of either his life (1644-1694) or his work. I did know a few of his haiku: the famous one about the frog jumping into the old pond; the one about the dreams of warriors growing back as summer grass; another about the sound of cicadas retreating into the rocks on a hot day; and the one he wrote about Sado. I thought of him as a generic figure, a poet who was both sage and fool, a rhapsodist of the natural world, a hermit, a man outside the world who nevertheless comments upon the world. Shirane's book described a different figure, cosmopolitan, sophisticated and intricately connected to the milieux of his time, both politically and in terms of his influence upon, or differences with, other writers. Meanwhile his masterpiece, called in this translation (by Hiroaki Sato) *Narrow Road to the Interior*, is a work which includes within the narrative of the journey a wealth of allusions, literary and otherwise, most of which I was unfamiliar with. Behind the simple yet artfully constructed persona, then, stood a figure of some complexity.

Oku no Hosomichi is also a work in a genre Basho invented and named himself. Like many of its Chinese and Japanese precursors, *haibun* is a mixture of poetry and prose. However, it has a broader range than most and can include, as well as verse, autobiography, diary, essay, prose poetry, short fiction and travel writing. For Basho, haibun combined 'classical prototypes, Chinese prose genres and vernacular subject matter and language' as well as being a genre which highlighted his favourite poetic form, the haiku. The *Oku* was not his first attempt at haibun — it was preceded by *Nozarashi Kiko* ('Travels of a Weather-beaten Skeleton') (1684) and *Oi no Kobumi* ('Knapsack Notes') (1688) — but it is the best known and most achieved, and it was after making the journey recorded therein that he coined the word haibun to describe what he had been doing.

Basho was perhaps what we would now call a gay man and on his journey to the north had with him a companion, Kawai Sora (1647-1710?), who is himself a figure of some complexity. I'm not suggesting they were lovers; I don't know. Basho loved women too; but he never married and had no children, though he did bring up one of his sister's sons. More to the point, Sora also kept a diary and, when that came to light in 1943, it changed forever people's understanding of Basho's work. Sora's diary, which is an unadorned account — dates, times, places stayed, distances travelled, people met — shows that Basho's *Oku*, which until then had been read as a realistic description of their journey, is a highly wrought literary artefact which includes fictions, inventions, evasions, elisions and even deliberate misattributions alongside its many classical references. If Sora's diary is documentary, Basho's is artifice; one he spent four years perfecting.

Even more interesting is the speculation that Basho was a ninja and the two sojourners were engaged on a clandestine mission of some kind. I first came across the ninja suggestion in a brief online biography of the poet. Basho was born and grew up at Ueno in Iga Province, in a family which was of samurai descent but in decline; the poet's father was probably a *musokunin*, a class of land-owning peasants retaining some of the privileges of samurai, including the right to a family name. The biography also said, without giving a source, 'the Matsuo were a ninja family and Basho trained in ninjutsu'. In other words he was educated as a *shinobu* (an invisible one) and so learned various martial arts techniques and other methods useful in warfare by stealth. Most shinobu came from Iga Province and Ueno was a centre of the profession.

If this was the case, he would have done his training when he went, perhaps after his father died in 1656, perhaps later in his teens, into the service of the local lords, the Todo clan, where he worked in the kitchen or, alternatively, as a page to the head of the family, Todo Yoshitada. Or both. Yoshitada's poetry name was Sengin, and from him Basho began to learn the poetic arts, including the one, *haikai*, at which he excelled. Haikai, rather than the writing of discrete and individually authored works is, like renga, from which it is descended, a process of communal composition of linked verses amongst a group of poets. Basho's apprenticeship with Yoshitada ended abruptly after his patron's sudden death, aged 25, in 1666. Basho had to leave the Todo house, thereby severing his formal connection with the samurai class.

There are many theories, including two alleged affairs with married women, to explain this sudden change of circumstances;

the most likely cause is the simplest. Yoshitada was succeeded as clan leader by his younger brother, who had no room for a poet in his entourage. Basho went back to live with his family in Ueno and moved between there and Kyoto for the next five years. This was the period during which, he said, he became interested in sexual love between men. He also pursued his studies in poetry. The family connection would remain strong for the rest of his life; as the second son he did not inherit the land but maintained a good relationship with his older brother, who did; with their four sisters (one older and three younger); and with his mother, whose death in 1683 occasioned the first of his poetic journeys.

In 1672 he moved to Edo; in some versions he was sent there by the Todo, close allies of the ruling Tokugawa, and remained under an obligation to them for the rest of his life. It may be so. He was certainly intending to embark upon a literary career, hoping to become a haikai master, a *soshi*, a leader of group poetry sessions, who could charge for their services. In Edo he came under the influence of Nishiyama Soin, the head of the Danrin school of haikai, with whom he was composing by 1675. And he found a patron, Sugiyama Kensuke, a supplier of *koi*, live carp, to the Tokugawa. The fish were not for eating but for stocking ornamental ponds. Basho lived with the Sugiyama family and became good friends with Kensuke's son and heir, Sugiyama Sanpu, who was, like his father, a poet and who in time took over the business. Basho also worked for four years as a clerk in the water department, and probably had other jobs as well.

By 1680 he was established enough to move, with Sanpu's help, from central Edo to Fukagawa on the banks of the Sumida River on the outskirts of the city where he lived in what had once been the caretaker's cottage on the Sugiyama fish farm. Fukagawa was his home, insofar as he had one, for the rest of his days. In 1682, however, his house burned down in the great fire which consumed Edo in that year; he had to take shelter in the river with a mat over his head to escape the flames. A new house was found for him but, after the conflagration, and his mother's death, which followed hard upon it, he seems to have felt a sense of the impermanence of things. In 1684 he embarked upon the first of the journeys that would take up most of the remaining decade of his life.

The ninja speculation is interesting but it seems to me that, even if Basho did train in the secret arts, he probably abandoned them for poetry while still a young man, perhaps at the time he left the employ of the Todo; it's unlikely he was a spy in later life. A more promising candidate for espionage is his companion on the journey north, Kawai Sora; and, I thought, any further suppositions about a clandestine mission should probably concentrate upon him. But sources for the life of Sora are difficult to find and those that do exist are almost exclusively in Japanese. Even his diary, that crucial document, has not yet been translated into English; although there is a machine version online which, while sometimes difficult to follow, is nevertheless, if intermittently, illuminating.

The other problem we had with retracing even a small part of Basho and Sora's journey is that we would have to do it backwards. They left Edo in May 1689 and headed north, travelling inland roads before arriving at the eastern city of Sendai and going on to visit coastal Matsushima and the harbour town of Ishinomaki. Then they went to Hiraizumi, site of the Battle of Oshu in 1189, before crossing over the mountains of Honshu to the other coast, making several side trips along the way. Their furthest point north on that coast was Kisakata — like Matsushima accounted one of the most beautiful places in the country. After that they travelled south and west along the shores of the Sea of Japan as far as Tsuruga before turning inland and ending their journey, five months later, in mid-October, at Ogaki near Nagoya.

A great loop, then, which we could most easily pick up at Joetsu, formerly the castle town of Takada, about forty kilometres away from Shinanomachi. From there we proposed driving up the coast as far as Kisakata, if we could do it in the time available, before crossing the island, going the other way, east not west, to Matsushima on the Pacific coast. From there it is a relatively short drive to Togatta Onsen in the foothills of the Zao Ranges in the Ou Mountains. We gave ourselves a week, leaving Shinanomachi on Monday July third and intending to arrive at Zao on Monday July tenth. Along the way we would visit as many Basho sites as we were able to (there are dozens of them) and make whatever connections we could.

A crucial concept in the *Oku no Hosomichi*, and in Japanese poetry generally, is *utamakura*; literally 'song pillow' or perhaps 'bed of song'. Utamakura are words, often place names, which convey. in a kind of shorthand, a wealth of poetic associations. Sora's diary includes a list, made before they departed, of utamakura along their route. He and Basho visited many of them and composed their own poems to add to the accumulated associations of the places. We would, in our own way, be trying to do something similar: adding our small contributions to the lore of these ancient poetry places. Although I didn't know it then, Mayu's project during her residency in Zao would also involve utamakura.

One other thing. Basho's title has usually been awkwardly translated into English and its meaning thus misunderstood. It occurs in the text as the name of an actual path he and Sora walked down when they were in Sendai: a narrow way leading along a ridge flanking a rice field, with sedge planted on the other side. Using this farmer's name for a local feature might be understood as an attempt to create a new utamakura; an extremely successful one. But it was also a reference to *Tsuta no Hosomichi*, the narrow path of ivy, a much older utamakura dating back to the *Ise Monogatari*, the Tales of Ise, a collection of waka poems and associated prose narratives from the Heian period, most likely compiled in the ninth century CE.

The commonest English translation is *The Narrow Road to the Deep North*. *Hosomichi* does mean narrow road or alley or path; but *oku* doesn't mean north and nor does it mean the interior, or not in a geographical sense; it is more of a direction. Furthermore, the title doesn't signal a journey *to* anywhere; *no* is a possessive; the title means *oku's hosomichi*, its narrow roads. What then does oku mean? Its primary sense is derived from Zen Buddhism and refers to 'what is deep and hidden.' The space at the heart of the house, for instance. A temple in the mountains may be oku with respect to its pair in the town. Women, in the old days, were sometimes said to be oku, that is, spending most of their time inside. The kanji character means private, intimate and deep; exalted and sacred; profound and recondite.

This esoteric meaning is complicated by the fact that, in Basho's time, northern Honshu was sometimes referred to as Michinoku, which may be translated as 'the end of the road.' It was also known as Oshu and then the 'O' was written with the same kanji character used for 'oku'; *'shu'* means state. The region in question included present day Fukushima, Miyagi, Iwate, and Aomori prefectures, and part of Akita prefecture. Basho and Sora didn't go to Aomori; they stepped briefly into Iwate and Akita; and travelled extensively through Fukushima, Miyagi and what is now Yamagata. It would be characteristic of Basho to have come up with a title with multiple resonances. I assume that all of the associations mentioned above are evoked in *Oku no Hosomichi*; also that Basho and Sora, whatever else they might have been doing, were seeking both intelligence and enlightenment along the back roads of the heartland.

Day One

Kurohime to Teradomari via Izumozaki

It was a misty morning in the mountains above Shinanomachi. We packed up and left our house in Kurohime a bit before 11.00 am, filled the car with gas at the Apollo Station on Highway 18 and took the freeway north and west to Joetsu, where there is an ancient junction of two major roads. The Hokurikudo, running parallel with the coast, intersected here with the Hokkokukaido, leading inland towards Nagano and ultimately to the Pacific coast of Honshu. The Hokurikudo, sections of which still exist, was established after the Taika reforms of 645 to connect the imperial capital of Kyoto with the northern provinces; parts of the Hokkokukaido, down which the gold convoys went, became present day Highway 18. The junction is sometimes called the Takada interchange, after the old name for Joestsu. During the *Oku* Basho and Sora stayed three days at Takada with a doctor called Hosokawa Shunan because Basho had fallen ill.

We continued north on the freeway and, at Yoneyama, Rice Mountain, turned off onto the coast road. If it was misty in the mountains, it was hazy by the sea. The flashing lights on the communications towers of the nuclear power station at Kashiwazaki trembled out of a murk of thick hot air but that was all we could see of it; that, and the gleaming razor wire on two parallel security fences, interspersed with pylons and guard towers, snaking silver through the greenery beside the road. The facility is built on a promontory reaching out into the Sea of Japan and it looked as if the entire headland had been cordoned off against threats of terrorism or insurgency. A majority of the local people do oppose its presence here. A sinister place; even though it wasn't operating at the time, there was a lot of traffic at the front gate. I guess maintenance is ongoing.

In fact the power station, built 1980-85, with seven reactors, all using the so-called 'advanced boiling water method', and once the largest nuclear generating plant in the world, has been shut down (mostly) since the Chuetsu offshore earthquake of July 2007. The station suffered some damage in the quake, which also exposed a number of safety issues: there was a fire in one of the transformers, drums containing radioactive waste fell over and their lids came off, spilling the contents. Contaminated water leaked into the ocean. A subsequent, more searching examination of that section of the coast of the Sea of Japan discovered several hitherto unknown fault lines, one of which runs beneath the power station itself. Under pressure, the regulatory authority changed the criterion for quiescence along a fault: from the last known movement being 120,000 years ago to the much longer period of 400,000 years. About time.

Somehow the owners, TEPCO (Tokyo Electric Power Company), negotiated all the regulatory requirements and gained approval to re-start the plant. It was just beginning to generate power again when the 2011 Tohoku earthquake and tsunami devastated its sister facility at Fukushima on the Pacific coast. Kashiwazaki was closed again, along with the rest of Japan's fifty-four nuclear power stations; and has not since re-opened. Only ten of the thirty-three currently operable stations have. There were security as well as safety concerns; staff were in the habit of using each other's cards to enter restricted areas of the facility. TEPCO agreed to spend a large amount of money to further secure the premises. The razor wire fences, which look more appropriate for a high security prison, are one result of this upgrade. The bureaucratic method by which closure is enforced is curious: the power station authorities are not permitted to shift nuclear fuel from one place to another within the complex and so cannot operate the plant.

☗

The old town of Izumozaki, where the gold came in, like Sado, and for the same reasons, was administered directly from Edo. It is now a small fishing village standing on a narrow plain beside the sea, with steep cliffs rising up behind and featuring many houses and warehouses painted in Black Japan, the dark stained timber we had seen so much of on the island. On a loop behind the main road was a narrow stone bridge which was a remnant of the *Kaido* that led to Edo. Nearby, up the hill, was a bare space like a car park which, a notice board assured us, was where the bugyosho, the magistrate's house, had once stood. There was a shrine behind that, reached by an old stone staircase. It was flanked on one side by a row of red banners and, in the dappled light, looked quiet and peaceful; in stark contrast to the next place we visited.

This was the execution ground where those found guilty of crimes against the state were beheaded; although the actual death site was not identified. A crooked path led to a graveyard remarkable for its many small shrines in which cloaked, red-capped figures presided over rank upon rank of tiny stone buddhas, each representing the soul of one or other of those condemned men and women. Not all of them would have been criminals in the way we understand the term today: if a village proved refractory, for whatever reason, the authorities might choose one of its principal residents as a scapegoat and, as a warning to the others, lop his or her head off. There were individual graves too, attended by more of those tiny buddhas. One had lost its head and someone had replaced it with a flat, oval stone. This was one of those places where you hear, plainly, helplessly, the sound of the unquiet dead wailing in the air.

The park where Basho's visit to Izumozaki is commemorated was over the bridge and a few more steps down the same road. A green thought in a green shade, with moss and grass and maple trees, inscribed stones and a bronze statue, half life-size, of the poet, which had a patina of an attractive aqua-grey colour. Basho was standing with his legs apart, sandals on his feet, wearing a robe, with his staff planted before him on the ground and the hands with which he was holding it concealed by the round sun hat he usually wore over the bandana on his head. His face was worn and his gaze somehow occluded, as if he was focused upon something deep within. The execution ground perhaps.

Everything about his visit to Izumozaki is obscure. It coincided with a period during which, in the *Oku*, Basho says he was ill and for nine days made no entries: 'Due to the heat and rain, the spirit is exhausted, and in addition, the physical condition deteriorates. Therefore, he has no record to write,' is one version. Donald Keene's translation reads: 'During these nine days of travel I was worn out and depressed by the heat and the rain. I had a bout of illness and wrote nothing.' Sora is more succinct: 'Sunny. Depart Yahiko around 8:00 am. Arrive at Izumozaki around 4pm. Heavy rain overnight. July 5. Night rain continues until morning. Depart from Izumozaki around 8:00 am. It started to rain on the way.'

Scholars say the silent journey actually took them sixteen days. They are also fond of pointing out that the haiku mentioning the Milky Way stretching, above a rough sea, over Sado Island, cannot have been written at Izumozaki because, from that part of the coast, the stars along the River of Heaven don't appear to incline over the island. This is of course nonsense and has no bearing on the place of the composition of the poem; poets don't have to be geographers, although they might be. Basho's prose note, however, written later, does throw some light upon the haiku and what he was thinking about when he wrote it. He called it *Ode to the Galaxy*:

> From the place called Izumozaki in the province
> of Echigo, Sado Island, it is said, is eighteen li
> away. With the cragginess of its valleys and peaks

clearly visible, it lies on its side in the sea, thirty-odd li from east to west. Light mists of early fall not rising yet, and the waves not high, as I look at it, I feel as if I could touch it with my hand. On the island great quantities of gold well up and in that regard it is most auspicious. But since from past to present it has been a place of exile for felons and traitors, it has become a distressing name. The thought terrifies me. As the evening moon sets, the surface of the sea becomes quite dark. The shapes of the mountains are still visible through the clouds, and the sound of waves is saddening as I listen.

On our way to lunch we heard singing. Down by the sea, a man of about forty, wearing sneakers, jeans and a T-shirt, sat on the top step of the concrete terraces with a white mask of the fox god Inari pushed up over the top of his balding head like a hat. He sang soulfully and in tune and loud enough, it seemed, that his voice might carry as far as Sado, silhouetted, pale blue, on the horizon. When he finished the song, he cried out to the sky: *Arigato! Arigato Gozaimasu!* then began to sing another one. They were both songs made famous by the actor and singer Nomura Masaki, born 1952, a crooner who'd recently turned seventy. The man in the fox mask was paying tribute to him and thanking him for the songs he had sung and all the pleasure he had given to people.

We could still hear him singing while we ate in a restaurant up above the beach. Afterwards we went to the museum next door, focussed upon the gold and silver convoys which left from Izumozaki on their way down to Edo. Most of the displays had an audio component. At the entrance, where some of the sturdy wooden boxes in which the gold and silver was transported were stacked, when you pressed a button a bowed figure, representing a samurai, creaked upright into ghostly life and instructed you in a sepulchral voice to go further. Inside stood a half-life-size model of a kitamaebune, the ships which carried the precious metals over the sea from Sado, and when you pressed the button on that display you heard the sound of a storm and the voices of sailors shouting above the howling of the wind and the crashing of the waves.

The most illuminating offering was a recreation of one of the convoys which took the treasure down Route 18 to the capital. It used miniature models, each about ten centimetres tall, in single or double file: horses with their loads and handlers, men lugging boxes on their backs or balanced on shoulder poles, musicians, singers and dancers, dignitaries in their finery, palanquins carrying important people, armed soldiers. The whole panoply was ordered as it would have been in life and was so long it stretched around three sides of the large central room. You could hear the blare of the trumpets and the beating of drums. I could easily imagine them wending their way through Shinanomachi and on down through the mountains towards Nagano and beyond. Such convoys might consist of 200 horses and more than twice that number of people; they might take an hour to pass.

Upstairs was a recreation of the old town, with mannequins attending storefronts containing simulacra of the artifacts or services that would have been for sale. A screen which lit up showed you, behind shoji, paper blinds, the silhouettes of Basho and Sora in profile. Basho sat with a brush pen in his hand in the act of inscribing characters onto a tablet; Sora sat behind him, with his head slightly bowed, as if honoured to be allowed to sit in the presence of greatness. This was of course a fiction invented by whoever had made the silhouettes; once again I wondered who Sora was and what he was actually doing on the journey. The day before they left Edo he had shaved his head and taken to wearing the black travelling cloak of a Shinto priest.

We were staying the night up the road in Teradomari, 'resting place with temples' — of which there were many, lined up along the steep cliffs above the streets of the town. A statue of Nichiren, the iconoclastic Buddhist priest who had been exiled to Sado, stood just behind the hotel. Larger than life-size, his face a mask of severity, if not rage, he had a *japamala*, a string of prayer beads, in one hand and the other held out, palm first, in interdiction, presumably against all ways that were not the way of the Lotus Sutra. The hotel was U-shaped and consisted of two buildings linked by corridors; as if we were in Fawlty Towers, we had to walk up and down this absurd connection every time we came or went; when we did so, at the bottom of the U, without fail, there was Nichiren, glaring balefully down upon us.

We ate at a fish restaurant on the main road, where half a dozen men in their sixties were getting boisterously drunk. The waitress, who was also the proprietress, had her hands full dealing with them, especially one skinny fellow who seemed to need to go to the bathroom every five minutes or so: what was he doing in there? Whatever it was, I think it involved her cleaning up after him each time. When at last they roistered away, and we were paying our bill, she relaxed and told us this was a family business and they had been running restaurants in Teradomari for a very long time. In the old days, she said, they used to cook for the brothels which lined the cliffs behind the town, on the third level, up above the temples and the shrines.

They did a roaring trade back in the day, she said, although we weren't sure what days she meant? Of the bakufu and the convoys? The Meiji? Or the boom times leading up to the Pacific War? Maybe even during the Occupation. Teradomari, she said, was closer to Sado than Izumozaki, but for some reason that was where the port had been built. The administration and all other official business happened down there; this was the entertainment quarter, where people came to unwind and to enjoy themselves.

Whatever time she was referring to, it seemed likely that the complementary roles of the two towns probably date back a very long time, perhaps as far back as the inception of the gold and silver shipments out of Sado in 1603.

Day Two

Teradomari to Murakami

Because Basho didn't write anything about the two weeks and two days it took them to travel between the Nezu barrier in the north of the province then called Echigo, and the Ichiburi barrier in the south, we had to rely on Sora's diary to work out what route they took and where they stayed. We also had to make allowance for the tendency of people to claim a connection with the famous poet where none, in fact, existed. Mayu had been diligent in her researches and she had found two places, both temples, which they had certainly visited, even if they had not actually stayed in either place. One was the Saisho temple inland from the city of Nagaoka, about an hour south of the capital, Niigata. The other, Oppo temple, is about the same distance north of the city, at a place called Tainai near the mouth of the Akagawa River. We intended visiting both temples, skirting the metropolis, so far as we were able, on the way through.

Saisho-ji stands high upon a forested ridge above the sea. You reach it by driving up a narrow, twisting road and going through the temple gates. It was still quite early in the day, about 10.00 am, when we arrived and found it closed. We parked the car anyway and went for a walk. Down the side of the main building were hundreds of tiny stone figures standing row upon row on terraces, watched over by larger figures and adorned with offerings of flowers, both real and artificial, coloured plastic pinwheels, white cloth bonnets, T shirts with smiley faces upon them. These represented the souls of *mizuko*, water children: those who died in the womb, were stillborn or died shortly after birth. Mizuko may also represent foetuses which were aborted or children who became victims of infanticide, once common amongst the rural poor.

In Japanese Buddhism, such children are thought to have been unable to accrue enough good karma to allow them to cross over into the afterlife. They are also thought (no matter how they died) to have caused grief to their parents by pre-deceasing them. Mizuko thus exist in a kind of limbo and need help to move on to the next stage of their journey towards reincarnation. The larger figures are Jizo, bodhisattvas, compassionate beings who have chosen to delay their own enlightenment in order to help others. Jizo are protectors of children and travellers as well as guides for those who have died before their time. Mizuko are required to stack stones as a means of attaining entrance to the afterlife; but each night a demon comes and tries to knock over the cairns which they have built or which have been built by pilgrims on their behalf. Jizo act as protectors of these children, hiding them in their sleeves or beneath their robes until the demon goes away.

These gatherings of mizuko were very affecting; but Saisho-ji is famous for something else. It is the home of a *sokushinbutsu*, a mummy monk, 'a buddha in his very body.' This form of perfection is the result of a process a monk completed over a period of some 3,000 days, involving a strict diet called *mokujiki* (eating a tree), in which he consumed only pine needles, resins and seeds in order to eliminate all fat from his body. The monk would also, over time, slowly reduce his intake of liquid, dehydrating himself and shrinking his internal organs. Sokushinbutsu, ideally, would die meditating, perhaps chanting a mantra, and their physical body would continue to exist, naturally preserved as a mummy, with skin, teeth and hair intact, and without the need for any form of artificial preservation of the flesh.

The one here, according to the official version, was about 600 years old. Knowing that his time was near, he entered a small chamber dug in the earth somewhere up on the mountain, where he chanted and rang his bell until the end arrived. After he fell silent, the chamber was sealed to limit oxidation and prevent insects eating the corpse; which was then left in situ for several years before being extracted and carried down to the small compartment in a wooden building in the temple grounds where, a very holy relic, it now sits. That, at least, was the story. Those who have studied the matter analytically tend to the view that the process of live mummification, so called, is a fiction and the bodies of these monks have been preserved by other more conventional means after they starved themselves to death.

Mayu was relieved the temple was closed and we could not therefore see the mummy monk; she does not share my taste for grotesqueries. The display is suitably bizarre: you are supposed to approach the monk by visiting, in sequence, various other relics: a skull, resting on a pillow, of a man decapitated for trying to push his finger into the mummified flesh of the monk; the body of a cat, also mummified, allegedly from an extinct species of unknown provenance; two stuffed Chinese wolves in a glass case; and a series of X-rays of the mummy himself. Unable to see any of these things, we wandered instead through the peaceful bamboo groves behind the *hondo*, the main building, listening to the repeated cry of a single crow, *karasu*, talking to itself somewhere in the trees overhead.

The place seemed entirely deserted; but once I saw a solitary monk, dressed in brown, bent over, crossing the carpark. And in the distance I could hear the voice of another, haranguing somebody in one of the administrative buildings beyond the temple. I spotted him eventually, through an open window, also bent over; but I could not see his interlocutor. Strangely, or perhaps not, both of these men's posture imitated that of the giant statue of the mummy monk (I never learned his name) which stood in a small park above the road to the temple entrance gates. You were supposed to sprinkle water over his feet and ask him to grant you good health; but we had neglected to do so.

It was a somehow desultory experience. When we returned to the car, Mayu pointed in the direction the solitary monk had come from and said that behind those trees was a graveyard for those who, for whatever reason, could not or did not want to be buried in the family plot. They might be estranged from their people, they might have no children who could look after their graves, they might not want their descendants to continue bearing the cost of maintaining the grave generation after generation. This way, everything was organised beforehand, a small fee was paid to the temple authorities and it was the monks who tended to the graves and looked after the souls of the deceased, insofar as it is possible to look after dead souls.

Although it is home to only about three quarters of a million people, Niigata is very spread out, with the largest land area of any Japanese city; to avoid driving through the centre we decided to take the coastal route. This involved making our way through an unprepossessing industrial landscape surrounding the port, crossing several rivers and canals, and circumventing the airport; all of which we accomplished. It was a hot day and, since we were still in the rainy season, humid too. Niigata is an old port on the Sea of Japan, at the mouths of the Shinano and the Agano Rivers, both of which flow through the town. It is sometimes called the water city; there was once a large lagoon, long since drained. Basho and Sora did come through here but all Sora says is that the weather was hot and sunny.

When, however, Basho resumed writing his account of their journey, 'a place called Niigata' featured. They were staying at a roadside inn just before the Ichiburi barrier, one of the military checkpoints all travellers in Edo period Japan had to negotiate. Basho was weary after a day's hard journey, mostly along a rocky shore, and went early to bed; but lay awake, he says, listening to a conversation in the adjoining room. Two young women and an older man were talking. The man, having escorted the women thus far, was returning to Niigata in the morning; they were dictating a message to their people back home. Basho quotes, or perhaps paraphrases, thus: 'as if cast up on the beach by white waves, living lowly lives like those of fisherman's children, forced to have faithless relationships, we are, to our great misfortune, committing sinful deeds day after day — such was their talk and while listening to it I fell asleep.'

The next morning the two women, whom Basho identifies as *yujo* — 'play women' — who are on their way to Ise to worship at the shrine of the sun goddess Amaterasu, introduce themselves and ask if they may join he and Sora on the road. They say they will cause no trouble and walk modestly behind. Evidently, because the travellers are wearing monk's robes, that is what they take them to be. Basho refuses their request; they will be making too many stops along the way to be good companions, he says, then adds he is sure that if the women take their chances with the rest of the pilgrims, they will arrive safely at their destination. The great shrine at Ise, as mentioned, is rebuilt every twenty years; that year, 1689, was the year of its next re-incarnation and people from all over Japan would be making their way there to pay their respects to the goddess.

Basho follows his prose account with a haiku:

hitotsuya ni | yujo mo netari | hagi to tsuki
in one house | prostitutes also slept | bush clover and moon

The passage has, predictably enough, excited a great deal of commentary. It was one of the things that suggested to some scholars, even before Sora's journal came to light, that Basho might have fictionalised parts of his *Oku*. This was because many readers found it improbable that play women from Niigata would have known the tanka Basho has them paraphrase: 'I spend nights on the beach where the white waves roll in, a fisherman's child with no place to settle.' This appears under the category 'prostitutes' in the *Wakan Roei Shu*, an anthology compiled seven hundred years before. Some translators find the paraphrase so implausible they make Basho quote the poem out of sympathy for the plight of the poor beleaguered women, but this isn't what the text says. Others think it was the poem which inspired the vignette. There is no mention of the incident in Sora's diary.

Leaving aside its status, fictional or otherwise, which we can't know, how likely is such an encounter? The women are not geisha and, even if they were, would not be identifiable as such: they would have been wearing pilgrim's robes. If they were play women they had probably been sold as teenage girls by their families to a brothel owner and would have had to pay off the money he had spent on them by working for him. It's conceivable that they have run away, in which case they could never go back. It's also possible that their owner has allowed them leave, because the twenty-year anniversary of the rebuilding of the shrine at Ise was a significant national event and one that might have persuaded him to let them take a holiday. Perhaps they're aging and so losing their usefulness to him. Or maybe they've paid him off already.

It's also likely they were nervous about their ability to pass safely through the Ichiburi barrier and this is why they made the request of Basho. They would have had good reasons for feeling that way. Women were always examined carefully at military barriers, usually by another woman employed specially for that purpose. This was because they might be runaways from a brothel, a castle, or some other form of servitude; concubines being illegally trafficked; noble women in disguise trying to return to their families; couriers carrying clandestine messages; even men in drag. Their hair would be searched for letters, their hands and feet scrutinised to see if they bore marks of manual labour, their robes opened to ascertain their sex.

Basho's refusal to allow them to join him, too, has been interpreted in different ways. Some say he showed, not selfish unconcern, but the compassion of Buddha, a wise understanding that we are all pilgrims on the road of life, alone and at the mercy of fate: though in fact he commits the women, not to the protection of Buddha, but to that of Amaterasu. By the same token, many commentators read the haiku hierarchically: Basho is the moon, the play women petals of bush clover; how poignant that they should be sleeping under the same roof! But there is no male voice in the poem and the meaning seems to be that all travellers are scattered like petals along the highway and all sleep soundly, this night at least, under the moon.

The Oppo temple, inland on the plains north of Niigata, in a nondescript suburban townscape, was a complex of buildings on flat land in the lee of a low hill, under spreading trees, a place of worship for both Buddhists and devotees of Shinto. There were many graves scattered among the cedars and the pines. It was a torpid Tuesday afternoon, peaceful enough, but when we climbed out of the car I smelled a strange smell which I couldn't get out of my nostrils for the whole time we were there. Cat shit, I thought, only not quite so acrid as the real thing, with a vegetative underlay, the way some Australian wattles smell of piss. I never worked out what it was.

There were hardly any people about and most of the buildings were closed; we wandered amongst them, looking for the monument to Basho which was said to be here. We found it eventually: a round stone with the inscription upon it so worn as to be unreadable; next to it was another stone with a haiku cut into it. That too turned out to be difficult to read. Mayu thought the subject matter had something to do with mountain cherry trees but that was all she could construe. Nearby was a magnificent, somewhat decayed, three storey wooden pagoda built by the local lord between 1614 and 1620. The unpainted wood had gone a beautiful silver-grey colour. It stood alone in a small glade, seemingly untended and unvisited.

A map of the grounds showed the way to 'The Red Lake'. A pond rather than a lake, this was where the bodies of still born or aborted children, or those who were victims of infanticide, after some hair had been cut from their heads, were ceremonially thrown into the water. It received its name because, after each sacrifice, the water turned red and remained that way for three days. There was a mossy green buddha sitting down by the side of the water with a sombre stone child at its feet. The surface of the pond was a murky, purple grey colour, with green weed growing upon it and a strange plant, with flowers that looked like eggs, hanging pendulous over it. It seemed an afflicted place.

There was a fellow sitting on the ground near the buddha, apparently meditating. About thirty-five or forty, he had some kind of rash on the skin of his face and papers in plastic folders placed on the moss next to him. Mayu asked him if he knew the name of the plant with the egg-like flowers. He said he did not. It turned out he was one of the teachers of a class of eleven and twelve-year-olds who were staying in the village and visiting the temple that day. Both boys and girls were full of laughter and lifted the gloom of the place into something more cheerful. We met two other teachers, both women, and several posses of kids who were, it seemed, free to roam at will around the temple complex. Japanese school children love to practice their English upon you and will continue calling out even after you have met and greeted and passed: 'Today is July! I am Sagittarius!'

It is of course difficult to track down a particular haiku, by Basho or anyone else, which mentions cherry blossoms. Mountain cherry narrows the field and there is a rare variety, with a double bloom, which grows at Oppo-ji; and this is perhaps what Basho is referring to in the haiku which I did, eventually, locate:

urayamashi | ukiyo no kita no | yama-zakura
how enviable | north of the world | mountain cherry

Basho didn't write this during the *Oku* but a couple of years afterwards, in 1692. It was included in a letter to a man called Kukii, a hermit living in a temple somewhere in the north; I don't know if it was Oppo-ji or another one. Many Basho memorials include poems that have only the slightest connection to their location, if there is any connection at all. Maybe the temple chose this haiku because they already had those unusual mountain cherry trees growing there.

We stopped again, late in the afternoon, to the north of the city of Murakami, at a beach where Basho and Sora had reputedly also been on their route south, during which they often had to walk beside the sea. Alternative transport was expensive and sometimes difficult to find. It cost a lot to hire a horse, even for half a day, even if you could get one; boat travel was available, both by river and by sea, but again it had to be found and paid for. Most of the time they just walked, down forest paths, over mountain passes, along narrow roads or, as here, along the sands of the shore.

Like just about every other Japanese beach I've been to, this one had been extensively altered, in this case with the addition of a concrete terrace with a promenade at the top and wide, shallow steps leading down to the sand. The beach itself was deep and long, tending from ochre to grey, with many distinctive black and white pebbles upon it. I picked up a couple of these to use as paper weights; and another small clay-like rock which had marks upon its flat surfaces which resembled hieroglyphic writing: katakana or hiragana rather than kanji. When I gave it to Mayu, she remarked that it would probably take her the rest of her life to figure out what it was saying.

After cooling my feet in the waters of the shallow sea, I walked back up the steps to the promenade to look for her; she had gone off to take photographs. There she was, further down the strand, in the company of two leather clad bikies, doing something inscrutable. When I got a bit closer I saw that the young man and the young woman, both stylish and a bit raffish, were posing for a picture. They were standing before their bikes, their backs to the camera, showing off their patches and looking soulfully out to sea. Mayu came upon them having trouble setting up their phone camera for a selfie — the wind kept blowing it over — and offered to do it for them.

We were staying the night at Senami Onsen, a rusty slab of a hotel built on a ridge overlooking the ocean. Opposite was a ruined skateboard park festooned with vines beside a disused educational institute, also overgrown, which had a hollow 1960s Op Art statue of a woman and child standing before it. The car park, long and narrow, faced these derelict structures. After I'd locked the car and was walking back to reception I saw a row of nine or ten dark brown fish suspended on hooks under the hotel's eaves, swaying gently in the evening breeze. They were a local specialty, salmon caught in one of the two rivers which flow through Murakami, salted by hand then hung out to dry, a process that might take a year to complete.

The hotel was elegant, old-fashioned, a bit worn. Our room looked out, through large square windows, past a red discharge pipe, to the island of Awashima in the Sea of Japan. Once the haunt of pirates from Kyushu, now a nature reserve, it was a pale blue line on the horizon. A solitary walker moved slowly along a path through the marram grass; another man spent a long time preparing his rod and then cast his line into a shallow pool between the tetrapod breakwater and the shore. These Euclidean breakwaters, ubiquitous along the coast of the Sea of Japan, are made out of concrete cast into a variety of geometric shapes which fit together as in a child's puzzle. They are there to break up the tsunami which so often trouble this earthquake afflicted land.

Day Three

Murakami to Sakata

Mayu ascribed the excellence of the hotel food at breakfast, as at dinner the night before, to the quality of the salt they were using. She bought a packet of it from the hotel shop. After checking out, we drove into the city of Murakami, made our way to the castle ruins on Mount Gaygu, an isolated peak to the east of the town and walked up a winding path, through low scrubby forest, in delicate green light, towards the summit. The stones under foot were loose or broken, the steps crumbling, puddles of water stood here and there. At each bend in the zig zag there would be a bench to rest upon and a tattered straw broom beside it for those who wished to sweep clean the seat or the place where they set down their feet. We didn't stop once, because the insect life was ferocious and it was better to present them with a moving target. Both on the way up and on the way back down, we met lean, lithe, fit, cheerful older men and women who use this walk as their daily constitutional.

Murakami castle, like so many others, was decommissioned and partly demolished after the Meiji Restoration. Its stones were given to people in the town below as building blocks until some of the more historically minded residents protested and managed to get the site protected. Some partially demolished castles have since been restored but not this one. As at Takeda, all that remains is the massive stonework, which would once have supported the three, five, or seven tiers of the *tenshu*, the keep, and the many *yagura*, the watch towers. Most of this wooden superstructure was destroyed by fire after a lightning strike in 1667; after which the tenshu and the yagura were not rebuilt. However, the complex remained the seat of power and, when Basho and Sora came through here in 1689, it was in the hands of the Sakakibara clan.

People from the town below would retreat here in times of war; there were places were rice could be stored; there was a well inside the walls. Although it didn't seem like a very high hill, only 135 metres, the views from the top, unimpeded by any other structure or landform, were extensive. You could look out over the city below, the two rivers running to the sea, the littoral hazy in the humid morning air, the cloudless blue skies over the Sea of Japan. We could even see our hotel from the night before. Somewhere out there, in the far distance, lay the coast of North Korea, the Hermit Kingdom. A single crow, like the spirit of the place, hopped through the torii gate leading to the shrine where Shinto worshippers paid their respects, flew up onto an inscribed, square stone standing on a plinth, and cawed loudly, twice. We turned to go back down.

We were eating in a salmon restaurant in the old town, Komachi, at 11.00 am. So early because the management insisted they were busy for the rest of the morning and the whole afternoon too. And yet, when we arrived at about ten to eleven, there was only one other booking, another couple, also for 11.00 am, written in the schedule out the front. Nevertheless, the woman sent us away, politely, and told us to come back once they were officially open. Nearby, we knew, in Teramachi, was a temple which Sora had visited, evidently because a man called Itoko, a friend and colleague from the days when he was stationed here and worked as a government messenger, was buried there.

Jiyonen-ji was, however, closed. We could go through the heavy wooden front gate and look at the outside of the small hondo;

but that was all. There were some graves, but nobody to ask questions of and several notices forbidding further exploration of the grounds. A blue, white-spotted umbrella with a red border, open, stood on a lawn of flowering clover, with the effigies of seven rabbits sheltering beneath it; what it signified I do not know. Mayu said she thought this was one of those rare temples with beams made out of compacted dust, not wood, but we were unable to confirm this possibility either. We gave up and went back to the restaurant.

A small, two-storey place on a corner, made out of wood painted in Black Japan which had, over the years, faded to a luminous silvery grey, it had once been a ryokan — and the very place where Basho and Sora stayed in Murakami. The entrance was from the street at the front but there was another door, leading into a small courtyard garden, down the side. When we were seated in the cool, dim interior, we looked out into this garden and I could just about see the two wayfarers, at the end of the day, coming wearily through the low wooden door, up the curving garden path and, after slipping off their sandals and removing their hats, going in through a second low wooden door to the ryokan.

It is said that in Murakami there are a hundred different ways of preparing salmon; we tried a dozen of them, including salmon sperm, called *shirako* or white children; a mash up of a whole fish's head, pickled for so long the bones were soft as boiled beans; dried, grilled skin; along with more conventional dishes of salted flesh served with various condiments and accompaniments. Each dish came with an explanation, delivered by the young waitress. It was a set menu and, after a while, the other couple who'd booked in at the same time as us, sitting at an adjoining table in the otherwise empty restaurant, were included with us in an audience of four. The food, including the rich flesh and bones of the pickled head, was delicious.

After we had finished eating, Mayu came back from the bathroom and showed me a black speck on the skin of her neck which, for some reason, she couldn't brush off. It was in what Japanese call the *nodobotoke*, the Buddha spot, the depression just below the Adam's apple. I couldn't get it off either. I put my glasses on and had a closer look: whatever it was, was alive. I managed to get the nails of my index finger and thumb around it, gave it sharp tug, and away it came. A tick. Still alive and apparently none the worse for wear after its violent extraction, it set off to try to find some soft place on my wrist where it could re-attach itself.

I coaxed it onto a paper napkin, crumpled it up inside and, after we left the restaurant, released it into a low hedge on the other side of the road. It must, I thought, have fallen into her hair when we were visiting the castle ruins and made its slow way down to that spot on her neck. It didn't seem to have been there long enough to have injected her with its anaesthetic, which can contain various nasty bugs, including the bacteria which causes Lyme Disease. We watched anxiously for the rest of the day but no inflammation appeared, no itching, no symptoms at all.

After lunch she wanted to go down the street to buy some smoked salmon to send to her mother in Tokyo. The shop looked like an ordinary deli, with a counter and open, refrigerated shelves where packaged products were displayed for sale. However, out the back, through a sliding door, where I was invited to go, was a different world. Here were the drying and storage rooms in which hundreds of brown leathery fish hung in rows from the ceiling. Shelves held galvanized iron buckets or small wooden barrels. Bigger barrels, in which salt water was stored, stood on the floor. Directly behind the ranks of drying fish was a square wooden opening into a light well containing a tiny garden, with two miniature trees, a flowering plant in a pot, a metal lantern and several stones placed on a bed of white pebbles. There was a hillock of green grass growing behind. A wooden stool stood before this shrine, where you could sit in contemplation.

On the other side of the room was a low raised bare stage with an altar where offerings were made. To the left of that was a formal reception area, with tatami mats on the floor, a low polished wooden table, a large free-standing grey ceramic jar and, on the wall behind, a painted screen showing a salmon leaping up a waterfall. The complex rendition of the water of the fall was reflected, shimmering, in the table top below; another smaller vase to the left, before a black bamboo screen, held a bunch of pink roses. The mixture of the ceremonial and the mundane; the way the salting of fish took place among altars, gardens and shrines seemed both salutary and wise. It felt like a space that had not changed, in essentials, for hundreds of years.

Sora was busy over the three days the poets spent in Murakami; the detail is in his diary. On the evening of their arrival in town, for instance, he went up to the castle in the company of the owner of the ryokan and three others, all old friends of his. The next day he received a sum of money, in gold, from a man called Tatewaki who worked for the daimyo, the local lord. He was evidently liaising with people from the Ogaki clan in order to finance, and facilitate, the next stages of their journey. He also went, as mentioned, to the temple to visit the grave of his friend Itoko and afterwards, by pre-arrangement, met someone by the name of Suzuki. They ate cold noodles together at the ryokan and then a gift of food arrived 'from the mountains.' Some sweets and melons were brought over by the wife of a friend. On the morning of their departure, light rain was falling.

Sora was, clearly, much more than a junior poet who happened to be Basho's friend and companion. He was also his secretary, his business advisor and his road manager. His diary frequently notes letters he has sent on ahead, either to secure accommodation or to organise haikai sessions; and his irascibility is evident, and pungently expressed, when someone doesn't reply or doesn't reply quickly enough. Haikai sessions were complex: gatherings of poets would perform renga, group composition, sometimes over a period of days, usually at the house of someone wealthy enough to offer them food, drink, a bed and a fee. All this had to be organised beforehand, either by word of mouth or by correspondence. Japan under the Tokugawa already possessed a sophisticated mail system; Basho was famous enough for someone to quip, with what degree of seriousness I do not know, that he had what amounted to his own postal service.

Mail in those days was carried by messengers called *hikyaku* ('flying legs'); parcels and heavier freight went by horse. There were three main systems, one run by the shogunate, one by individual daimyo, and one by private companies, using regularly spaced relay stations along the main highways. There were more specialized services as well: couriers who carried news about the latest rice prices from Osaka's Dojima Rice Exchange to anywhere in the land; others who ran money orders. Daimyo needed their own postal services in order to communicate with different parts of their domains and also because they were required to spend every other year in Edo, where their woman and children lived as virtual hostages, necessitating regular, reliable communication both with the family there and the administration at 'home'.

Official messengers ran in pairs, one carrying on his shoulder a black lacquered message box on a bamboo pole, the second with a lantern to light the way after nightfall; he was also the reserve in case of misadventure or an injury to the other. The pole carrying the letter-box had bells attached, giving rise to the name 'chirin chirin no machi-bikyaku' (jingle jingle town couriers). They had right of way — even over daimyo — and were allowed to pass at night through barriers, something forbidden most people. Machi-bikyaku, an independent, commercial network of couriers first organized around 1664, was the most commonly used private service. Like other hikyaku, regardless of the weather, their couriers wore a loin cloth and straw sandals. This gave them greater comfort running, especially during the months of intense humidity. In the extant illustrations they are usually shown to be extensively tattooed. These pictures also suggest they used the ipsilateral gait rather than the contralateral method adopted by all modern athletes.

It was an efficient system. By the end of the 1600s, a message took about six days to cover the 500 kilometres between Edo and Kyoto. Letters were not delivered to the people they were addressed to but deposited at way stations, de facto post offices which sometimes also served as hotels; the addressee had to apply for them there. Responses were handed over on the hikyaku's return trip. There were no stamps. Coins were pasted on to a letter in payment for the cost of transmission. In Edo, on the morning after the arrival overnight of the express messenger from Osaka, a straw bag would be tied to the railings of the Nihonbashi Bridge and those who wished to send a letter to Osaka would place it, with a coin attached as payment, in the bag. Next evening the hikyaku would pick up the bag of mail and start on his return journey.

It isn't clear what system Sora was using for his mail. If it was a daimyo's couriers, they would change from domain to domain; if it was a commercial service, it would have to be paid for. If Basho did have what amounted to his own postal system, details of how that operated are unrecoverable now. The Tokugawa shogunate was a military government. This meant, on the one hand, a highly efficient communication system throughout the land; on the other, that everyone, regardless of who they were, had to pass through the regular military checkpoints, the barriers. Another possibility is that Sora had been granted some kind of official status and therefore carried an inscribed wooden permit, which allowed them safe passage everywhere he and Basho went.

After leaving Murakami we drove inland, north and east, looking for the park which commemorates the place where Basho and Sora came down from the mountains of Dewa to the western plains. Dewa is the old name for the prefectures now called Yamagata, where we were, and Akita, in which we would soon set foot. This was after the two poets had visited the three sacred mountains of Dewa: Haguro, Gassan and Yudono. We were going there too, the following day. It took us a while to locate the park but we found it eventually, serendipitously, in an otherwise deserted spot among rice fields at a place called Ogoto. We spotted, across rice fields, a graffitied toilet block standing next to a children's playground with a path leading between the fields towards it.

This we took and discovered, past a rusty, faded, rainbow-coloured jungle gym, a broken see-saw and a moribund, miniature flying fox, a faint track leading further up the hill to where some inscribed stones were set in a grove of cypress trees with a stand of bamboo behind. There were noticeboards but it was a long time since they had been readable. Someone had tried, inexpertly, to construct a pond; the rubble that remained was empty and dry. There was a haiku written on one of the stones; again, we weren't sure which one it was — it mentioned the moon — but it may have been this one, written during their visit to the mountains:

suzushisa ya | hono mikazuki no | Haguro-yama
coolness | faint crescent moon over | Black Wing Mountain

Before we left to go down the stone steps which constituted the real (and effectively hidden) entrance to the park, I went to use the boys' toilet. It had not been cleaned for a long time; the urinal was clogged with the bodies of black ants. At the bottom of the stairs a wooden sign had been nailed to a dead tree, with the characters for '*Oku no Hosomichi*' written vertically upon it in white paint: as if that desolate and melancholy spot were indeed the entrance to the interior's narrow roads; as perhaps it was.

⛩

We were going to the city of Tsuruoka to look for the place where Basho and Sora boarded the river boat in which they travelled to Sakata to the north. It was in an old part of town called Izumimachi and to get there we drove down a long street in which a glittering brown dust lay along the centre and banked thickly on both sides of the road. The wheels of passing cars threw it in clouds into the air: particles of rusty iridescence which had fallen from the roofs and the walls of shops and houses lining the road, most of which were made of corrugated iron gone silvery brown with the years. This was not the only street of rust we drove down in the north. They are eerie, like the future of some alternative past we do not know about. Or like something on a colonized planet which is not our own.

We crossed a bridge over a stream and parked above the river. Mayu went one way and I the other. I came across two wooden boats of traditional design moored together under another bridge; she found the notice board confirming that this was indeed the place. It was entitled *Oku no Hosomichi Uchikawa Embarkment Place* and gave the dates Basho and Sora had stayed here, after descending Mt Haguro, at the house of one Nagayama Juko. Three days later they left, by boat, from the wharf that used to stand here, on a seven li (twenty-eight kilometre) journey along the Uchikawa and Akagawa rivers to the mouth of the Mogami at Sakata, a trip which took them half a day.

The Uchikawa was slow-moving, placid, flowing between green banks; quiet enough for a kind of purple-green weed to grow along the meniscus of its backwaters. The bridge under which the boats were moored appeared to be painted with a startling, op-art design, in black and white, resembling waves. When I got closer, however, I realized that the black parts were actually negative spaces between sculpted white concrete curves. The boats were long and narrow with a shallow draft, each with their long oars shipped. Something about the post they were moored to gave you the illusion of the head of a boatman about to cast loose the ropes. There were blue hills behind and, without any city buildings in view, it looked uncannily like a sight you might have seen three hundred years ago.

Nagayama Juko's house was, we had been told, still extant. It was a few hundred metres away, in the neighbouring district of Sannomachi: walking distance. We went down narrow alleyways, past small blocks of flats and smaller houses, the rear entrances of shops and restaurants, until we found the place. Alas, the house was long gone, replaced by a tiny park which, another noticeboard assured us, was the actual site of Juko's former residence and his garden. Though he had left the area not long after the poets' visit, the street was still called Nagayama Alley. The park was neglected, overgrown with weeds, the solitary pine tree dead, its needles sere and brown. However there was an elegant old wooden shelter at one end, roofed and shady; the inevitable haiku inscribed on a stone; and, unusually, an account of its composition.

> Due to his pilgrimage to the Dewa Sanzan, Basho was exhausted and took a rest. At night, during a gathering of Haikai poets, he was served a bite of egg plant called Minden-nasu which caught his curiosity. Along with Sora, Juko and Romaru [another disciple / poet] he was inspired by this local delicacy and composed a Hokku:

mezurashi ya | yama o ideha no | hatsu nasubi
how rare | leaving Dewa mountains | the first eggplant

The minden eggplant is small, round and tasty and is often used to make pickles. Others have asserted it was the purple-black colour of the *nasu*, not its flavour, which caught Basho's eye. The *hokku* would have been the first of the haikai session which would then continue on from it. As tradition demanded, it establishes the season (summer) and compliments the host (on his food). Sora suggests the session lasted all of the three days they spent at Juko's house. He also mentions a few names but not much else. But memory can take different forms.

As we walked away, Mayu pointed out that the adjoining apartment block, painted a pinkish orange colour, was called Banana House. Basho means plantain, specifically a kind of banana plant native to Japan; he had one growing outside his house in Fukagawa and used it as his poetry name because its torn and tattered leaves and its fruitlessness reminded him of himself.

We walked back along the main drag, passing a bicycle repair place with the words 'Heartfelt Cycle Shop' written in green on a white board outside. Further along was a second-hand bookshop called Abekyu Books with a sign out-front saying that it had been doing business on the same premises since the Meiji Era. We went into a dusty old interior where the shelves overflowed with books and stacks of them sat in every spare spot on the floor. Mayu asked the tiny, ancient woman behind the wooden counter if they happened to have a copy of Sora's Diary? She said she didn't know but would ask and produced a mobile phone that was thicker than her arm and almost as old as she was: one of the bricks we used to use last century. She could only just get the fingers of her right hand around its bulk. After the call she told Mayu there might be a copy upstairs but she didn't know where. Perhaps in the poetry section. She said we would have to turn on the lights at the top of the stairs.

Upstairs old neons hissed and crackled into life, illuminating a space as dusty and cluttered as the downstairs was. Through a half open door I saw a figure sitting bowed over a table, examining a ledger, whether man or woman I could not say. They did not look up. Nothing seemed to be in any particular order. We could not find the poetry section. However, at the head of one of the rows of shelves, under a paper window through which pale yellow afternoon light fell, I came across a stack of art books on the floor, new but not recent, all still in their slip cases and their plastic wrapping. They were a full set (there are 25) of *Gendai Sekai Bijutsu Zenshu / L'arte Moderne Du Monde*, first published in the early 1970s by Shueisha in Tokyo, the largest publishing house in Japan, responsible for most of the Manga, for Playboy magazine, for popular novels, for anything really. I ran my name down the spines and chose #13, Paul Klee.

I took it downstairs and asked the ancient lady what it cost. She made another call. It was brief and afterwards she said ¥800, less than ten dollars; such a small amount I was tempted to run back up the stairs to choose a few more gems from the stack; but I did not. The book turned out to be a 1978 reprint of the original 1971 edition. The text was in Japanese, the information on the imprint page a mixture of French and German — and the colour plates were gorgeous. An unusual selection too. In the back there was an essay on the artist, a chronology, with black and white photographs, a memoir by Klee's son Felix and a catalogue, also illustrated. It was a find.

Day Four

Sakata to Mt Haguro

We had adopted a perhaps eccentric modus operandi. Before we left home, Mayu constructed an elaborate, comprehensive and somewhat speculative itinerary for us, of which I was aware only in broad outline. Each morning she would lay out the options for that day's travel and together we would decide what we would do. There were always more possibilities than we had time for. Once the destinations were determined, off we would go, I driving and she navigating, using Google maps on her phone to find the way. The only stressful moments came when we made a mistake, missed a turn, or found ourselves at a dead end. Fortunately wrong turnings didn't happen very often and some of them led us to places we would not otherwise have gone: a Jomon site, for instance, which we found up an obscure back road on the slopes of Mount Aoso near Zao.

In Sakata, in a swish hotel beside the library, we decided to visit a park at the mouth of the Mogami River — where Basho and Sora's boat from Tsuruoka came in — and then head further north along the coast to a place called Sixteen Buddhas which Mayu said she wished to go for reasons of her own. I didn't ask what these reasons were, since I would find out in due course anyway. I wondered if it had to do with her family. She had a connection through her mother's people with a temple in Tsuruoka but had not had time to track it down; perhaps she would find it on our way back (she did). And there were relatives of her father's in Shiroishi, the nearest big town to Zao, whom she would be meeting while we were in Togatta. I thought maybe there was something similar that needed investigating on the road to Akita.

Hiyoriyama Park, on the northern bank of the Mogami river near the mouth, was an island of calm in a cacophonous industrial landscape. There were tug boats nudging a freighter towards a pale green dry dock on the southern shore, cranes at wharves loading and unloading goods into and out of other freighters, container trucks coming and going, a dredge chuntering out past the bar to further excavate the sea bottom. In the distance the pale white spectres of wind turbines turned above a flat yellow shore. We missed the turn off the first time and ended up at some vast warehouse outside of which, inexplicably, in the desolation, someone's brand new late model black Lexus stood, driverless, but with its doors open and its engine running. We turned round and went back.

The park was over the road in a shallow basin at the top of a low hill; you climbed some steps and entered past a chalk-white, wooden, hexagonal lighthouse, once a guide for shipping and now a memento of the old days and a focus of prayers for safe journeys. Constructed in 1814, it had stood on the sand bar off the river mouth until it was de-commissioned, dismantled and resurrected here. Beyond, among lawns of green grass in which daisies and clover flowered, low, immaculately topiarized hedges, stands of pine trees, was a meandering path which led you past monuments to twenty-eight literary figures, with a bonus twenty-ninth reproducing a poem by an unknown poet. They were all writers who had visited Sakata at one time or another.

Basho was #4. His monument was a massive slab of grey granite with an inscribed metal plate affixed, overlooked by a stubby pine which had had several of its limbs lopped off, for what reason I do not know — plus a couple of wooden signboards. In Sakata, Basho and Sora stayed at the house of a physician, Ito Genjun, whom Basho in the *Oku* calls En'an Fugyoku: the first was his doctoring name and the second his haiku name. They held a haikai session; two of Basho's haiku from it appear, revised, in the *Oku*. The second, reproduced on the stone in the park, was written here:

atsuki hi o | umi ni iretari | Mogami-gawa
pouring hot sun | into the sea | Mogami river

The Mogami is over 200 kilometres long, rising south and east in the Ou mountains then flowing north and west into the sea at Sakata. It is accounted one of the swiftest of all of the hundreds of rivers in the country. Basho and Sora had sailed down a wild stretch of its reach, past precipitous mountains and through calamitous gorges, risking their lives, earlier in their journey; later in the day we were going to see the river station at Kiyokawa where they disembarked from that dangerous voyage before beginning their — and our — pilgrimage to the sacred mountains.

Past Basho's monument was a small pond with a model ship upon it, half size, with a white sail, furled today: one of the sea-going kitamaebune which carried the freight, mostly rice, south through the Sea of Japan. They were also known as *sengokubune* (1,000 koku ships) because they had space on board for that amount of rice. A koku, as mentioned, was enough rice to feed a single person for a year; and a measure of the wealth of a domain. This pond commemorated a rich burgher, with a text praising his generous shipments of rice to Edo during a time of famine. There was a statue of him too, high up on a knoll among the clover and the pines, a monument far larger than that to any of the twenty-eight literary men and women.

Sixteen Buddhas was not a family place but another site of pilgrimage. It is on a rocky point reaching out into the sea near the town of Yuza in the shadow of Mount Chokai. Confusingly, there are actually twenty-two figures carved into the lumpy volcanic tuff, the relic of a lava flow from the volcano. We picked our way down the rugged cliff path into a small sandy depression surrounded by outcrops — from which, one by one, and startlingly, the faces of the buddhas appeared. They are cunningly carved, accentuating natural features to find the heads and shoulders, hands clasped in blessing or in prayer, arms bearing a staff or a wand, amongst the living rock. Over the hundred-and-fifty years since they were carved, pilgrims have cast coins before these effigies and some had become part of the sculptures, as it were, their metal fused with and dissolving into the stone.

One buddha had been made on top of a rock so that its beatific face gazed skywards; another was in a mass that loomed over the pathway and looked down beneficently upon you as you walked beneath it; a third, weirdly, was shadowed by the profile of a vengeful demon, in such a way that I could not tell if it was an accident of nature or a deliberate piece of design. The central figures are representations of the historical Buddha flanked by three Bodhisattvas; around these the Arhats are gathered. In fact, the rocks were so worn down by wind and waves it was difficult to find all of the figures that are there and perhaps, in the end, unnecessary as well.

This remarkable place was the creation of Ishikawa Kankai, head priest of the Fukura Kaizen temple in nearby Yuza. Distressed by a series of maritime tragedies in the early 1860s — fishing boats blown away, ships sunk with all hands aboard, their cargo lost — that afflicted the Shonai community, which depended upon the sea for both food and trade, Ishikawa had the buddhas made as prayers for good fortune, charms to ward off evil, and in memory of those who had given up their lives to the sea. He would seek donations in Sakata and, when he had raised enough money, commission a local stonemason to carve, under his supervision, a buddha. When that was done he would begin raising money for the next; and so on until he considered the site to be complete. The process took five years, between 1864 and 1868; and, when Kankai saw that his work was done, and having as a consequence attained satori, he threw himself into the sea.

This would just have been a rocky point when Basho and Sora came past in the summer of 1689, on their way north to Kisakata; a bay full of islands which is accounted one of the most beautiful places in the land. It appeared as such in many poems and was also celebrated in legend: the Empress Jingu, who conquered Korea, was buried there. They found the passage north from Sakata difficult:

> We went over a mountain, walked along the coast,
> and trod on the sand, for about ten li until, about
> the time the sun was close to setting, almost
> hidden in the salty wind swirling up the sand and
> in the blurring rain, we saw Mount Chokai.

The rain got heavier and they took refuge in a fisherman's hut. Next morning, when the sky cleared, they were rewarded with glorious views of the bay. They took a boat out to one of the islands, named after the poet priest Noin.

As with so much of the *Oku*, the passages about Kisakata are so replete with references to other poets and poems it is difficult to determine what is narrative, what allusion and what fiction. Sora is more matter of fact. The weather was bad all the time they were travelling and, upon arrival, they had to hire fresh clothes because their own were soaking wet. They were hosting a haikai session and had to rent a ryokan to house their guests. He attended a performance at a shrine but doesn't say what it was. Basho ends his account on an equivocal note: 'Though its appearance suggested Matsushima, it also differed from it. Matsushima seemed to be smiling, Kisakata resentful. Sadness added to loneliness, the make-up of the place resembled a soul in distress.' Perhaps he was already out of sorts. It was after their return to Sakata that he fell ill and his account of the journey broke off, not to be resumed until he met the play women at the Ichiburi barrier, far to the south.

We didn't go to Kisakata after all — there wasn't time — but we did cross briefly into Akita, the prefecture in which it is located, in order to visit another Basho spot. It was a park on a headland where a walk had been constructed, a kind fractal *Oku*, like the one Basho and Sora had taken but in miniature and within the reach of day-trippers like ourselves. Another notice board gave a more lurid account of the problems and dangers they had faced on their journey to Kisakata: 'So they continued their difficult trek over rugged terrain in ghastly conditions with dull hearts and did finally reach their destination. Basho was moved by the beauty of the scenery that greeted him.' We didn't take the walk. We didn't even get out of the car. We drove a short way under trees, in cool green shade, photographed the notice boards then turned around and headed south again.

In the carpark outside the restaurant at the river station at Kiyokawa was a larger than life statue of the poet, hat and staff in hand, gazing across the river towards the other bank, now obscured by a busy highway. The restaurant, which doubled as a museum, had closed for the day but the woman who ran it was still there and she invited us in to have a look around. There was a beautiful water colour of two river boats like those I had seen moored under the bridge in Tsuruoka; and several models of this and other kinds of craft in a glass case. An actual oar, long and robust, leaned against a wall and a number of documentary photographs of sengokubune on the river were displayed, with their square white sails spread, like birds, sailing seawards carrying their kokus of rice.

Outside the heat was blinding. The restaurateur said she had never known it this hot before; it was the week during which record temperatures were reached and then surpassed all over the northern hemisphere, when Canada and Greece were burning, Sicily too. She fanned herself and told us what we had already read on one of the sign boards: 'At that time Kiyokawa was a busy and prosperous port of the river, and there was a barrier station in the vicinity. Now the things reminiscent of the bygone days are only an old nettle tree and a well beside the tree.' The tree was bunchy and non-descript, sclerotic with age; the well was capped with a solid wooden cover. A rack of weapons stood next to it, typical of *sika*, barrier houses, ready to be taken up and used against intruders at a moment's notice. The guard house stood next to the nettle tree and it was open.

It was one of those buildings which have been restored only insofar as the shell is concerned. Nothing inside betrayed its former function or gave any clue as to how it was set up or how it operated. It featured some beautiful wood grain in the window shutters and the doors, and it had a view, past the highway, of the cool green flowing river. And there was one remarkable, also fractal, exhibit. On a small corner table, in a V-shape, stood effigies of all the Basho statues in Yamagata prefecture. Thirteen little dolls, with varying attitudes and poses, all labelled, all gathered here together in silent colloquy, as if about to begin a haikai session of their own.

A pink train crossed electric green paddy fields as we drove over the plains towards Mount Haguro. Just under 500 metres tall, Black Wing Mountain is the lowest and least conspicuous of the three peaks of Dewa, but also, in some respects, the most sacred. It is the most accessible too; you can drive to the top. The road was wide and well-sealed, as befitted a popular tourist route, and we soon came to the place where the devout begin to climb the two thousand four hundred and sixty-six stone steps to the summit, passing along the way the famous Five Tier Pagoda, twenty-nine metres tall, made of unpainted unstained shingled wood. Said to be the oldest pagoda in the north, it was built (or more likely rebuilt) in 1372 by Muto Masauji, a vassal of the Shonai clan and the head priest at Haguro.

The pagoda was undergoing renovation and obscured by scaffolding. We decided to give it a miss. Though the afternoon was waning, it was still hot. We were tired, it had been long day. We returned to the car and drove, like limp moderns, to the top. Here was another statue of Basho; I remembered its miniature from the guardhouse at Kiyogawa. It had been right at the back, at the point of the V of the phalanx and it showed him with staff in hand and satchel round his neck, looking somewhat quizzically away to the left. The face was craggy, weather-beaten, old and somehow wise as well. I don't of course know what he looked like but here was a portrait of a man whose character was apparent: neither aesthete nor literary politician, but seasoned wayfarer.

Nearby was an inscribed stone set up by the Shonai clan which I found, in its mixture of buoyant pride and dignified humility, very moving. It said:

> We have lived in this part of the land for a very long time, since the earliest days: the kofun, dating back 1,500 years, to the west of here, are the resting places of our ancestors. We were the ones who helped to reconcile the beliefs of Shinto and Buddhism with each other, to which the shrines and temples all about us bear witness. We have given rice to the Tokugawa when they were in need of it; we have always stood for knowledge, peace, harmony and understanding and we always will.

The hondo stood on the other side of a small lake which reflected, among the lilies and the floating pond weed, the building itself. The plant we had seen at the red lake, with the strange egg-like flowers, grew here too. I climbed the stairs, paid my respects and made my wish. I saw three people sitting on benches within, two women and a man, while a priest, with his back to them, chanted softly on a higher platform. When he fell silent, another priest appeared, ushered the three up onto the higher level then drew a white curtain across, obscuring from view whatever was to happen next. This, the first of the three mountains you visit, is where you ask to be granted what you wish for in life. I asked only that our present happiness continue.

The two and a half thousand steps of the staircase ended not far from the temple; every now and then exhausted pilgrims would emerge from under the trees, joy and relief on their faces. We went down those stairs a short way to see the lodge where Basho and Sora stayed when they were here. You enter through stout wooden gates in a watch house roofed with blue tiles, the same one through which the poets would have passed — after they had climbed that immense staircase — 334 years ago. Before us stood a big old timber building, L-shaped, with the tiles on the roof orange with lichen. It too was undergoing renovation. Three workmen were joshing together at the end of the day, lounging, drinking tea, in the shade of their truck. The doors to the lodge were open, several pairs of shoes stood on the porch, and a faint smell of incense came from within.

The lodge was called Minamidani, and here, on the fourth day of their stay, in the grand hall, at the suggestion of the head monk, a man called Egaku Adjari, the poets held a haikai session; which Basho began with the hokku:

arigata ya | yuki wo kaorasu | minamidani
give praise | fragrance of snow | south valley lodge

In none of the commentary I have read is it clear what, exactly, the scent of snow is. Does snow even have a smell? I wonder if, as cold weather approaches, you might catch a whiff of the resins of trees readying their sap to withstand freezing temperatures? Or is he referencing wood smoke? Maybe he meant something completely different, what in another place he called *nioi-zuke*, 'link by scent', suggesting how, in a group session, a verse might pick up the aroma of its predecessor and transmit it to its successor, the way the scent of a flower (or of snow) is carried on the wind.

We returned down the stone path to the blue-roofed gatehouse, through the old wooden gates, then wandered back up, in the green stillness of the forest, past the grave of Prince Hachiko, who inaugurated mountain worship here in 593, to the car. Our own accommodation for the night was in Daishinbo Shukubo Pilgrim Lodge not far from the foot of the stone staircase.

Day Five

Mt Haguro to Yamagata

The Shukubo, a 350-year-old building, had a narrow frontage but extended a long way back. It also went up. Our room was at the rear, large, on the second floor, overlooking a small enclosed garden. There was a mini staircase, only two or three steps, at the beginning of the short corridor that led to our door and when I got up in the night to go to the loo, which was downstairs, I forgot these steps were there and, in my sleepy confusion, stepped off into space. I'm not sure how I managed to stay upright but I came to with my left hand jammed flat against the other wall and the muscles in my lower back spasming. It felt like the kind of thing that would happen to you in a Pilgrim Lodge: a leap in the dark followed by a shock which emphasizes, once again, the way in which we go through this world only half aware of where we are and what we are doing.

We had been invited, the evening before, to attend prayers in the chapel at seven o'clock the next morning, before breakfast. We woke early, about 4.30, when the first pale light of dawn began to infiltrate the room, drank tea and went about our business until the time came to go downstairs and join a dozen or so others in the chapel at the front of the building. Apart from a woman and her daughter, tourists like us, and a Japanese fellow who acted as interpreter, they were all neophytes of some kind, perhaps training to become *yamabushi*, mountain monks. This is supposition because I never spoke to any of them, nor they to me. With the exception of another woman in her sixties and a German in his forties, they were all young North American men.

Yamabushi practice *shugendo*, an ancient belief system in which elements of Buddhism, Shintoism, Taoism, and Animism combine. In shugendo, mountains are considered to be the abode of the gods, and by training in the mountains, adepts can attract the spirits of the gods into their souls. It is an exhaustive process which might take thirty years to complete. Part of the discipline involves eating *shojin ryori*, ascetic cuisine, without meat, fish or animal products. Both meals we ate at the Shukubo featured shojin ryori. Its local origins lie in the desire of the yamabushi to spend as much time as possible in the mountains, so they learned to eat, and to preserve, what was there in the forest: nuts, roots, grasses, bamboo shoots, flowers and mushrooms. The diet is supposed to purify as well as sustain; there are analogies with what the mummy monks subsisted upon. I noticed that all of the neophytes with us in the chapel had a lean and hungry look.

The head priest, the *Sendatsu*, the seventeenth in line, a Mr Hayasaka, was officiating. Robed in yellow, wearing an elaborate headdress, bespectacled, he came from a side room to begin proceedings. He blew on a conch shell and beat upon a drum before and after he spoke; he laid things upon the altar and moved other things around. He sat on the floor and then he stood up again. The prayers, which he led, were in two parts. First: '*Sango*, to purify ourselves and maintain sustainable relationships together with kami and nature.' Then: '*Ava ni*, to worship the kami.' The chants were both sonorous and repetitive and, so early in the morning, had a soporific effect.

We had been given a song sheet in case we wanted to chant along but I wasn't able to do that. The neophytes could, however, probably because this was a service they attended every morning. The names of eight kami were listed but I don't think we honoured all of them; I only counted four. The chants for the kami were guttural, melodic and strange and I much preferred them to those of the sango, which resembled, to my untutored ear, a series of Hail Marys or Our Fathers. Prayers for the afflicted, for disaster victims, for world peace, for health, for family followed. We heard both of our names spoken out loud and prayers were said for the fulfillment of our hearts' desires too.

After the formal part of the service was over, the Sendatsu addressed us directly, preaching a kind of sermon. His words were translated by the young Japanese man, rather more long-windedly, it seemed to me, than the way they had been spoken. Mayu confirmed that was the case. She said he added all sorts of extraneous matter to what the Sendatsu had said, anxious, perhaps, to editorialize in such a way that we would not miss the important message we were being given. To me the most resonant thing he said was that, whatever the politics of Shinto versus Buddhism may be — and they are complex, sometimes divisive, even violent — behind both systems of belief lies a more profound truth, which is the wisdom, indeed the necessity, of nature worship.

Breakfast was served after the prayers were over. We made our way towards the back of the building, heading for the room where we had eaten the night before; only to be called back by Mr Hayasaka himself, sans headdress, with his glasses perched upon the end of his nose, his robes swishing, hurrying in his white socks after us down the corridor. The breakfast room, he explained, was next to the chapel. Suddenly he seemed no longer distant and austere but human, companionable. Later we learned that the old, frail, self-effacing chap who had greeted us when we first arrived was not a house servant but Mr Hayasaka's father, the retired sixteenth head priest. And the smiling woman who had served us the night before, generously re-filling our saké glasses every time we emptied them, was Mrs Hayasaka. It was a family business, then, and they were pleasant and friendly people.

I wish I could say the same about the neophytes. While Mayu was inside paying, I waited with our luggage out on the porch in the sun, where they were preparing for their day's adventures in the forest. The discussion was first of all about their equipment, their walking shoes and other accoutrements; then it segued into talk about other walks they had made, in this and other places, the trials they had overcome, their injuries and accidents or near accidents. Although I was standing with them, at no stage did any of them seek to include me in any way in their conversation. I imagine this was because, as a mere tourist, I was beneath their notice. I couldn't help thinking that some people rate their spiritual accomplishments in the same way they do their hiking gear. For these fellows, top of the range, in both cases.

Somewhere in his diary Sora says that he and Basho visited many Buddhist places on their journey but only ever worshipped at Shinto shrines. Sora had in 1681 gone to Edo to study Shinto with a renowned master, Koretari Yoshikawa, and had become an adept. And he embarked on the *Oku* wearing the black robes of a Shinto priest. Even then, in the late seventeenth century, the two faiths had been intertwined for the best part of a thousand years and there are still many places in Japan where you will find Shinto shrines and Buddhist temples side by side. Sometimes, as in Nagasaki, there'll be a church in the precinct as well. There's a saying: born Shinto, marry Christian, die Buddhist.

The Tokugawa, who were Tendai Buddhists, in the 1630s and 40s initiated the replacement of Shingon Buddhist monasteries on Haguro with those of their preferred system of belief — which inclines to the view that, if you are born rich and powerful, that is a sign of good karma — and subsequently poured vast amounts of money into their temples. After the Meiji Restoration, the new government attempted to suppress, or at least curb the power of, Buddhism, by making Shinto the state religion. On Haguro, where there had once been twenty-eight Buddhist temples, there is now just one.

I always prefer Shinto places. They seem more tolerant, less severe, and without the obsessive focus upon decorum, on the one hand, and money, on the other, that you so often find at Buddhist temples. The Shinto kami, despite some affinities, are not, like the Greek gods, mired in tragedy. They are joyful gods and wish to be worshipped joyfully; the mirrors, ubiquitous in their shrines, are to remind you of how you look to them: and have the intention, it seems, of persuading people to put their best selves forward.

⛩

After we left the Shukubo, we drove halfway up Mount Gassan, Moon Mountain, along a narrow winding road, with a thick growth of plants encroaching on either side and sometimes making an arch overhead; every stick on the tar seal looked like a basking snake. At the Eighth Station, where the road ended, the carpark was full of buses and cars. Here you may leave your vehicle behind and walk the rest of the way to the summit, three or four hours away; as quite a few people were preparing to do. At 1,984 metres, Gassan is the tallest of the three mountains of Dewa. It was a lot cooler up there and those going further were kitting themselves out in mountain wear — hiking boots, thermal vests, stout walking sticks. You could see snow on the flanks of the mountain in the distance.

When Basho and Sora were here, they too climbed the mountain and spent the night at the top:

> Yushime (a necklace made of paper string) hung on our bodies, hokan (a white cotton cloth worn like turban) wrapped round our heads, and led by a mountain guide, we climbed about eight li through clouds and mists, treading ice and snow, wondering whether we'd entered the orbits of the sun and the moon. Breathless and frozen,

we reached the summit, when the sun set and
the moon rose. With bear bamboo spread and
short bamboo as pillow, we lay down and waited
for the day to break. As the sun rose and clouds
dissipated, we went down to Yudono.

We too changed our clothes and set off along a path made of
wooden slats gone silver with age, through fields of green grass
where yellow lilies grew; if you lifted up your eyes and looked
into the west, you saw lines of pale blue hills receding, horizon
upon horizon, towards the Sea of Japan. The Midahara shrine was
modest, unassuming. There were a couple of old fellows dressed
in white overalls gardening; white is the colour yamabushi wear.
Like the young men at the lodge, they neither looked nor spoke to
us. Perhaps I was being unfair to the neophytes, I thought; perhaps
a degree of aloofness is required of them. Mountain monks are
supposed never to initiate contact but are obliged to give you their
full attention should you ask anything of them. No wonder they
prefer to remain, so far as possible, remote. I would too.

Gassan is named after the moon god, Tsukuyomi, the brother of
Amaterasu, goddess of the sun; his attributes include a love of
order and beauty; and of rectitude where etiquette is concerned:
a rectitude so extreme he is prepared to kill those who transgress.
He is a mysterious god; he rules the night. In Buddhist thought,
the Midahara wetlands on the slopes of Gassan are the haunt of
Amida Buddha, who represents salvation in the afterlife in Pure
Land Buddhism. Thus, for both faiths, Moon Mountain lies at the
borders of the next world. Here you remember your ancestors and
say farewell to your dead. At the small wooden shrine I dropped
some coins in the slot of the collection box, bowed my head, shut
my eyes, and silently rehearsed the names of mine, or at least

those I could recall. I remembered others later. I was surprised how many of them there were, something Mayu also remarked upon. 'You were there a long time,' she said.

We passed through the fringes of the wetlands on the way down; they are home to rare alpine plants and feature small circular lakes, tarns, which are a mysterious golden black colour and shine like mirrors. At the eighth station we paused in a small café to have a cup of coffee before driving down the mountain again. The sticks which might have been snakes had all wriggled away, to be replaced by squadrons of dragon flies, zooming and humming in the air, seemingly on a collision course with the windscreen of the car only to veer away at the last moment. Basho and Sora walked along the ridge from Haguro to Gassan and then from Gassan to Yudono before returning to South Valley lodge; we went the long way round. At the bottom of the road we turned left and began the hour-long circuit of the massif to the third place, the future mountain.

Yudono, at around 1,500 metres, is smaller than Gassan but taller than Haguro; only yamabushi climb to the top these days. It is where they complete their training. The Yu in the word means hot water and dono means lord; but it can also mean bath. So the name might be translated as Lord Hot Water; or it might simply mean a place to have a good hot bath. A more resonant phrase calls the shrine on the mountain Oku-no-in, the temple of the deep. That *oku* is the same one as the one in *Oku no Hosomichi*. The temple, however, although it is surrounded by things people have made, is not a building. Rather, it is a natural feature of such strangeness, of such rare and unusual power, and so protected, that you are not allowed to photograph it and nor are you permitted to describe it in words. Those who visit Oku-no-in go through a series of elaborate rituals associated with this natural feature which are understood to constitute a ceremony of re-birth. Having pledged your wishes for the present at Haguro, honoured the spirits of the past at Gassan, you embark upon your future life at Yudono.

We turned off the main highway and drove, not far, until we came to a roadhouse overlooked by a large torii gate painted a resplendent red and leading to the path that goes up the mountain. A graveyard and a small temple stood to the right. You could walk up to the shrine or you could take a bus. We took the bus. It was full. Halfway up the mountain it stopped. We disembarked and, with the other pilgrims, walked in single file up a path, over a low ridge and then down the other side into a small valley through which a stream ran. The way was strewn with coins, some of which had, as at Sixteen Buddhas, fused with the earth. When Basho and Sora came here, you were not allowed to take any money to the shrine and so people would empty their purses or pockets of coins as they walked towards it. Evidently, some still do.

We crossed the stream and went a little further on to a low shelter resembling a bike shed where you took off your shoes and left them in a rack. Opposite that, a large man, robed in white, stood before a booth. You offered him money — ¥1,000 — and in return he blessed you and gave you a small white cut-out figure, a paper doll, which you dabbed upon the sweat of your brow, upon your arms, your chest and wherever else on your body you wanted to. Then you cast it into the water of a small hot stream which ran down towards the bigger stream below. Mine bobbed away for a bit then got caught into a logjam of other cut-outs. The paper doll takes with it all the bad karma you may have accrued, the sins which inhere in your flesh.

After that, you go through a wooden gate and walk along a stone path to the shrine itself, the natural feature I am not permitted to describe. I have seen many things in thermal and volcanic areas in New Zealand, the Americas, Indonesia, the Pacific Islands, Japan and elsewhere; but I have never seen anything like what I saw at Yudono. We prayed to it in the Shinto manner. Bow, clap your hands to attract the attention of the kami, pray, then bow again. After that we walked, bare foot, through very hot water, up beside and around the shrine to greet the kami there. There was a lookout with a spectacular view down the valley, the top of the red torii gate just visible above the green trees and before the blue hills beyond. When you come back down again, trying not to slip on the hot wet rocks, reborn, you go to pay your respects to the ancestors again.

We bought a flower, a candle, incense, and another paper figure, which you wet and paste to a rock face. I wasn't sure if this represented the ancestors or was another version of my sinful self. You light the candle, place it in a rack, light the incense from the candle then put it with other sticks in a small, smoking, fragrant pile. The flower goes into a basket and after that you fill a glass of water, pour it out, fill it again and place it on the altar. On the way back you bathe your naked feet again in a pool of hot mineral water. We were at times uncertain of the order in which to proceed with these complex observances but a genial fellow we met along the way, with an ironically conspiratorial manner and a comb over, helped us with them. Afterwards, while we were putting our shoes back on, he said to me in English: 'This is a strange country!' And then glossed that with 'mysterious!' We saw him again later, leaving the car park. He drove a smart red Subaru saloon with Tokyo plates.

We took the bus down again. After we disembarked, passing the graveyard, I stopped to photograph a beautiful stand of purple irises, the thin dark kind, flowering next to someone's grave. Just along from it, at the end of a short, dedicated path I saw, with a shock of recognition, a mummy monk. He was sitting upright, behind glass, with his domed head and shoulders visible, and the skeletal fingers of his hands, tiny as a child's, clasped in front of him. His skin had gone a rich golden-brown colour, tending towards black, as in those pictures you see of folk who have been dug out of the bogs of Northern Europe. It was also the colour of the flesh of the dried salmon we had seen hung up on racks in Murakami.

Yudono was a centre for the practice of sokushinbutsu; of the twenty mummy monks still extant in Japan, eleven are of men who trained on Yudono. I don't know who this one was but he will have a name and history. There is a temple on the mountain which is dedicated to Shinyokai Shonin, who became a mummy monk in 1786 at the age of 96. He would have been born about the time Basho and Sora came through here. His clothes are changed every six years, and the old ones cut into pieces to be sold as amulets; perhaps this was him. I didn't inquire.

When the Tokugawa decreed that all the temples on Haguro convert from Shingon to Tendai Buddhism, those on Yudono were expected to follow suit. They refused, arguing that to do so would be to betray their founder, the monk Kukai, who established the first temple here in 807, and thereby initiated the worship of Dewa Sanzen. However, in Shinto belief, it was Prince Hachiko, son of the assassinated thirty-second Emperor Sushun, fleeing Nara after his father's death, who began mountain worship here, much earlier, in 593. He whose grave we had seen on Haguro.

I'm not sure how the dispute between Tendai and Shingon at Yudono was resolved, if it was resolved; but sokushinbutsu is a Shingon practice. After the Meiji Restoration, there were violent pogroms against both sects, temples were burned and monks killed. The primary distinction between the two, to my mind at least, is that in Shingon Buddhism a person may achieve enlightenment, called satori, during their lifetime; in Tendai, you must proceed through all the weary cycles of death and rebirth until you achieve nirvana. Meanwhile in Shinto belief, when you die, if you do not become a demon of some kind, you will become an ancestor and thus a guide for the living. That's what I would like to be.

Basho's haiku on Yudono alludes rather to his awe than his grief:

katararenu | Yudono ni nurasu | tamoto kana
at Yudono | forbidden to speak | my sleeves wet with tears

While the more practical (or less sentimental) Sora focused upon the discarded coins along the way:

zeni funde yo | o wasurekeri | Yudono michi
on Yudono path | stepping over coins | I forget the world

Somewhere in the vast commentary on Basho's oeuvre is the suggestion that he understood the prohibition against describing the shrine on Yudono only after seeing it. It was, he said, because it resembles, in certain respects, a woman's sex. This is perhaps also why the shrine is popular with lovers and especially with women in love. On the other hand, Japanese are not particularly prudish when it comes to such things; rather the opposite, in fact. I suppose Basho, as a gay man, if he was a gay man, might have felt differently. I did not notice any such resemblance myself. However, when I relayed Basho's supposition to Mayu, she looked thoughtful and said: 'Now that you mention it . . .'

Day Six

Yamagata to Matsushima

The city of Yamagata (mountain shape) stands under a range of improbably symmetrical rounded hills, volcanic in origin, which rise up one behind the other like buns on a baker's tray. They are at the southern end of the Ou Range and on their other side lay our destination, Togatta Onsen in the town of Zao; but we weren't going there yet, we were going to Matsushima first. When I looked north east through the hotel windows, the green mounds of Ou were hazy in the early morning light; by the time we'd checked out and were on the road to Yamadera, it was raining steadily. There was no wind; silver water fell vertically from the grey sky, washing over the roads and fields, reducing visibility almost to zero: we drove in a watery bubble which moved as we did.

The town of Yamadera (mountain temple) is built on both banks of the Tachiya River. On one side, close up against Mount Hohu, stands the ancient temple Risshaku with its extensive network of smaller temples and shrines, a dozen or more, stretching up the mountain. There is a thousand step stairway leading to the top but it seemed unlikely, on a day like this, that we would be climbing that. Even though it was pouring with rain, because it was a Saturday many people had come to pay their respects and many cars, on the bridge over the river and in the narrow streets, were jamming the way to the temple. On a low hilltop on the other side of the valley is the Yamadera Basho Memorial Museum and we decided to go there first. Ours was the only car in the carpark.

The exterior of the building, from 1989, follows the *kurazukuri* style typical of Japanese clay-walled storehouses. It was low, restrained, ochre with brown boards. Inside you entered a clean well-lighted place with a spacious lobby that had floor to ceiling plate glass windows at one end, looking out over an artificial lake surrounded by curving green lawns to the wooded hills beyond. Suddenly the rainy day turned from a troublesome affliction into a view with a soothing, other-worldly aspect. Droplets slid lazily down the outside of the glass, saucer-shaped interior lamps reflected in the windows looked like UFOs hovering over the lake with its soft green shores.

We bought tickets and a catalogue and went through to the exhibition area, where the first thing that caught my eye was a pair of painted screens depicting, in sequence, the many stages of safflower production, from cultivation all the way through to shipment of the finished product to the markets in Kyoto for sale. It was painted late in the Edo period by Aoyama Eiko (b. 1817) and was a very beautiful thing, using reds and whites and yellows on an ochre ground beneath the green of the trees and the darker green of the mountains. Safflowers have been grown here for at least four hundred years. Basho mentions them in a haiku — inadvertently repeating the name of my beloved:

mayu haki o | omokage ni shite | beni no hana
eyebrow brush | bringing to mind | the safflower

It is one of humanity's oldest cultivars; pigment derived from the plant was used in Mesopotamia and by the ancient Egyptians. The herb, here called *benibana* or rouge flower, came to Japan from China. It was (and still is) cultivated intensively in Yamagata, and made into *hanamochi* (rice flower cakes), which in the old days were sent down the Mogami River and then by ship to the southern cities. The yellow flowers are picked, washed, trampled, fermented, pounded, then made into balls which are placed between straw mats and trodden flat to make the small round cakes; all of these processes may be seen in Eiko's screens. A range of pigments and dyes can be extracted from hanamochi, from palest pink through vivid reds to delicate yellows; they are used to dye fabrics as well as for make-up and in painting. It was their thistle-like flower, resembling cornflowers, which made Basho think of the brushes women use to apply cosmetics, including the rouge, *beni*, which gives safflower its Japanese name.

Elsewhere in the museum were treasures: a hand-written copy of *Oku no Hosomichi* transcribed by Naito Joso, a disciple, in 1697 (before its publication in 1702 such copies were the only way in which it was circulated); a complete, illustrated, miniature, bound copy of the *Oku* made as a tribute by a later artist; and a number of items in Basho's own hand, which was fluid and elegant, seeming to flow like words written on water down the page. These included three haiku plus his own commentary upon them; instructions for a haikai session ('the gathering should not devolve into drunken revelry'); a prose excerpt from a later work (*The Hut of the Phantom Dwelling*); a letter to a friend mourning another friend's death; and, finest of all, a poem and painting with Basho's calligraphy and an image by Morikawa Kyoriku. This was a minimal work of great delicacy and restraint, showing the moon over a plum tree:

haru mo ya ya | kesheki totonou | tsuki to ume
slowly spring | makes itself known | moon and plum

When we came out of the museum the rain had eased but it was still falling steadily as we crossed the river and went up to the temple on the other side of the valley. Risshaku-ji was founded more than a thousand years ago, in 860, early in the Heian period, when Emperor Seiwa sent the priest, Jikaku Daishi, also known as Ennin, north to what was then still a frontier region to build a temple. Ennin was a Tendai Buddhist and, as far as I know, that remains the teaching followed at Yamadera.

Here we were able to stow our umbrellas, take off our shoes and go inside the hondo; even inside the inside (the oku of the oku) where, in the dimness of a fenced wooden enclosure, on a raised stage, stood a collection of dusty old god figures from long ago. There were a dozen or more, all different shapes and sizes, men, women and other beings, standing together, facing forward, as if determined to enter the future together. Perhaps, I thought, they were older than a thousand years. Perhaps they had been brought here from China or even India. They seemed ancient, with paint peeling from their dusty splintered wood, dulled eyes and ragged robes — wise, and somehow barbarous too, as if they carried within themselves knowledge of the time when people were still able to shape shift from god to beast and from beast back to god again.

An enormous gingko tree, not tall but metres round, stood in the temple grounds; it had multiple trunks and was said to be 1,200 years old. It must be an extraordinary sight in autumn when the leaves turn yellow; today it looked hunched, beleaguered and solitary beneath the grey, misty rain clouds drifting up the valley of the Tachiya. Nearby, in a green glade, were statues of Basho and Sora, side by side — the first time we had seen them together since viewing their silhouettes in the museum at Izumozaki at the beginning of our journey. They were both sitting, rather far apart, as if estranged from each other, with a haiku inscribed on a stone standing between them.

Basho's plinth was higher than Sora's, to emphasize the master / disciple relationship I suppose. He wore a bandana on his head, the satchel slung round his neck was resting on his knee, with his right hand upon it, and he was looking slightly quizzically to the left, in Sora's direction but not at him. Sora, on his lower plinth, had his body leaning forward, his feet spread wide and firmly planted, a staff in his right hand, his round hat in the other, looking forthright and energetically ahead. Bare-headed, bald, in profile, he resembled the honest, uncomplicated servant he is so often imagined to have been. The grey metal of the sculptures, glistening with rain water, shone eerily in the green light of the glade where they sat. I felt briefly, unaccountably, as if I were in their presence. There was the visionary and there the functionary who helped him find his way to his visions.

It was very different weather the day they were here: hot and still. They arrived in the afternoon, found their accommodation for the night, then climbed up the thousand steps to the temple on the mountain top:

The mountain was made of rocks piled upon rocks, the pines and cypresses were aged, and the soil and the stones old and smooth with moss and the doors of the lesser halls all closed — we heard not a sound. As we went around the cliff, crawled over rocks, and paid our respects at the Buddhist sanctum, the splendid scenery was so hushed and silent we could only feel our hearts go clear.

The haiku he wrote here is justly celebrated, not least for its brilliant evocation of that moment, on a hot day, when everything suddenly goes quiet:

shizukasa ya | iwa ni shimiiru | semi no koe
silence | sinking into the rocks | cicada's songs

We drove on, in the easing rain, through the round wooded mountains of the southern Ou Range, stopping for lunch at a roadside restaurant where locals and travellers ate. The food was excellent and Mayu surprised then gratified a solitary diner by giving him the complimentary vouchers the restaurant had just given to her. Then we drove out onto the plains, following geometrically straight roads through the white heron haunted rice-fields north of Sendai until we reached Matsushima: a place so beautiful, Basho said, he could find nothing to say about it.

Day Seven

In Matsushima

Matsushima means island of pines. There are said to be over two hundred and fifty islands in the harbour, some quite large, most small, and they all seemed to have pine trees growing upon them. Large islands with tall pines leaning parallel in the wind; little ones carrying twisted ones that looked, from a distance, like they'd been bonsai-ed. Its beauty has been celebrated in poetry for a thousand years and it was one of the reasons Basho gave for embarking upon the *Oku no Hososhimi* in the first place. On the opening page, just before he sets out, having moxa burned over his knees, he writes: 'I thought of the moon over Matshushima.' His decision, or his inability, to write a poem about it has been taken as the ultimate accolade; but there is in the *Oku* a prose piece in which he speaks at some length about the place and the things he and Sora did there; and elsewhere another piece which includes a single haiku, perhaps written there, perhaps later:

> shimajima ya | chiji ni kukakete | natsu no umi
> islands shattered | a thousand pieces | summer sea

One of their visits was to the island of Oshima, which he calls Ojima. Oshima has been a place of training for adepts of Shingon Buddhism since the Heian era:

> The Ojima shore, connected to the mainland, is an isle jutting out into the sea. There are things like the site where Zen Master Ungo's detached residence used to be and his Zen meditation rock. I also saw under pine trees a smattering of people who had renounced this world quietly living in a grass hut from which smoke rose from a fire of gleanings and pine cones. I do not know who they were but I stopped by, feeling close to them. The moon shining on the sea gave a view different from that of daytime.

We too went there, almost by accident, on Sunday morning. White lilies with gold specked petals and red stamens grew wild beside the path. A small bridge with bright lacquered crimson railings connected mainland and island and on the shore side a thin woman holding a plastic folder stood as if waiting for us. She was a senior, a volunteer guide, and she seized upon us with alacrity and undisguised glee. I suppose my status as a gaijin suggested tourist and Mayu's presence as a native speaker meant opportunity. I would have happily wandered guideless around the island, which is tiny, but Mayu felt obliged by the women's interest to let her show us at least some of the way. We said several times that we were in a hurry (not true) and wouldn't be able to stay to see the next attraction; but in the event she conducted us around the whole island and told us many things we would not otherwise have known.

Before Basho, perhaps the most famous pilgrim to come to Oshima was Kenbutsu Shonin, who took up residence here in 1104 and stayed for twelve years, meditating and chanting sutras. He is said to have recited the Lotus Sutra 6,000 times over those twelve years and to have thereby attained the ability to fly. In 1119, Emperor Toba in Kyoto heard of his accomplishments and sent one thousand young pine trees as a gift. They were planted on Oshima and from there spread to the mainland and gave Matsushima its name. Or so the story goes; common sense suggests there must have been pine trees here long before Kenbutsu. Notwithstanding, the emperor's gift made the island so beautiful it was said to resemble, even to be, the Pure Land, the Buddhist paradise. Subsequently, from the twelfth century on, people have erected gravestones and carved memorial tablets on Oshima and it is now exceedingly crowded with such things. Among them is a Basho monument but our guide did not know where it was.

First we made our way out to a small headland on the southern tip of the island which is, at the right time of the month, a moon viewing platform. The full moon rises in a gap between two other islands at the mouth of the bay; islands which, incidentally, protected Matsushima from the worst of the 2011 earthquake and tsunami which destroyed the nuclear power station at Fukushima and devastated much of this coast, including the nearby port city of Ishinomaki. Nearer at hand was another pair of islands which, our guide explained, are called the whale and the turtle; they did indeed resemble those two animals. A monument erected here long ago is accounted so precious that it has had its own building built around it, and a high picket fence around that. You can hold your camera through the slats of wood of the hexagonal building, called a *sayadou*, and take a photograph of the inscriptions on the rocket shaped stone within; but that is all.

The stone is a memorial to another monk, Raiken, who spent twenty-two years on the island following ascetic practices. A Shingon Buddhist, he came after Kenbutsu and was sometimes thought to have been a reincarnation of him. His dates were 1196-1273 and the monument to him was erected by his followers in 1307. Over three metres tall, it was engraved with dragons, with abstract patterns called *raimon* (lightning) and *karakusamon* (scrollwork), with a one syllable seed mantra, a *shuji*, and some writings in cursive characters by Issan Ichinei (1247-1317) a Chinese monk of the Yuan dynasty who visited Japan at the time it was being inscribed. The sayadou itself was built late in the Meiji period, just before the First World War.

Our guide, who had been looking for it everywhere, found the Basho monument for us as we made our way back from the southern headland. It stood, with others, including a stone bearing a haiku by Sora, looking out to sea from an earthen bank among scrubby trees above the path. The stones were pleasingly weathered and covered with a creamy-grey lichen; they were more or less unreadable, which was true of many of the standing stones we saw on our journey. Their status seems to rely, not upon their scrutability, but upon their presence and their provenance. Beyond them we came to another headland, looking north, the path to which was lined by ranks of kannons, buddhas, and bodhisattvas, including one, bearing a staff and a globe but without a face, which I found very moving.

And on the way back from there we came to what I thought of as the heart of the island: a clearing surrounded by low cliffs honeycombed with caves made into stone cells in which monks or other ascetics endured and practiced their long years of discipline and abstinence. The ground of the clearing was moss-covered and the catacombs shaded by elegant maple trees, their spring growth of leaves a lovely soft green. I felt sure this was where Basho had seen those who had renounced the world living in their grass huts and burning pine cones. It seemed as if some of them might still have been there; or rather I mean that their spirits were.

We parted with our guide at the same place where we had met. She said goodbye regretfully, her eyes bright with emotion; and gave us, from the voluminous plastic folder of information she carried, two bookmarks with coloured cotton tassels showing the island from the beach to the south, with the red lacquered bridge on the left and the moon watching platform on the right. We left her among the lilies, hopefully awaiting her next pilgrims, and made our way back to the hotel, which was, we had been assured, situated on the very street Basho and Sora had walked up when they left Matsushima, on foot, for Ishinomaki, a journey which they seem to have made in some confusion.

We were staying another night and decided, instead of doing any more sight-seeing, to take it easy. Mayu had found a book about Kawai Sora, written by poet and scholar Inui Sachiko, and downloaded it to her Kindle. Inui had made a detailed study of Sora's diaries and derived from her readings an alternative theory as to who he was and what was going on before, during and after the journey he made with Basho. Her book title, *Sora No Shotai 'Oku No Hosomichi' No Shinjitsu* translates as *Sora's True Identity — The Truth of 'Oku no Hosomichi'.* I couldn't read it, but Mayu selected certain passages and read them aloud to me, translating as she went, while I made notes. So passed the afternoon.

The story Inui reveals is complex and fascinating and although it relies, at times, on supposition, this she freely admits. The core of her argument is that Sora was not, as the biographers say, the eldest son of merchant and saké maker Takano Shichibei, born in 1649 in the village of Shimokuwabara on the shores of Lake Suwa, Shinano Province, but someone else entirely. She believes his mother was already pregnant with him when she married Takano Shichibei and that his true father was Matsudaira Tadateru, the errant sixth son of the first shogun of the Edo period, Tokugawa Ieyasu. Tadateru had fallen out of favour with his father and, after 1616, was exiled, first to Ise, then to Hide, finally to Shinano, where he spent, effectively, the rest of his life. He died in 1683.

Matsudaira is the clan name of the family who re-named themselves Tokugawa when they attained the shogunate; they claim descent from the Minamoto who defeated the Taira in the Genpei War. If Sora was in fact a scion of the Tokugawa, albeit the bastard son of a member of a disgraced minor line, that changes everything. It also explains certain anomalies, for example his elevation to the samurai class, an unusual trajectory for one of his ostensible birth and background. Most biographies record that, after the death of his parents, he was adopted by his aunt (in some versions his grandmother); and after her death, when he was twelve, taken in by Fukaizumi Yoshinari, the head priest of a temple in Nagashima, Ise province, who may have been his uncle.

From 1668, when he was nineteen, he served Matsudaira Yasunao, the daimyo of Nagashima (and also Lord of Sado). Later still he was at Murakami, evidently as a retainer of the Sakakibara clan (who succeeded the Matsudaira in 1667). During this period, he travelled widely as a messenger. It is this elevation to a retainer, with samurai status which, if he were a commoner, marks him out as unusual. All daimyo had their own mail and messenger services, both to communicate within their own domain and to and from Edo, where they had, perforce, a city establishment to run. Sora, with diplomatic status, was one of these messengers. Perhaps he had this status on the *Oku* too.

His interest in poetry is harder to trace. His first attested haiku seems to have been written in 1676: 'Spring is coming out of the sleeves – Matsuba-sen.' It evokes a new year gift of money to children. In 1681 he went to Edo and studied Shinto with Yoshikawa Koretari, a teacher whose reputation was on the rise; some accounts suggest he worked for him rather than studied with him. Yoshikawa was an advisor to daimyo like Tokugawa Yorinobu of Kii and Hoshina Masayuki of Aizu, and had been introduced to the shogun, Tokugawa Ietsuna. In 1682, shortly after Sora began to work with him, Yoshikawa was appointed to an hereditary position in the bakufu as 'Shinto kata' or Shinto councillor. This was the period during which Basho, having established himself as a haikai master, left Edo and went to live on the Sumida River.

Basho said he met Sora because they were neighbours on the river at Fukagawa, where he lived in the remodelled caretaker's lodge at the fish farm run by the Sugiyama family, whose business was supplying live carp for the ornamental ponds of the Tokugawa. Both Sugiyama Kensui, Basho's first benefactor in Edo, and his son Sanpu, were haiku poets. In time Sanpu inherited the business from his father; he remained a close friend and benefactor of Basho's until the poet's death in 1694. Basho's letters to Sanpu, who was deaf, are notable for their warmth and tenderness. I don't know if it was Sanpu who introduced Sora to Basho but it may well have been. With their extensive connections to the Tokugawa, all three of them are likely to have been something more than just poetry friends.

Many scholars have remarked upon the fact that Sora was a late comer to the *Oku*. Basho was originally going to go on the journey with the wandering beggar poet Yasomura Rotsu; Sora replaced him at the last moment. Subsequently Inui focuses upon a delay of ten days, during which the poets were marking time at a Mito clan house north of Edo. The Mito were, with the Kii and the Owari, one of the Gosanke, the three honourable Tokugawa houses from which shoguns were selected. The Mito had less land and less money than the other two but, crucially, were the keepers of the annals and, in the 1680s, were compiling a history of Japan which emphasized the place of the Tokugawa, as descendants of the Minamoto, at the heart of the nation's story.

Inui thinks the Mito were involved in the planning of the poets' journey and probably provided them with funds; her detailed analysis of income and expenditure reveals that the trip wasn't viable without some sort of capital investment. They wouldn't have been able to survive on the fees paid for haikai meetings, which anyway were never guaranteed to occur. She thinks there was a further injection of funds at Murakami, when Sora went up to the castle and was given a sum of money in gold; likely a reward for services rendered as much as an investment in future activities.

Inui suggests the ten-day delay was because the poets were waiting for an official letter to arrive, which they were to take with them on their journey north. It was brought by their poetry friend Sanpu, and, she says, came from the Seisui temple at Asakusa in Edo and was addressed to the head priest at Nikko Toshogu, where there is a shrine dedicated to the first shogun, Tokugawa Ieyasu. The letter included detailed instructions for the renovation of the shrine, which the Tokugawa in Edo expected the powerful Daté clan, the local lords, to carry out. The Daté were dragging their feet on this project, which entailed a great deal of expenditure in money, materials and time. From the point of view of the Tokugawa, this was the point. One of the ways they kept rival clans weak was by imposing vast expenditures upon them and the renovation of the shrine at Nikko was a means of doing this to the Daté.

There was more to the mission than the delivery of a letter however. Inui thinks, as other scholars do, that Sora was a government agent and that his duties also involved gathering intelligence about the state of waterworks in the Daté domain. The politics of water have always been central to Japanese culture, not least because the economy depends upon wet rice cultivation and therefore upon irrigation. However the management of water was not a national matter but the responsibility of the local daimyo. This was an area where Basho also had experience. He had worked for four years (1677-81) as a clerk in the water department in Edo and had a background in water works construction going all the way back to his time with the Todo in Iga as a young samurai. The Todo clan were specialists in the building and maintenance of water works.

Furthermore, it is likely that the trouble he and Sora got into at Matsushima had its roots in Basho's connection with the Todo. Some scholars believe Basho was, in the first instance, sent to Edo by Todo Takahisa, the daimyo of the clan. Takahisa, who was responsible for large scale irrigation works and the development of new rice lands in his own domains, was married to a daughter of Sakai Takakiyo, a powerful man who had fallen abruptly from favour at court in 1680 and died suddenly, possibly poisoned, the following year. Previous to that, he had attempted, with Takahisa's support, to break the power of the Daté. After Takakiyo's fall, the Todo, just as abruptly, changed allegiances, a move which attracted derision at court at the time. The Daté, it seemed, had long memories and had not forgotten Todo Takahisa's complicity in intrigues against them, nor Basho's history as a retainer of the Todo clan.

They had other, older grievances against the Tokugawa. In 1646, Daté Mitsumune, the heir apparent, grandson of the ferocious, one-eyed warrior Daté Masamune, founder of the clan, died, aged nineteen, in Edo castle. He was a young man of great promise, skilled in military matters as well as in literature and associated arts; the clan had high hopes for him. His family thought the Tokugawa had him poisoned because of the threat his future leadership posed to their power. Mitsumune is still venerated, and mourned, among the Daté to this day; there is a shrine to him next to the temple in Matsushima. If, as seems likely, the Daté knew about Basho's and Sora's connections with the Tokugawa, knew they had carried a letter to the Head Priest at Nikko (even if they didn't know its contents) and suspected their visit to Sendai and beyond had more than poetic significance, that might explain what happened next.

Basho's account of events after they left Matsushima is confusing, to say the least; he became disoriented:

> On the twelfth we meant to go to Hiraizumi, but because we had heard about Aneha Pine and The Thong-Breaking Bridge [both utamakura], we took a road seldom used by people but frequented by pheasants, rabbits and woodcutters, and pushed ahead, until we took a wrong turning and ended up in a port called Ishinomaki. Wondering how we ended up in a place like this, we tried to find lodging, but no-one was willing to take us in. Finally we managed to spend the night in a poor small house, and as day broke, we resumed wandering along an unknown road.

Sora mentions an incident on this journey which Basho omits: they asked for hot water at a house along the way and the request was refused. Then a samurai, a man by the name of Konno

Gentazaemon, from Neko, appeared, took them to his own house, gave them hot water to drink and afterwards found them a place to stay. Sora's account also mentions an interrogation, outside Matsushima, by four soldiers. One of the commentaries records that the incident of the refusal of the water made such an impression on Basho that he brought it up again, much later, in a letter to Sora. The same commentator also suggests the road frequented by pheasants and rabbits (and woodcutters, who were thought of as a kind of legendary being) was a fiction designed to dramatize the perils of travel and that Basho and Sora always meant to go to Ishinomaki and went there, not along wild back roads, but using the normal route.

Inui Sachiko has an alternate explanation for this imbroglio. She says things began to go badly wrong for Basho and Sora at Matsushima and they had to leave town in a hurry. Hence, perhaps, the interrogation by the soldiers. The fact that they had fallen out of favour with the Daté became known along the route they were taking and thus no-one dared give them water to drink, let alone a place to stay. They were, she suggests, in some extremity when the samurai, Konno, appeared and offered them help. His advent, she further suggests, was not an accident. She says he had been sent after them because it had been decided by the Daté that, while Basho might have been persona non grata, Sora was not. And the reason for that was the fact that his putative father's first wife, who was a Daté, is buried at Matsushima and is still esteemed there.

There is quite a bit to unpack here. The Daté princess was Irohahime, the first born child of Daté Masamune, who had been given a boy's name because that was what she was expected to be and retained it (albeit with a feminine pronunciation) because she had so many of the attributes traditionally considered masculine, in particular her intelligence. Matsudaira Tadateru married her in

1606; a union arranged as part of Tokugawa Ieyasu's strategy of strengthening relationships with daimyo by making liaisons such as these. It was another of his attempts to circumscribe the power of the Daté.

It was a happy marriage but there were no children and, when Matsudaira Tadateru was sent into exile in 1616, Iroha returned to her father in Sendai, where she became known as Lady Nishikan, after the west annex of the castle where she lived out her days. She was valued for her counsel by her younger brother, Daté Tadamune, who became daimyo when their father died in 1636. Lady Nishikan did not marry again, despite her family's wish that she do so, and died childless in 1661 at the age of 68. In some versions of her story she is said to have converted to Catholicism, hence her disinclination to re-marry. It's true that the Daté clan flirted with Christianity in the early years of the seventeenth century: in 1613 they sent an envoy, via New Spain, to the Pope in Rome. Matsudaira Tadateru, Sora's alleged father, was also interested in Christianity, probably for political reasons.

Tadateru's guardian in his early years, and the man who arranged his marriage with Irohahime, was none other than Nagayasu Okubo, the Noh theatre aficionado who became the first magistrate and controller of the mines on Sado Island. He served the Tokugawa well, in a variety of capacities, until his death from a stroke in 1613; but he was a proud and ambitious man who tried to build a power base of his own through his connection with the Daté and made many enemies as a result. It is likely that Tokugawa Ieyasu's confiscation of his estate after his death and the forced suicide of his seven sons had nothing to do with financial chicanery — an invention put about by Nagayasu Okubo's enemies — but was done in order to destroy the power base he had built up.

Nagayasu contemplated a future in which Matsudaira Tadateru, with the support of the Daté (and perhaps also the Pope), replaced his father as shogun. This would have been a proto-Christian regime with strong support from the Portuguese Jesuits. If so, Tadateru's exile after 1616, the year Ieyasu died, makes perfect sense. Ieyasu was succeeded by one of Tadateru's older brothers, Tokugawa Hidetada, who was an enthusiastic persecutor of Christians and had no good reason to keep his younger brother, and rival, around. One final detail: Nagayasu Okubo loved luxury, lived opulently and wanted to be buried in a gold coffin. When Tokugawa Ieyasu heard this he remarked, sardonically: 'And where would this gold come from?' Out of the mines of Sado, of course.

If Sora's distant connection to the Daté princess, the first wife of his alleged father, saved the poets' bacon on the road to Ishinomaki, that wasn't something either of them was going to mention; but it might be a reason, apart from the beauty of the landscape, why Basho wrote nothing while he was in Matsushima. It's almost certainly the case that, despite what he said, the trip to Ishinomaki was always part of the plan. Ishinomaki was the main port of the Daté clan; it was from there that their ships came and went on their trading voyages, both nationally and internationally. The envoy to the Pope left from, and returned to, Ishinomaki. Basho wrote in the *Oku*: 'several hundred freight ships gathered in the inlet, houses vied for the land, and smoke kept rising from the ovens.'

If a survey of the port was part of Sora's brief, that was probably the last official duty he had to carry out on the journey, at least insofar as gathering information about the Daté was concerned; he had more to do disseminating what he had learned. Afterwards, at Hiraizumi, mission accomplished, they were free to concentrate on poetry, as they did for the rest of their travels. There were many haikai gatherings in the weeks to come — but here too Sora's work continued. After all, such gatherings are perfect opportunities for the exchange of intelligence as much as for the composition of poetry.

It was at Hiraizumi that Basho wrote his famous haiku:

natsukusa ya | tsuwamono-domo ga | yume no ato
summer grasses | all that remain of | the dreams of warriors

He was remembering the defeat of the northern Fujiwara by the army of Minamoto Yoritomo in 1189, exactly 500 years before, and the death of Minamoto Yoshitsune, who had himself been responsible for the earlier death of his cousin, Minamoto Yoshinaka, a man Basho revered to such an extent he asked to buried next to his grave at Otsu in Omi, as indeed he was, in 1694, after dying, aged fifty, from the stomach ailment which troubled him for years and probably caused the interruption in his writing while they were travelling down the coast of the Sea of Japan.

Two more things. Inui Sachiko notes that when, at Fukushima on June thirteenth, Basho wrote the only letter he is known to have written during the *Oku*, to their poetry friend in Edo, the koi merchant Sugiyama Sanpu, and the man who had bought the message to the Mito clan house at the beginning of their journey, he spoke of Sora 'in honorific and humble language.' In other words he did not use those forms of address typically employed when referring to a pupil or a disciple, or indeed to an equal or a friend, but those appropriate to a person of higher status: as if Sora were a samurai or even a Tokugawa — a fact, if it was a fact, which would have been known to Sanpu as well.

Later on their journey, Basho and Sora had a falling out, at an onsen in Yamanaka, where Basho became enamoured of the proprietor's beautiful teenage son and Sora, impatient with his frivolity or perhaps just jealous, left. In the *Oku*, however, Basho says that Sora had developed stomach trouble (his own ailment) and went to recuperate with relatives in Nagashima. Basho, who soon found another companion, mourned their separation, writing: 'We were like single ducks after parting, lost in clouds.'

And: 'The separation of a single night was equal to a thousand li.'
They were re-united several weeks later, outside of Ogaki, towards
the end of the journey.

Kawai Sora, who was five years younger, outlived Basho by more
than fifteen years. His activities in later life are obscure but he
seems to have remained in the service of the bakufu until the
end of the first decade of the next century. The official story
is that he fell ill and died in 1710, aged 62, while travelling as a
government inspector on Kyushu under the orders of the new
shogun, Tokugawa Ienobu; and was buried at Noman temple on
Iki Island in Nagasaki prefecture. However, there is another grave
at Suwa, in what is now Nagano prefecture, suggesting, not that he
died twice, but that the first death was faked. Or so Inui Sachiko
believes.

She quotes from a letter Sora wrote to a family member in
Suwa in 1709, mentioning his appointment by the new shogun as
a *goyounin* — 'a manager, steward, person next in rank to the chief
retainer and in charge of general management and accounting in
a samurai family' — entrusted with a special mission to Kyushu.
Sora also said he had been given a large sum of money to spend
on the mission. This elevation to full samurai status could only
have occurred, Inui believes, if Sora's putative father, Matsudaira
Tadateru, had been pardoned, posthumously, for his alleged
crimes. Tokugawa Ienobu was a reforming shogun — in his short
reign he is credited with beginning the transition of the shogunate
from a military to a civilian government — and did issue an
amnesty which freed many suspects from the imputation that
they were or had been criminals.

Sora's mission, upon which he embarked under an assumed
name, was to inquire into the conduct of the Kuroda clan's
dealing with the Koreans. In the lead up to the goodwill mission

of 1711, during which the Korean delegation would formally acknowledge the new shogun in Edo, their envoys had been housed, at government expense, in specially built accommodation on Ainoshima Island off the coast of Fukuoka. The Tokugawa suspected that the Kuroda clan, who held Fukuoka, of skimming off some of the bakufu's money for their own private purposes; and otherwise failing in their appointed task of implementing the shogunate's policies with respect to Korea.

There hadn't been a mission from Edo to Tsushima Island, in the Korea Strait, where diplomats from the Hermit Kingdom were usually received, for many years; after visiting Fukuoka, that's where Sora was going to go next — to see how matters stood with the ruling So clan. He was delayed on the island of Iki, halfway to Tsushima, by the machinations of the So envoy, who kept changing protocols, inventing delays, or proffering maps which had been strategically altered, probably to buy time in which to conceal evidence of corrupt practices. It was during this period that Sora, after a short illness, is said to have died. But the diary of the So envoy makes no mention of the death of the goyounin; and the mission proceeded to Tsushima three days after the death is alleged to have occurred: which is unlikely. If the party's leader had just died, funeral arrangements would have had to have been made; and these would surely have been noted in the So envoy's diary.

Inui Sachiko suggests another scenario. She points out that, in his letter describing his mission, Sora says he requested to be allowed to take his pilgrim's robes with him and that the request had been denied. But what if he took them anyway? Or found another set? Perhaps, she says, he went on ahead of his party, incognito, disguised as a pilgrim, with a pass from the bakufu, to make his own reconnaissance and come to his own conclusions as to whether or not the So clan were administering government funds honestly and otherwise implementing the shogunate's

Korean policy. He would also have surveyed ports and shipping, doing much the same kind of work he did when he was with Basho at Nekko, Matsushima and Ishinomaki.

Half a dozen years later, at Joshu in the onsen town of Ikaho, now in Gunma prefecture, two colleagues of Sora's, who had studied with him in Edo under the Shinto master, Yoshikawa Koretari, saw a white-haired old man coming towards them and recognised him as their friend. They embraced, joined hands and celebrated. Sora had retired from government service and was living as an ascetic on Haruna mountain, overlooking Ikaho, where he had ancestral connections. When he died, not long after, he was buried at Suwa City in Nagano prefecture. I have been to his grave and paid my respects. Every year on the ostensible day of his death on Iki, ceremonies are held jointly at the temple on the island and at Suwa; which was, after all, where he was born.

Day Eight

Matsushima to Zao

The next morning we saw irrefutable evidence of the grandeur of the Daté clan in their prime. The Zuigan temple in Matsushima was founded in 828 by Jikaku Daishi of the Tendai sect and converted into a Zen temple during the Kamakura period, after which it fell into disrepair until it was rebuilt between 1604 and 1609. Daté Masamune used cypress, cedar and zelkova wood from Wakayama and employed over a hundred master carvers in its restoration; as well as artists to paint its spectacular sliding screens. It had recently undergone restoration and the paintings in all of the rooms in the hondo, save one, had been restored and appeared as they would have done when they were completed in 1622.

Each of the ten reception rooms had different motifs; you can visit the hondo, circumnavigating clockwise, peering into room after room; but you cannot go into any of them and nor can you take photographs. My favourite was probably the room where doctors waited to be called, decorated with gorgeous panels, almost abstract, featuring peonies, chrysanthemums and other flowers in bloom. Other rooms included the one where the people who performed the tea ceremony waited; two adjoining rooms where guests of greater and lesser importance waited; the room in which women were entertained; and the *Sumie no Ma*, the ink painting room, with its black and white panels, where the head priest received his visitors.

This was the only room whose paintings had not been replaced with replicas. I say black and white but that is not quite right. Small amounts of red ochre had been mixed in with the black ink, giving the pigment a slightly rubicund tinge which was initially disconcerting and then made the imagery seem radiant and glowing, almost dream-like. Next to that was a very strange room where two cohorts of samurai, sixteen and twenty strong respectively, who had committed seppuku upon the deaths of their masters, were memorialised as mannequins wearing the armour and bearing the weaponry the actual warriors would have used.

The chief glory of the hondo was the main hall where the peacock panels, painted by Sendai family painter Sakuma Shuri, were displayed. They lined three sides of this room; but I won't attempt to describe them. Like Basho at Matsushima, I am better off saying nothing. Further, any qualms I might have had about their status as replicas were allayed when I saw, in the museum next door, examples of the original panels. They were so faded you could hardly make out the imagery upon them: the hawks, the pheasants and peacocks, the green pines and blue rivers, the cranes and moons, the plum and cherry blossom, the robed and gowned figures processing on festival days, all reduced to grey shapes to which just a few scraps of fugitive pigment still clung.

Nothing of the gold ground upon which these things originally appeared had survived.

The Daté rebuilt the temple at the end of a long period of civil war and it includes features more commonly seen in castles, including a watch tower and an *uguisubari*, a nightingale alarm floor, whose timbers squeak as you walk over them. The *uguisu* is not, however, a nightingale, it is the Japanese bush warbler; the boards squeak because they are built in such a way that the flooring nails rub against a jacket or a clamp when trodden upon. It is thought this was a chance discovery that was afterwards used deliberately as a form of warning that intruders were in the building. The hondo also had, as castles do, a special entrance for distinguished guests, like the daimyo himself, with his retinue, who came in through a side gate and across a floor made of chipped granite pieces, lined with plain wooden benches, into the south wing.

Along the northern side of the hondo, you looked out to the intricately raked white sand, the placed rocks and the miniature pines of a Zen garden. The form followed here is Rinzai Zen which was popular amongst the samurai class because of the rigour of its practices — its martial spirit. Rinzai is often contrasted with Soto, a gentler practice, thus: 'Rinzai for the shogun, Soto for the peasants.' Zuigan-ji was the family temple of the Daté clan but it isn't clear how often they came here. One of the attendants, while showing us the celebrity entrance, suggested it was used only rarely. The hondo felt more like an art gallery than a temple and after spending half an hour or so there I did have that fatigued feeling that sometimes comes over you in galleries.

The veritable museum and art gallery next door included a life-sized figure of Daté Masamune wearing his black and gold armour. He was sitting on a small stool, legs spread wide and feet planted flat on the floor, arms akimbo, glaring out at us ferociously with his one eye; he had lost the other to smallpox while still a child. He was in a glass case and looked to have been quite a small man. Japanese armour was complex, elaborate, difficult to put on and was worn by infantry as well as men on horseback. The different clans all bore different insignia on their helmets, so they could tell each other apart in battle. The Daté's was an extravagant asymmetrical crescent moon-shaped piece of metal, worn affixed to the top of the headpiece, with the concave side upper most and the longer horn of the moon projecting out over the left shoulder. It must have been problematic in some circumstances, for instance when riding under trees.

After leaving the temple, we went looking for the grave of Irohahime, aka Lady Nishikan, the first wife of Sora's putative father but, although we found the cemetery where she was interred, we could not find her tomb. It would have been interesting to see if there was any Christian symbolism upon it. There certainly was at the Sankeiden, the mausoleum for Daté Mitsumune, the young man of promise poisoned by the Tokugawa at Edo in 1646. It was at the back of the temple grounds and approached over moss gardens and under spreading trees. The day was hot and humid but it was cool there, in the lee of high rocky cliffs. The mausoleum was a small wooden building whose interior you had to peer at through a grill made of heavy, twisted wire. Daté Mitsumune, or rather his effigy, rides a white horse, behind him stands a kannon, and around him range statues of the seven samurai who killed themselves after his death.

The interior walls are coated with gold; hence, I suppose, the grill. On the right hand door there is said to be a painting of rose, and on the left, one of a narcissus with white petals and a bell-shaped yellow corona; I couldn't distinguish either of them. Both narcissus and rose, or rather images of them, were bought back by Daté Masamune's papal envoy, Hasekura Tsunenaga, when he returned from his seven-year sojourn in Europe in 1620. There were also images of the hearts, diamonds, clubs and spades from the deck of playing cards. Elsewhere, the linked crosses and diamond designs on tiled floors were alleged to be clandestine Christian symbols, disguised because of the extreme persecutions of the 1620s and 30s. Perhaps. Nothing I saw there seemed particularly Christian to me.

Behind the mausoleum the path meandered under cliffs honeycombed with cells like those we had seen on Oshima. These were natural caves hollowed out for use as retreats, for prolonged meditation or as places in which to live. Sometimes ashes from cremations were scattered here, and there were freestanding monuments, of uncertain provenance, at the mouths of some of the caves. The area seemed oddly neglected and somehow relaxing too; everything else was so minutely curated. We passed a cedar grove, a rose garden and a heart-shaped pond on our way back to the entrance. The main hall was originally Daté Masamune's summer house in Edo. His son, Daté Tadamune, had it removed and rebuilt here when the temple was established in mourning for his own son in 1647. The English on a bilingual sign by the path advised: 'Please don't get into the moss.' I did not.

We left Matsushima mid-morning to drive to Zao, a couple of hours away. Our actual destination was Togatta Onsen in what is sometimes called the Village of the Dolls. *Kokeshi*, the cylindrical, armless, painted and varnished wooden dolls are said to originate there, although other villages and towns in Tohoku have their stylistic variants; and there are many stories about where the dolls come from and who first made them. I'd asked Mayu at the outset of our journey what she was going to do during her two-week artist's residency and she had said: 'I don't know.' An answer which startled me. I would never go to a residency without a clear idea of what I was going to write.

Not far from our destination we stopped for lunch at the Michinoku Centre, a rest house and restaurant set up on a hill overlooking Kamafusa Lake — actually a dam. In the course of the meal Mayu remarked, casually, that she now knew what she was going to do. She would use the time to identify poetry places, utamakura, in the vicinity of Zao; and to track down poets, past and present, who have written about them or written, more generally, about the area. If there weren't any utamakura to be found, she said, she would invent some, for current and future poets to use. There would be specific, tangible outcomes: with the help of her friend Muraoka Chie, a designer in Sydney, she was going to make a website and print a zine based upon it.

She said she also intended to keep a diary like the one Sora had written. It would record facts only — weather, time, destinations, roads taken or not taken, activities, people met, food eaten and so forth — without comment or elaboration.

'No flowery language,' she said. 'I'll leave that to you.'

'You mean you want me to be Basho?' I asked.

'Yes,' she said. So that is what we did.

Mizuho

Shinano | Winter | 2023-4

Kurohime is *yukiguni*, snow country. Properly speaking, the name ('black princess' but also 'secret iron') belongs only to the mountain and the railway station. The larger town is called Shinanomachi and the village we are living in, Kashiwabara. Even more confusingly, Mayu's mother Yoshie's house, just down the road from ours, is in Kumakura, 'bear's larder' but we are in Mizuho, 'lustrous shoots'. Mizuho refers to an abundant rice harvest and is an old name for Japan as well as the modern name of a bank. Kumakura, and Mizuho too, are names derived from shrines which have come to define the localities where they stand. But it's still snow country, which means that, from December to February and sometimes for longer, snow falls and drifts rise one or two metres high, perhaps even reaching past the windows of your house.

Shinanomachi is surrounded by mountains: Madarao to the east, a long sinuous rounded range, once a cone, overlooking Lake Nojiri, formed 70,000 years ago when a volcanic landslide dammed a river; Iizuna, Kurohime, and Myoko in a line to the west; Togakushi in the hinterland behind. The five mountains are collectively known as the Hokushin Gogaku, and you get spectacular views of them driving up from Nagano, the nearest big city. Iizuna, Kurohime and Myoko, like Madarao, are or were volcanoes; Togakushi, a great wall of granite upthrust from the earth, is not. But of those four, only Myoko is still active and, even then, its activity is solfataric, that is, the escape of mineral rich gasses from fumaroles near the lava dome at its summit, where sulphur used to be mined. There are however a great many hot springs on its slopes and thus many onsens where you can go to bathe.

Shinanomachi is built along the rivers running down from these heights, in an upland valley remarkable for its fertile, black soil. In summer the farmers grow rice, soba (buckwheat), corn, sunflowers, blueberries, onions, beans, cucumbers, pumpkins, tomatoes, eggplant and much else besides. There are always flowers blooming at the margins of their unfenced fields or outside their houses, from crocuses, daffodils and irises in spring to poppies and lilies in summer, to tall yellow and orange daisies and red hibiscus in autumn. In autumn, too, the rice fields, elegantly symmetrical, usually rectangular, with raising mounds running between them, turn from electric green to pale yellow as the stems flower and then go to golden seed. After the grain is harvested the plants stay rooted in the ground and there is a brief spurt of second growth, which does not yield any grain, before snow covers the fields in a carpet of luminous white. These roots will be ploughed back in, as fertilizer, when spring comes again.

Mayu has been visiting here for fifty years, ever since her mother bought a house near Nojiriko with her second husband, Tominaka Satoru, a businessman, whom Mayu calls her second father. Like her first father, Kanamori Kaoru, he's dead now too. The house, which Yoshie bought with the alimony money after her first marriage ended, was a besso, a second home where they could escape the Tokyo heat during the summer months. That house has gone now, resumed by the authorities when they were putting a highway through from Nagano to the coast; but with the pay-out she built another one on the slopes of Kurohime. Yoshie still comes up here from Tokyo at regular intervals in the summer months to stay. I'm not sure exactly how long ago her new house was built but at the time it was the last one on the road and she had to pay for the power pole, which stands at the head of her drive, to be installed.

Subsequently, houses built further up the road used to pay her a small fee to run their own electricity off that pole and I think that arrangement continues today. Our house is one of those later dwellings, built by Sato Constructions, the same people who built Yoshie's house; like hers, it is maintained by them too. It was originally a companion to the larger house that stands behind it, a besso for a family who lived elsewhere. Their daughter, a nurse who was single mother, used to stay with her son in the little house when they all came up on holiday but she stopped using it about ten years ago. When Mayu first looked at it, it had been empty for that long. She bought it for the equivalent of $15,000 and spent as much again making it liveable. The nurse's parents are both in care homes. A few years ago they sold the big house to a young woman from Joetsu, Sakura, who lives there still.

We are just at the edge of the forest of birch and cedar intermixed with pine and fir trees which covers the lower slopes of Kurohime. The larch trees are deciduous but the others are evergreen; we mostly have larches on our land but there is one cedar behind the house and numerous seedlings in the yard, plus a few maples, *momiji*, and a large-leafed magnolia, which, although substantial, isn't old enough yet to have begun flowering. The momiji are deciduous too and glorious in autumn. The magnolia also drops its broad veined leaves to the ground. It has a cousin, called the white magnolia, which grows wild in the woods and when we first came up here you could see its blaze of white fire here and there amongst the delicate green of the new growth on the larches and the darker green of the cedars. On one occasion, walking around a lake near Togakushi, I saw a large monkey climb backwards down a tree then amble across the track in front of me with a flowering branch of white magnolia in its mouth.

Our section is on a corner and, although it isn't large, when I tried to count the trees upon it the other day, I reached thirty before I became confused as to which ones I'd already counted and which I had not. Next to us is another corner section which isn't built upon and there the ground cover, mostly bear bamboo, is waist high in the warmer months, gone wild amongst the creepers and vines and native hydrangeas with their pale blue flowers. A walnut tree leans over our house and, in autumn, you'll sometimes hear a sharp crack, like a gunshot, when a nut falls onto the roof then rolls down the slope and off onto the ground below. Many of these nuts end up buried under the snow to be retrieved in spring by squirrels, which sniff them out, dig them up, then retreat up into the bend of a momiji to crack the case and eat the contents.

Over summer I try to clear the creepers and the bear bamboo and the other ground cover off our land, hoping to encourage a kind of soft green grass which grows in clumps so as to make, if not exactly a lawn, a kind of park. A variety of wildflowers grow here, most of them unfamiliar to me though Mayu, who has made it her business to learn their names, knows how to identify them from photographs. She has already gathered a library of pictures and their accompanying nomenclature, not only from here but also from beside the roads and at the People's Park, a stand of cherry trees between our house and her mother's where, for a year, she went every morning to take photographs which she later compiled and edited into a single work of visual art. Flowers we think of as garden varieties are common in the woods: violets, irises, a yellow lily, a daisy which resembles a sunflower, the hydrangeas. Meanwhile wild strawberries, with their tiny bright red sharp-tasting fruit, carpet the ground beside the waterways.

If you walk up the hill behind our house you are, almost immediately, in the woods. They are not however trackless wastes; the streams which run incessantly off the mountain have mostly been diverted into channels, like small canals; and even where the stream bed is intact the banks have been shaped and sometimes, in spring, they are mowed. I don't know how far up the mountain this network of waterways reaches, just that it is further than I have so far gone. There is a small lake up there, which I've seen on maps but haven't yet visited. The existence of these waterways emphasizes something it might otherwise be easy to miss: although it appears to be in its natural state, this is in fact a profoundly altered landscape and the major alterations are mostly to do with the management of water.

The checkerboard of rice paddies down in the valley, for instance, is sustained by a largely invisible network of irrigation channels, with water gates that can be opened and closed to regulate the flow; up here in the woods, similar gates have been built which can also be opened and closed. You come across these water gates in the most surprising and out of the way places; they look rusty and derelict but most of them still work and can be used for flood control or water diversion when necessary. Furthermore, this network of pipes also includes, as well as our household supply, a system of fire hydrants, one on every block, to be used in the event of a conflagration. This is such a watery place it's hard to imagine forest fires; but when you look at what is happening elsewhere on the globe, maybe not.

One reason, perhaps the main one, that the water ways are so healthy and the water so pure and clean, is that Japanese do not build on the hills: there are very rarely any houses nor other kinds of building (except temples, shrines and communication towers) standing any higher than the gentle slopes. This means that the mountains are still forested, much as they would have been thousands of years ago, and also that the kinds of wild life which prefer a forest environment still live there. Even here, which is remote but still well populated, there are bears and wild boars, sika deer, serow (a goat-like antelope), foxes, monkeys, badgers (called *anaguma*, hole bear), a small wild canine called tanuki, squirrels, weasels and moles — and then there is the prolific bird, reptile, amphibian and insect life.

There are owls, pigeons, several kinds of woodpecker, blue-winged magpies, the ubiquitous crows, jay birds, raptors such as the black kite and the peregrine falcon, ducks, herons, thrushes, shrikes, minas, and a variety of smaller birds like finches and robins.

In spring and summer it's common to see rat snakes, which eat the green and brown frogs as well as rodents. And, though I haven't encountered one yet, the pit viper, *mamushi*, which is venomous, lives here too. It is an ambush hunter so you need to be careful where you put your feet when you're out walking in the woods. In fact there are forty-seven different kinds of snake in Japan, four of which, all vipers, are poisonous. As you walk along beside the creeks in summer the big brown frogs hop into the water and breast stroke away; the small green ones you find, unexpectedly, all over the place.

In summer, too, the dragon flies, damsel flies and grasshoppers are thick along the water ways, where there are also enough butterflies to keep even a Nabokov happy; and the number, and kinds, of moths that come out at night make you doubt stories of the insect apocalypse — despite the probable over use of pesticides and fertilizers in the valley below. Beetles range in size from the horned rhinoceroses, big as a small bird, to the tiny shiny black ones which snuffle industriously in the leaf litter. In season, cicadas start up before dawn and go on until dusk. The huge sparrow wasps, *osuzumebachi*, are not aggressive, not even when you remove their nests, as we had to do for one under the eaves of the house; but the stinging March flies are; and there are any number of little, stingless native bees. Last autumn there was a plague of *kamemushi*, stink bugs. Mosquitos are not nearly as common as I thought they would be but there are still plenty of them too. And so on.

None of this wildlife represents any threat to humans, apart from the mamushi, and possibly the bears and boars. I have seen wild pig sign in the woods and sometimes their muddy footprints on the road or precisely imprinted in the snow; and once spotted one trying, unsuccessfully, to cross Highway 18. Bears, meanwhile, are a constant concern, almost an obsession. If one is sighted there will be public service announcements on the loudspeaker network for the rest of the day. One morning I woke around 5.30 am to find a police car with its lights flashing down on the corner. There were two cops and they were talking to some holiday-makers from another vehicle, a wagon with a roof rack. A man, a woman and a boy of about ten. Clearly it was not a criminal matter — they were being far too polite to each other. While I watched, everybody bowed several times, the family got back into the wagon and reversed a few metres to let the cop car out. It drew away, still with its lights flashing, and then stopped a bit further down the road and made an announcement.

At this point Mayu woke up and said: 'Bear!' When she looked at her phone, there was a missed call from our neighbour, Sakura, which included a video. She'd woken up at 5.00 am, seen the bear out her bedroom window and rang the police (though it wasn't clear to me what the police could actually do). In the video, the bear is sitting on its haunches in the bear bamboo growing between her house and ours, eating; then it stands up and ambles away into another neighbour, Mr S's yard, past the extension he was building, and into the street upon whose corner I saw the cop car. It looks completely unhurried and totally at ease — and why not? It lives here too. A few days later the same bear, or a different one, was filmed by a neighbour on the other side, at Ven's Kitchen, an intermittent pizza restaurant, leisurely climbing up a tree beside their deck.

They're black bears, called moon bears, *tsukinowaguma*, because they have a crescent of white fur upon their chests. In early summer they're inclined to come down from the mountain because food is still scarce up there then. Bear attacks are rare but they do occur; usually by females when someone inadvertently gets between a mother and her cubs. One evening around dusk, from the car, we saw a mother bear with four cubs just down the road and the look she gave me left no doubt in my mind as to her intentions if I tried to come closer. The farmers used to shoot them on sight but now, if one becomes troublesome, it is more likely to be tranquillised and returned to its habitat in the mountains. Every place in the local area where a bear has been seen in the last ten years is logged and entered onto a map which you can get a copy of at the town office. Our street now has a new sign down the bottom announcing the recent sightings here.

Consideration of bears, and of waterways, reminds me that this is an anciently inhabited landscape. Wet rice cultivation in Japan is about three thousand years old, though these high valleys were probably first farmed more recently; but people have been here for much longer than that. When they were building the motorway which necessitated the demolition of Yoshie's first besso, workers unearthed fragments of a Jomon pot estimated to be 6,500 years old — that is, from the middle Jomon period. Some years before that, in 1948, a fossicker in the mud along the shallow shores of Nojiriko found an elephant's molar tooth. This turned out to belong to an extinct variety of pachyderm called the Neumann's elephant, after the German scientist who was the first to describe them. Along with a kind of woolly mammoth and a giant elk, these beasts lived in the archipelago until about 28,000 years ago. And they cohabited with humans.

Since then, every year at the end of winter, when the level of the lake drops as water is taken out to run hydro-electric power stations, archaeologists and volunteers gather on the exposed shoreline to dig for artefacts and bones. More discoveries have been made. One is an exquisite ivory statuette of a woman carved from the tip of an elephant's tusk; another is a complete tusk laid beside a branch of an antler of the giant elk. Called 'Moon and Star', this arrangement is believed to have been deliberately made, for ritual purposes, by the people who lived here then. Their tools have been found in great numbers, from tiny obsidian scrapers and bone points to larger hammer stones and hand axes. The so-called Lake Nojiri people were big game hunters who, in the Pleistocene, followed herds of the great beasts into the archipelago along the land corridors that used to connect Japan, north and south, with the continental land mass to the west.

More than a hundred years ago, at a place called Cheddar Gorge in Somerset, England, labourers digging a ditch in a cave found, buried beneath a stalagmite, the nearly complete skeleton of a male in his twenties. Cheddar Man was about ten thousand years old and died from a bone infection after a blow to the face which fractured his cheek bone and eye socket. Many years later, DNA was extracted from his remains and he was given, tentatively, a phenotype. Dark skin, dark hair, blue green eyes, a typical profile for a Western European hunter gatherer of the Mesolithic period. Then someone had the bright idea of comparing his DNA with that of people living locally and soon came up with a match. A history teacher, Adrian Targett, from a family who had lived a long time in the area, was found to have shared a remote maternal ancestor with Cheddar Man.

When I told this story to Mayu, she wondered if there might be people around here, for instance her mother's boyfriend Kitamura-san, who are descended from the Jomon or even from the Lake Nojiri people. Kitamura-san has lived here all his life; he farms ancestral land on the other side of Nojiriko, although these days he lives in town. Like many of the local people, Kitamura-san (the name means 'north village') is short in stature and strongly built, with a large head and large hands. Some of the older folk, and especially the women, are bent double from their lifetime of labour in the fields and can no longer stand upright, but not Kitamura-san; he remains straight and strong and active. The other day when we called in on him he was pulling a large boulder out of the soil of the garden next to his house. I don't know how old he is but imagine he is, like Yoshie, well into his eighties.

The appellation 'boyfriend' is ironic. Kitamura-san was a drinking partner of Yoshie's second husband Satoru and, after Satoru-san died, took it upon himself to provide her with companionship and other kinds of support. He would take her out for lunch and, because she no longer drives, if she needed to go somewhere, he would drive her there. His own wife was for many years an invalid and he cared for her devotedly. She died recently but there are children and an extended family for him to look after and to look after him. There is something honest and good and true about Kitamura-san which is uplifting. He is a wise man, whose advice may be depended upon in any circumstance which pertains locally. He is also a man of strong principles. Between the time Satoru died and the death of his own wife, he never once set foot in Yoshie's house. I was there when he came back in for the first time in years; I saw the look of curiosity and wonder on his face.

There doesn't seem to be any compelling reason why such continuity of human occupation, human ancestry, should not exist in a place like Shinanomachi. Even over a period of 40,000 years. Despite the vicissitudes of its history, especially recent history, this is a country which, although it has been several times invaded, has never been colonized, meaning that a continuity of generations of people living here over millennia may yet turn out to be something we can attest has actually happened. Paradoxically, it is also a place which has always welcomed knowledge, and visitors, from the beyond the sea. Look at how much of the culture — including the written language and one of the major systems of belief — has come from China. And, more recently, how much from Europe and the United States. And the food, from everywhere.

People still go on about how mysterious Japan is, how outsiders can't really understand what happens here or how Japanese people think. They say it is an alien place, and that its exoticism makes it, at the same time, both seductive and unknowable. This has not been my experience of living here. Partly, no doubt, because I have been welcomed into Mayu's family, who opened a place for me amongst them without a trace of prejudice or suspicion. This kind of welcome has also been offered me in the wider community, both amongst those I have ongoing interactions with and those I meet casually. I have not witnessed here the casual racism against outsiders you see so often in Australia and New Zealand. The nearest I have come to it is a sense of wordless hostility I've sometimes encountered from other men, usually urban types, usually younger than me, when bathing in an onsen. But because it is always left unexpressed, I am unsure if it is indeed hostility or something else entirely. Incomprehension, perhaps.

People also say the Japanese are very polite, which is true — but what is wrong with that? It is often said, I think, with the implication that politeness is a form of insincerity or at least a kind of masking. As if politeness in the West were not exactly the same thing and often in a far more toxic way. True good manners, and the ability to behave in a mannerly fashion, is something else. Why not assume the best of someone until or unless you find out otherwise? Why not present yourself in the best possible manner? Why wouldn't you go out of your way not to give offense to strangers? Sometimes I think the so-called Christian nations of the West have incorporated their own hypocrisy about religion into their daily interactions and assume, as a matter of course, a concomitant hypocrisy in people of other faiths whom they meet. Japan is, however, still a faith-based culture and that faith, while various and complex is, so far as I can tell, also genuine.

When we were in Takachiho on Kyushu in March we heard the story, told in the first part of this account, of how the sun goddess Amaterasu, after a dispute with her brother Susanoo the storm god, hid herself away in a cave; and how the other gods, led by

Omoikame, god of wisdom, devised a plan to entice her out. The goddess of dawn, Uzume, performed an erotic dance for the delectation of the other gods; and when Amaterasu looked out to see what was happening, Tajikarao, the god of power and strength, picked up the stone which had closed the cave entrance and threw it so far away that Amaterasu couldn't use it to sequester herself inside again. Togakushi — 'hiding door' — is where that rock is said to have come to rest, forming the mountain range of that name. It's the same Togakushi which is one of the five peaks of Shinano, only a half hour drive away from where we live; and when you go there you enter another world.

They are five shrines along the great wall of granite that is Togakushi, all of which have a connection with the story of Amaterasu's extrication from the cave. No doubt we will go to all of them in time but have so far visited just three. The first one we went to was the so-called Middle Shrine, Chusha, built in 1087 and dedicated to Omoikame. The administrative centre for all the other shrines, it stands above a busy road surrounded by huge old cedar trees. We queued to pay our respects outside the main building. When we reached the front, I saw in the depths of the interior a pair of priests chanting while half a dozen acolytes sat upon a bench before them. Outside, an old couple danced a two-step to the drum beats that followed the chanting.

The second and third shrines are at Okusha, on the slopes of Togakushi itself; we've been there quite a few times. Before you take the path up to visit them you have to cross a small river, the Sakasagawa, which is the border between the human world and that of the kami, the gods. If you are riding a horse, a stone set up on the left tells you, you must dismount here and go forward on foot. The wide path leads gently upwards through mixed forest; when you enter an avenue of tall cedar trees standing on both sides of the way, in some indefinable manner the atmosphere changes. These three hundred odd trees were planted early in the Edo period, that is at the beginning of the seventeenth century, and are thus about four hundred years old. Where a tree has fallen, a new one has been planted in its place; and this too has been going on for centuries.

The avenue they make is aligned with the rising sun at the vernal and autumnal equinoxes; it shines down upon you if you are lucky enough to go there on either of those days. Even on an ordinary day like the one on which we first went, misty and cool, you walk between them as though through a cathedral of trees. Not quite halfway along the two kilometre track you pass through the Zuijinmon Gate, an ornate wooden structure with a rich growth of ferns and other forest plants on its thatched roof and two god figures either side of the entrance. The path begins to rise more steeply after that. Off to the left, perhaps as encouragement for the faint hearted, there are four Jizo, or maybe they are two pairs of *Dosojin*, in a small grotto overlooking the path. Both Jizo and Dosojin are tutelary gods of travellers.

Then you come to the steps, which are disintegrating, crumbled away in places, and steeper again. They lead to the top of the hill where suddenly you see sky above you: no vistas, just the ubiquitous vivid greens and deep browns of the forest beneath the white of the clouds or the blue of the empyrean. The first and larger shrine, built hard against the rough granite wall of the mountain, is dedicated to Tajikarao himself, he who threw the door. The other, off to the side, houses a local deity, Kuzuryusha, who takes the form of a dragon with nine heads and is a god of water. Needless to say, or perhaps not, there is the sound of water everywhere you go: rice farmers come to Kuzuryusha's shrine to pray that the life-giving liquid continues to flow. Hence the barrels of saké stacked up before his altar. He is also, somewhat improbably, the god of bad teeth and you can ask him to relieve you of the pain of tooth ache and even to heal your cavities.

Kuzuryusha is an old god, who was here before Tajikarao or his rock arrived: you wonder how old? What gods did the Jomon worship? Or the Lake Nojiri people before them? Dragons are usually associated with volcanoes, of which there are many around here. In the event, Kuzuryusha greeted Tajikarao amiably and made him welcome, providing him with a place for his shrine. His own shrine is less imposing and within it there are four small, mysterious paintings on wooden panels leaning on a shelf against the back wall. One is a painted relief of a winged figure holding upright a sword or a wand and standing upon a fox's back: Inari Okami, the fox god or goddess of fertility, rice, tea, saké, of agriculture and industry and, more generally of prosperity and worldly success. Inari gives special protection to blacksmiths and one of the local industries in Shinanomachi is blacksmithing: here they make the best and sharpest kitchen knives in the country.

Next to that is a painting of a figure, Buddhist in origin, with pale skin, a green robe, a red skirt and one hand raised in blessing. The third painting shows a young man or woman in a striped robe and a black headdress riding a spotted horse and attended, on foot, by an aged monk wearing white robes and a tall white hat; they are passing before the cone of a volcano like Fujiyama. Apart from the green ground upon which the horse prances and the white of the monk's robes, most of the pigment has faded to a warm brown. I don't know who these two people are nor what they signify; nor even if they represent figures out of the Buddhist or the Shinto pantheon. Shinto has no holy book and no scriptures, only stories. It doesn't have any dogma either, nor a founder who must be worshiped. It is a practice before anything else: 'the way of the gods.'

The fourth and last work is also badly faded, so that only the green, some patches of red and the whites remain. It is a painting of a group of figures engaged in some kind of drama, in a bare landscape of rocks and pines and shows, I think, Uzume dressed in red dancing before the cave where the sun goddess sequestered herself; Amaterasu, also wearing red, presiding above; and on the right Tajikarao waiting to pick up the door — or has he already thrown it? At the centre of the composition is a round dark hole representing the cave mouth; and all about, seated on the ground or standing on rocky outcrops, the assembled gods are watching. In the immediate foreground a rooster, with its beak open, like those we saw at Amanoiwato, is crowing.

All four paintings, despite their decayed and neglected state, transmit considerable power. It is hard to think of them as art per se because they are clearly in some sense functional and furthermore in specific ways which those who understand their significance would be able to elucidate. For those who do not, but still believe, they would also have meaning, especially the relief of Inari, who is one of the most popular of the gods and whose shrines, generally painted a bright red, are found throughout the land. She is thought to have been originally a female deity:

> Inari descended from the sky riding on a white fox and in her hand carried sheaves of cereal or grain. Ine, the word now used for rice, was the name of this cereal, but what she carried was not rice but some cereal that grows in swamps. According to this legend, in ancient times Japan was water and swamp land.

Swamp land indeed. It was raining that day at Togakushi but even when it is fine, as it was the next time we went, there is still the incessant sound of water. A stream runs beside the path and in several places you can cross over into open green glades beyond, where groups of people gather to do spiritual exercises. The sound of water flowing always makes me think of one of the most beautiful stories in Shinto, that of the creation of the land. The twin creator gods, Izanagi and Izanami, brother and sister, later lovers, whom we also met on Kyushu, looked down from the floating bridge of heaven at the ocean below and, finding it dull, took up a jewelled spear and began churning the waters with its blade. When they raised it up, drops of sea foam fell from its tip and they became the islands of the archipelago of Japan.

One of the pleasures of visiting places such as these — quite apart from the majestic surroundings and the sense of otherworldly awe they inspire — is the company of other pilgrims. People climb up in a spirit of cheerful anticipation and, having made their devotions, come back down in a state of happy satiation. You see all sorts — young and old, women and men, groups of teenagers, solitary wanderers. People with walking frames or leaning on sticks. People who look as if they are on the last walk they will ever take. That first time, on the way up, going ahead of my companions, I kept passing and re-passing a family of four, a man and a woman with two young boys.

The elder boy, about four or five, was a dawdler who investigated, with rapt absorption, the contents of the creek running beside the road and anything else he came across; occasionally he would look up, realise he had fallen behind, and let out a cry, which was always answered immediately, reassuringly, by his mother or his father; then he would resume his investigations. The other, about two, was a busy cheerful kid who ran around his parents, but especially his father, the way a dog runs around its owner. Both boys walked the entire two-kilometre distance up to the top where, later, I saw them giggling in the shrubbery with their pants down having a pee.

On the way down my companions were four women in their forties perhaps, walking abreast on the wide path, laughing and talking, sometimes carolling like birds, sometimes literally jumping for joy. Now and again one or other of them would run off into the forest to get a better view of something, then run back with news of what she had seen. Whatever the precise status of

Shinto belief, I thought, a faith which inspires such pleasurable engagement in its adherents can't possibly be denied. It is about as far away as can be from the grim puritanism of my Presbyterian forebears, who gathered to worship on a Sunday, it seemed, only to confirm their status as an elect who would, apparently, sit out eternity in the same miserable and forbearing manner in which they sat through those interminable church services.

Faith of course takes many forms, some of them secular. The insides of the cloudy windows in the bathhouse opposite our studio apartment at Togatta Onsen, for instance, had a moisture line along their base which resembled the profile of a mountain range. Sometimes I thought I could see the peaks and valleys of the Zao Range; sometimes it seemed the profile represented the whole of the Ou Ranges, which include the Zao and are the longest on Honshu; and sometimes I remembered the blade dripping sea foam which created the archipelago in the first place. I used to stare at this feature while I lay in the hot brown water of the big pool during my evening bath. Or else I would gaze upwards into the cavernous spaces of the interior of the high peaked roof and wonder at its extravagance. The water in the smaller pool, contiguous with the big one, was too hot for me. I said this once to our host, Satoh-san, and he replied that he only used the very hot pool when he felt confused or uncertain about something: it cleared his head instantly.

Most of the men who came in the evening to bathe were getting on in years; most of them, after showering, took a short dip in the small hot pool before soaking for longer in the large one. Then they would industriously soap their bodies and shampoo their hair (if they had any) to a lather until it seemed not a speck of dirt could possibly remain. I was more casual. I just showered before getting in and again after getting out. These men regarded me benignly, as a curiosity perhaps, or as someone who might need occasional guidance in the protocols of bathing in public baths. One of them once gave me an unopened bottle of a very sweet green fizzy drink. They were kindly but unconcerned, probably because they had other things on their minds. The evening bath wasn't just about washing and relaxing, it was also a time to discuss what had happened in the town that day: to exchange, recount, examine, analyse, laugh about or exclaim over local events.

There was one fellow in particular, a skinny old chap, who was held in particular esteem by the others. I wasn't sure if this was because he was in some position of authority, whether naturally or socially acquired; or if they simply appreciated his ability as a raconteur. We were all of course stark naked, which leads to a kind of physical equality. No-one has the status clothes can give, everyone shares the vulnerability of an aging and imperfect body. Anyway this fellow was holding forth one night to a dozen or so others and I was listening without understanding what he was saying — when it suddenly occurred to me that I had heard something like this before. Not the words, the rhythm. He was intoning, I realized, in much the same fashion as the actors in the Noh play I had seen on Sado; moreover, those who were listening to him showed the same rapt attention the audience on that occasion had. I think he was probably telling a story rather than laying down the law but of course I don't know.

I had a similar experience one evening after we returned home, having dinner with Yoshie at her house up the road. We were sitting outside on her deck, with moths battering the screen door or dive bombing the portable tungsten lamps. Dinner was over, the dishes had been cleared away and she had just poured herself another glass of saké when she began to speak about the life she wanted to lead, in what was then her eighty-ninth year. Again I didn't know what she was saying but recognized the rhythm of her words. I had been reading a lot of poetry in romaji, romanised

Japanese, and her words fell naturally into that five – seven – five – seven – seven syllable pattern which characterizes both haiku and the tanka upon which it is ultimately based. It was about her desire to enjoy the pleasures of the senses: to eat food that was tasty and fresh, drink good saké, see the moon set behind the trees, hear the wind in the branches, watch the little creatures come and go about their business . . . and somehow, as she spoke, her speech turned into poetry.

Poetry is of course ubiquitous here. In Shinanomachi the local poet is the renowned Kobayashi Issa, ranked alongside Basho, Buson and Shiki as one of the four pillars of haiku. He was born in Kashiwabara in 1763, of a farming family and died here, aged sixty-five, in 1828. The place in which he lived out his last days, an old storehouse built in traditional style, is still standing just off Highway 18 in town and I have been there on several occasions. His grave is in the local cemetery and I have paid my respects to him there too. However, although he grew up here, he spent the middle decades of his adult life elsewhere, in Edo, or on the road in various parts of the archipelago. He is a paradoxical figure, at once charming and irascible, who left a huge body of work behind him: an estimated 20,000 haiku (Basho wrote about 1000) as well as numerous prose works, including voluminous diaries from the later period of his life.

Issa has the earthiness of someone raised upon the land as well as the clarity that may be a consequence of a life lived in poverty. He can be sardonic too:

harusame ya | kuware-nokori no | kamo go naku
spring rain | ducks quacking | those that haven't been eaten yet

When he is looking out over Matsushima, whose beauty left Basho lost for words, he writes (surely with the elder poet in mind):

nomi domo ni | Matsushima misete | nigasi zoyo
look fleas | Matsushima | why don't you hop off?

suggesting that his fleas might like to leave him now and go to live in this lovely place instead. Perhaps my favourite image from his vast oeuvre is that of a branch floating down a flooded river — with a cicada singing thereon.

Issa's most famous poem, as well known as Basho's one about the frog and the old pond, still retains its emotional resonance:

tsuyu no yo wa | tsuyu no yo nagara | sari nagara
this dew drop world | is just a dew drop world | – and yet, and yet . . .

The dew drop world is the world of appearances which a true Buddhist must learn to disregard as the transitory illusion it is; while the 'and yet' is our inability to leave our shared and imperfect humanity behind. The haiku was published in *The Spring of My Life*, (*Oraga haru*), the haibun he wrote after the death of his daughter, Sato, aged two, from smallpox in 1818.

Today is a fine winter morning, with about a foot of snow lying on the ground outside and blue sky above. Mrs S, who lives diagonally behind us, is over at her in-law's house next door, having called an ambulance for her ailing father-in-law. We found out later in the day that he had a fall and suffered minor bruising. Mr S, her husband, normally a busy, cheerful, active man in his fifties, fell off the roof of the house opposite while he was doing maintenance there one day, injured his ankle and is now on crutches. We watched him instructing his wife in the use of the snow blower the other day, bellowing lustily and waving his sticks. His parents are old and his father, at least, quite frail. They have a dog as ancient as they are which on occasion they walk.

The house opposite, where Mr S fell, is a besso where a couple from Tokyo we call The Two Ladies come and stay during the holidays. They too are ancient and venerable and somehow intimidating; one of them plays the piano. On the next corner live the dog-walkers, a couple, who always wave cheerily as they pass our house, twice a day, with their three *shiba inu*. The man of the pair is the tree-lopper who took down the dead spike behind our kitchen. Then there is the house of the people who ran away; the house whose roof cracked because of the weight of snow upon it; the house of the man who died; and the house whose east wall is full of holes made by woodpeckers. These are all empty.

Another house I can see from here used to belong to a single man who lived alone and whom we called the Zombie because of the shambling way he walked. He wasn't liked by the other residents in our little corner of the world because he was in the habit of burning his rubbish in his back yard, letting toxic black smoke billow into the air. The foxes we see sometimes in the evening live somewhere in that wild back yard of his and we used to joke that he was not a zombie at all but a shape shifter who manifested as a fox when he wanted to go wandering. For all that, on one occasion he did us a kindness and our nickname for him was given from affection not dislike. Now, however, he has departed, having sold his house to a fellow from Toyama who comes up here to ski.

I've already mentioned Sakura, the young woman who lives in the house behind ours. She has a busy life and goes out every day, working at her friend's soba restaurant or on the ski fields; she has been a radio announcer and an MC at live events. One day she said to Mayu: 'You guys go to bed so early!' She herself is a night owl and sometimes when I wake up in the wee small hours I see the light from her front room blazing and, very occasionally, see her silhouetted there, doing what I do not know. Some kind of dance or meditation or martial art perhaps. That room used to be where she looked after her cat, Fersen — named after the Swedish lord who was the lover of Marie Antoinnette — until Fersen died. Now she has a twenty-four-year-old, one-eyed, ginger rescue cat who, on occasion, yowls mournfully in the evenings and who will certainly die soon too.

Yoshie doesn't come up here in the winter, which means Mayu doesn't have to drive her out shopping every day, mainly for food. Over the autumn she made preserves — huckleberry, blueberry, rhubarb — which are delicious. Yoshie grew up in the period just before and after the Pacific War and suffered displacement and other privations as a result. It's probable that her obsession with food goes back to when, as a little girl, she was often hungry, if not actually starving. One day she found a kind of melon which was all they had to eat at one point when she was young and I saw the avid way she devoured it. Despite her healthy appetite she is exceptionally thin, to the point where I can scarcely believe the amount of food she puts away. She must have an extremely fast metabolism.

I don't know Yoshie's life story in detail but do know she was part of a hip young scene in Tokyo in the 1950s and 60s. I've seen her image, in various poses and permutations, on the cover of a literary magazine from the late 1950s. She looks as elegant as Jean Shrimpton. During those years she was the girlfriend and muse of a lesbian poet who still has a reputation today, obsessively overseen by her son, who has dedicated his life to conserving his mother's memory. But if you mention the poet to Yoshie she will say, dismissively: she only ever wrote about herself. She is, generally speaking, not inclined towards nostalgia or sentimentality or dwelling on the past.

Even in her late eighties she is forward looking, an admirable trait, even if it does preclude reminiscence. She always walks very quickly in whatever direction she wants to go. Mayu has a story about how once, when she was a little girl, her mother boarded a suburban Tokyo train so precipitately she left her daughter behind on the platform. Mayu had the wit to catch the following train and they were reunited at the next station. Yoshie, who is now quite deaf, during the summer and autumn evenings likes to sit out on her deck and look into the trees as light fades from the sky and night comes on. She remains alert to changes in the weather and maintains an interest in the living creatures that come around her house when she is here: the frogs and snakes, the beetles and the moths, the squirrels who run and jump between the trees.

It isn't necessarily the case that with age comes wisdom; on the other hand there are some things you only learn chronologically. It would be foolish to claim that Yoshie, any more than Kitamura-san, is the inheritor of the knowledge of the Jomon or indeed of whoever the Lake Nojiri people were: but something is handed down the generations and it is probably more than just genes and superstitions. Speaking of which, Yoshie has a collection of sloughed-off snakeskins which are supposed to bring good luck. Sometimes, with her long face and heavy-lidded eyes, she can look rather ophidian herself; and especially when she is contemplating the answer to some question I might have asked. Those answers are almost always suitably gnomic.

Her first husband, Mayu's father, Kanamori Kaoru, was a theatre designer who worked with some big names, including Mishima Yukio and Hijikata Tatsumi. One of Mayu's mother's boyfriends collaborated with Kurosawa Akira and if you look at Kurosawa's 1970 film *Dodes'ka-den*, you'll see behind the opening credits Mayu's drawings of trams. She was about seven years old at the time. Both of her parents had affairs and eventually separated and divorced; both married again and had children with their new partners. Mayu's father died young, aged forty-nine, of cancer of the oesophagus. Recently we saw, at a museum in a nearby town, an exhibition which included a number of three dimensional models of his elegant and innovative stage designs for various productions by Asari Keita's Shiki Theatre, including Jean Giraudoux's *Ondine*, Chekhov's *The Seagull*, Bernard Pomerance's *The Elephant Man* and *Hikarigoke*, 'Luminous Moss', a drama set on Hokkaido during the Pacific War.

One thing which surprises me about living in Japan, even for the short time I have, is how pervasive memories of the war are here. The fact that sixty-seven Japanese cities were repeatedly fire-bombed by the Americans between 1944-5 is one reason; the atomic bombs dropped on Hiroshima and Nagasaki is another; but there is a deeper history. In the last millennium Japan has experienced three long periods of military government: the Kamakura shogunate from 1192-1333; the Ashikaga shogunate from 1338-1573; and the Tokugawa shogunate from 1603-1868. That's 641 out of 831 years. Only the last of these periods, the Tokugawa bakufu, was peaceful: during which the state-salaried samurai class turned from warriors into bureaucrats. Ironically, it was after the re-establishment of Imperial rule that extreme nationalism ran out of control and the country attempted to establish a veritable empire, with disastrous consequences.

Perhaps these long periods of military rule and the endemic conflict they engendered or threatened made people docile, obedient and fearful of the consequences of doing wrong. Certainly most people are well-behaved, almost to the point of regimentation; great shame is attached to wrong-doing of any kind, especially if it involves public disclosure. It's also the case that most people arrested under suspicion of committing a crime will confess immediately, whether or not they have done it. This has made the Japanese police notoriously inefficient at tracking down real criminals. On the other hand, as mentioned, Japanese jails have a reputation as fearsome places, full of cruelty and squalor, where you wouldn't want to end up for any reason whatsoever. When the authorities, about twenty years ago, instituted prison terms for drink driving, the offence disappeared overnight.

Around here, as in most parts of Japan, there is a system of loudspeakers through which public announcements are made. This is obviously valuable in the case of natural disaster warnings but it is used for much more than that. At 3.15 pm every weekday, for example, we are reminded that the school day is ending and to watch out for kids walking home. Sometimes an announcement will concern a bear sighting, even if it took place several villages away. And sometimes, or rather often, it will be notice of a rehearsal of emergency procedures. The prevalence and ubiquity of these announcements lends a sense of incipient crisis to the most ordinary of days and, presumably, keeps everybody on the alert for possible catastrophe. It might be an exaggeration to say this means we live in a community perpetually on a war footing; but it can feel like that.

Our system also broadcasts the Westminster chimes at 12 noon; but the thing I most like about it is the regular repetition, at 5.00 pm every afternoon, of a tender, melancholy rendition of the tune of a popular song, 'Yuyake Koyake', Kusakawa Shin's setting of a 1919 poem by Nakamura Ukou. Kusakawa was a local, from Nagano, who went to Tokyo where he became a high school teacher. The lyrics of the first stanza are about the sky turning red in the evening, the temple bells ringing, children making their way home hand in hand as the crows, too, fly back to their nests. I have my own version which I sing to myself: 'Now the war is over / We can all go home / The sun is sinking in the sky / The crows are flying home too.' Childish enough, but it is a children's song.

However, it turns out this particular broadcast is not considered by the authorities a signal that the working day is over and we can all relax. Rather, it is a test — a way of reviewing, on a daily basis, the town's disaster warning system. As the official explanation puts it:

> In a country where earthquakes, tsunamis, and typhoons occur on a regular basis, speakers are used in times of emergency to give directions and warnings to the residents. Since a catastrophe may happen any time, it is crucial to make sure the system works perfectly, as it can make the difference between life and death.

Since a catastrophe may happen any time: there we are again with that sense of incipient disaster just around the corner on even the most ordinary of days.

I don't live my life as if it is about to end tomorrow in some natural or man-made disaster; and I'm sure those around me don't either. Rather, it is a sort of backdrop, a reminder if you like, of the impermanency which is a fact of our condition. And perhaps it is better to be reminded of that than to live in the complacent expectation that things will continue inexorably on just as they are today. That sense of an unchanging round of the seasons, and the human activities that accompany them, is often thought of (particularly by city people) as characteristic of rural, peasant or village life. All three descriptions — rural, peasant, village — may be applied to Shinanomachi, although it is also a resort town in winter, when the ski fields open and expensive vehicles driven by bearded outlanders or their lycra-ed partners invade the streets.

I grew up in a remote part of New Zealand, in what is now another ski town, in the midst of the scars of the felling of an ancient forest; and the attempted destruction of the people who cared for it and whom it had sustained for hundreds of years. Some of what we called the bush remained, however, and more of it is now growing back. The village of Ohakune, home then to about a thousand souls, is at a slightly lower elevation above the sea than Mizuho. Both places are on the slopes of a volcano: Ruapehu, looming over Ohakune, is active but Kurohime is not — or not so far as we know. These physical and geographic resemblances might have some bearing on why I feel at home here; or they might not. Perhaps for me home is just a place where I am free to read and write and to be with the people I love.

Nevertheless I do feel as if we live in a village, with all of the ordinariness that implies — and its occasional extraordinariness. What I mean by that is that here I do the same things every day, and see the same people, who are also doing the same things they do, day after day. It can feel as if the only thing that changes is the weather. This feeling of the essential sameness of life is characteristic of the whole archipelago, insofar as I have seen it. Some people might find it tedious; I find it comforting. Sometimes I entertain the notion that what charms me most about living in Japan is that the whole country is a village which became a nation; and yet remains a village, albeit one with about a hundred and thirty million inhabitants, some of whom live in other countries.

Not many people think of Japan as a socialist country but in some ways that's just what it is. This probably comes from the preservation, despite many vicissitudes, of the village structure. Health care is cheap or, for seniors like me, free. Dentistry is high quality and eminently affordable: a filling costs the equivalent of $20.00. Food is fresh, inexpensive and abundant; saké too, which some people think has medicinal effects. Beyond that, there's a larger sense of the intrinsic value and right to life of every single person, whoever they may be. This respect extends to property: theft is more or less unheard of and anything you lose will be, if humanly possible, returned to you. The sense of freedom you get from being a member of a just society is one of the great joys of living here: a buoyancy, a calm, a daily thanksgiving. It does also incline you to love your fellows.

Among other subtle effects, this means reality is fractal: each corner of the land you investigate opens up into worlds which appear, even if they are not, infinite. Also that, while Tokyo is the centre, the country is cosmopolitan in the sense that you can uncover great sophistication — of craft, technology, food, thought, history, tradition, worship — anywhere. When we visited nearby Noto Peninsular, for instance, we found a salt farm out on the tip of the promontory harvesting the sea the way it has been done for thousands of years. The Noto earthquake and tsunami on New Year's Day 2024 inundated the salt farm but it will no doubt return. And just up the road from here you can see a rock in which the horse of Basho's hero, the warrior lord Minamoto Yoshinaka, left its hoof print long ago; while over the hill, at Togakushi, is a museum displaying artefacts and memorabilia of the Togakure line of ninja operatives, still active, which Yoshinaka established in the 1180s.

Now, suddenly, I look out the window, and see a *kasasagi*, a magpie, investigating the bark on one of the larch trees. Its mate is doing something similar over the road. Their heads and necks are glossy black, like crows, but they are smaller, with longer tails, white bellies, blue wings, green and purple iridescence in their darker feathers. Their cry is hoarse and repetitive: *kasha-kasha-kasha*. The one I am watching is plucking small insects from the folds made where a branch stems off the main trunk of the tree. The blue of its wings shines like shards of the sky against the brilliant white, mica-glinting snow, the black of the trunk of the larch. While I am looking, it finishes whatever it was doing and, accompanied by its mate, wings away down the hill towards the main road. I see the flash of the blue of their wings as they fly through a band of slanted sunlight as if through a door in the sky; and then they are gone.

Notes on Sources

Stories of the Gods

Some of the matter related in this and subsequent sections of the book comes from brochures we gathered and bulletin boards we read along the way. Local versions of history or myth are never definitive; but neither are those in books. Nevertheless I have augmented the ones we found on the road from sources which may claim a greater veracity for their accounts.

They include *A History of Japan* by R H P Mason and J G Caiger (Tuttle 1997); and *The Christian Century in Japan, 1549-1650* by C R Boxer (Carcanet 1951/1993). I also read *Prehistoric Japan: New Perspectives on insular East Asia* by Keiji Imamura (University of Hawai'i Press 1996); and *The Glover House of Nagasaki: an Illustrated History* by Brian Burke Gaffney (Flying Crane Press 2015). *A Diplomat in Japan* by Ernest Satow (Seeley, Service & Co. Ltd 1921 / Forgotten Books 2018) is an eye witness account of the Meiji Restoration. Some of Felice Beato's photographs of Japan may be found here: holdenluntz.com/artists/studio-of-felice-beato/

Island of Silver & Gold

There are several good online sources for information about Sado Island. The best of them is here: visitsado.com/en/view/history/ with links to the history of the gold and silver mines, to shrines and festivals on the island and to the Toki recovery project. I used *A New History of Medieval Theatre in Japan: Noh & Kyogen 1300-1600* by Noel John Pinnington (Palgrave McMillan 2019) for my overview of Noh theatre.

Eight Days in the Oku

Basho's Narrow Road by Hiroaki Sato (Stone Bridge Press 1996) is the source for the prose excerpts from *Oku no Hoshomichi* quoted in the text. Other translations I read were *The Narrow Road to Oku* by Donald Keene (Kadanshusa 1996) and *Narrow Road to the Deep North* by Haruo Shirane (in *Early Modern Japanese Literature: An Anthology, 1600-1900*; Columbia UP 2002). Shirane's *Traces of Dreams: Landscape, Cultural Memory and the Poetry of Basho* (Stanford UP 1998) is a key reference.

All of these works translate the poems as well as the prose; but my primary source for those haiku I quote is *Basho & His Interpreters: Selected Hokku with Commentary* by Makoto Ueda (Stanford UP 1992). Each of the 255 haiku in this compilation appears in three versions: a poetic English translation followed by the Japanese in romaji and then a word for word English version of that. Commentaries upon every poem by a number of Japanese poets and scholars are appended.

I also consulted *Basho for Humanity* by Jeff Robbins and Sakata Shoko: basho4humanity.com/index.php; *Basho: The Complete Haiku*, by Jane Reichold (Kodansha International 2008): thehaikufoundation.org/omeka/files/original-/4b7e705b2aa76b4a77e-51fa5e09cc6d9.pdf; and *Matsuo Bashō's haiku poems in romanized Japanese with English translations* edited Gábor Terebess (Hungary): academia.edu/40839613/Basho_in_romaji_and_english

The Japanese haiku reproduced in the text follow the romaji in *Basho & His Interpreters*; the English versions are mine.

Mizuho

For Kobayashi Issa see: *The Spring of My Life & selected haiku*, translated by Sam Hamill (Shambhala Publications 1997). Another source is *The Haiku of Kobayashi Issa* by Daniel G Lanoue: haikuguy.com/issa/index.html. As with the haiku of Basho, those of Issa included here are in my own versions.

The website Mayu Kanamori made after her Togatta residency is here: mayu.com.au/togatta/

Photographs

Front Cover: Torii Gate, Aoshima

Part One: Horse Demon, Aso; Tanker, Amakusa

Part Two: Beshima Mask, Sado; Lighthouse, Naoetsu

Part Three: Bridge, Tsuruoka; Oil Drums, Sakata

Part Four: Table & Chairs, Mizuho; Shed, Kashiwabara

Back cover: Blue Door, Kurohime